Microsoft SharePoint 2010 Power User Cookbook

Over 70 advanced recipes for expert End Users to unlock
and apply the value of SharePoint

Dr Adrian Colquhoun

BIRMINGHAM - MUMBAI

Microsoft SharePoint 2010 Power User Cookbook

First published: October 2011

Production Reference: 1121011

Published by Packt Publishing Ltd.
Livery Place,
35 Livery Street,
Birmingham B3 2PB, UK.

ISBN 978-1-84968-288-6

www.packtpub.com

Cover Image by Jon Hancock (jonhan@blueyonder.co.UK)

Credits

Author
Dr Adrian Colquhoun

Reviewers
Robert Crane

Michael Nemtsev

Richard Paterson

Acquisition Editor
Stephanie Moss

Development Editors
Neha Mallik

Hithesh Uchil

Technical Editors
Kedar Bhat

Merwine Machado

Project Coordinator
Leena Purkait

Proofreader
Martin Diver

Indexer
Tejal Daruwale

Graphics
Geetanjali Sawant

Production Coordinator
Shantanu Zagade

Cover Work
Shantanu Zagade

About the Author

Dr Adrian Colquhoun is a SharePoint consultant, developer, and trainer with over 15 years of enterprise software development experience. He has been working extensively with SharePoint since early 2007.

He is the founder and Managing Director of Intelligent Decisioning Ltd (id), a SharePoint-focused Gold Partner with offices in Nottingham (UK) and Brisbane (Australia). Adrian migrated permanently to Australia in early 2009 where he now leads the Australian business from their beautiful Raby Bay office (http://www.id-live.com.au).

Adrian's multiple roles as business owner, consultant, developer, trainer, and SharePoint end user give him a unique insight to pass on as an author. You can find Adrian's latest thoughts, hints, and guides on his blog at http://www.sharepoint-mentor.com or follow him on Twitter at @spmentor.

When he's not working, you can find Adrian spending time with his family, socializing with friends, fishing, indulging his passion for Rugby League, and generally taking advantage of the great lifestyle and opportunities that Australia has to offer.

I would like to thank my wife Gail, daughter Alice, and son Liam for their continued patience, support, and inspiration through the production of this book. Thanks also to Mark Macrae for drafting the BI chapter and thanks to all my id colleagues (particularly Sam, Jamie, Peter, Alex, Dion, and Tony) for their help in the proof reading and production process. Thanks to Corinne and all my friends in the Brisbane Bayside for keeping me topped up with beer and my feet on the ground throughout the authoring process.

Perhaps one day I will write another book, but not today. It's time to fire up the barbie and then hit the beach!

About the Reviewers

Robert Crane has a degree in Electrical Engineering and is a Master of Business Administration. He is also a small-business specialist and Microsoft-certified SharePoint Professional. Robert has over 15 years of IT experience in a variety of fields and positions, including working on Wall Street in New York. He continues his involvement with information technology as the Principal of the CIAOPS.

Apart from resolving client-technical issues, Robert continues to present at seminars locally and internationally, as well as write on a number for topics for the CIAOPS. He has been the President of the SMBIT Professional community in Sydney since 2009 and can be contacted directly on `director@ciaops.com`.

Michael Nemtsev is an ex-Microsoft MVP in .NET/C# and SharePoint Server 2010, a status he held 2005 to 2011.

Michael's expertise is in the areas of Enterprise Integration and Platform & Collaborations, and he is currently working as Senior Consultant at Microsoft in Sydney, Australia, helping clients to improve business collaboration with SharePoint 2010 and Office 365.

Richard Paterson is a co-founder and director of the international SharePoint consultancy BrightStarr, a Microsoft Gold Partner with offices in the UK and US (`www.brightstarr.com`). He provides technical and architectural leadership to a team of consultants, architects, and software developers. Richard has been involved in web development since its inception and is passionate about its application in the business environment.

He has worked as a developer and architect in a broad range of industries including weapons modeling and psychometric profiling. In 2009, he was selected as one of the United Kingdom's top 30 young entrepreneurs in recognition of the rapid growth of BrightStarr.

Richard has an honors degree in Physics and is a Microsoft Accredited Software Developer. Outside of work Richard is a committed family man and an enthusiastic runner and cyclist.

www.PacktPub.com

Support files, eBooks, discount offers, and more

You might want to visit www.PacktPub.com for support files and downloads related to your book.

Did you know that Packt offers eBook versions of every book published, with PDF and ePub files available? You can upgrade to the eBook version at www.PacktPub.com and as a print book customer, you are entitled to a discount on the eBook copy. Get in touch with us at service@packtpub.com for more details.

At www.PacktPub.com, you can also read a collection of free technical articles, sign up for a range of free newsletters, and receive exclusive discounts and offers on Packt books and eBooks.

http://PacktLib.PacktPub.com

Do you need instant solutions to your IT questions? PacktLib is Packt's online digital book library. Here, you can access, read, and search across Packt's entire library of books.

Why Subscribe?

- ▶ Fully searchable across every book published by Packt
- ▶ Copy and paste, print, and bookmark content
- ▶ On demand and accessible via web browser

Free Access for Packt account holders

If you have an account with Packt at www.PacktPub.com, you can use this to access PacktLib today and view nine entirely free books. Simply use your login credentials for immediate access.

Instant Updates on New Packt Books

Get notified! Find out when new books are published by following @PacktEnterprise on Twitter, or the *Packt Enterprise* Facebook page.

Table of Contents

Preface   1

Chapter 1: Getting Started—SharePoint Essentials   7
  Introduction   8
  Creating a SharePoint list   8
  Creating a site column   12
  Creating a content type   14
  Creating and accessing my My Site   16
  Updating my user profile   18
  Tracking colleagues using my My Site   20
  Viewing the SharePoint sites I am a member of   23
  Tagging a SharePoint page so I can find it again later   25
  Reviewing the tags and notes other users have posted on a
  SharePoint page   28
  Adding an alert to a SharePoint page   29
  Managing my alerts in SharePoint   32
  Determining my permissions in a SharePoint site   34
  Checking another user's permissions in a SharePoint site   39
  Applying unique permissions to a SharePoint list   41

Chapter 2: Working Together—Using SharePoint to Collaborate   47
  Introduction   48
  Creating a Team Site   48
  Adding users to a Team Site   51
  Adding a new page to a Team Site   55
  Adding a link to the Top link bar of a Team Site   57
  Adding a slide library to share PowerPoint slides   60
  Adding a slide to a presentation from a SharePoint slide library   64
  Creating and tracking a discussion item   66
  Managing a Team Site Calendar with Outlook 2010   70

Creating a task and assigning it to another user   73
Using the datasheet to bulk-edit tasks in a task list   77
Managing a SharePoint task list in Outlook 2010   80
Creating a SharePoint contact list and connecting it to Outlook 2010 84

Chapter 3: SharePoint as the Data Hub—Storing and Integrating Data   **89**
Introduction   89
Creating a custom list   90
Creating a custom list view   97
Creating a term set using the managed metadata service   103
Creating a list column based on a term set   106
Creating an external content type   110
Creating an external list   117

Chapter 4: SharePoint Document Management Deep Dive   **123**
Introduction   124
Uploading an existing document to a document library   124
Uploading multiple documents to a document library   126
Creating a new document in your My Site   130
E-mailing a link to a document in SharePoint   132
Downloading a copy of a document   134
Creating an alert on a document to be notified when it is updated   135
Requiring users to check out a document before they can edit it   137
Enabling versioning on a document library   139
Publishing a major version of a document   141
Restoring a previous version of a document   143
Enabling content approval on a document library   146
Take SharePoint documents offline using Outlook 2010   150
Co-authoring an important document   152
Use content types to store different types of document in the same document library   155

Chapter 5: Getting the Message Out—Using SharePoint to Communicate   **161**
Introduction   162
Adding an announcement to a Team Site   162
Creating a blog in my My Site   165
Posting to my blog from Microsoft Word 2010   167
Creating a new page on a publishing site   171
Changing the page layout of a publishing site page   175
Publishing a publishing site page   177
Using web analytics to see which are the most popular pages on your site   182

Chapter 6: Where's My Stuff?—Finding Things with SharePoint — 185
Introduction — 185
Performing a basic search — 186
Performing an advanced search — 190
Finding experts using a people search — 192
Saving a search as an alert and being notified when the results change — 193
Using search analytics to see what people are searching for — 195

Chapter 7: Gaining Insights—Using SharePoint for Business Intelligence — 199
Introduction — 199
Creating a chart using the Chart Web Part — 200
Creating a Key Performance Indicator (KPI) — 206
Creating an Excel spreadsheet to run on the server — 212
Creating a report using Report Builder — 217
Creating a chart using the PerformancePoint Dashboard Designer — 224
Building a PerformancePoint business intelligence dashboard — 230

Chapter 8: Automating Business Processes—Recipes for Electronic Forms and Workflows — 237
Introduction — 237
Creating an InfoPath Form for a SharePoint List — 238
Creating a holiday request InfoPath form and publishing it to a form library — 246
Using the Collect Feedback workflow to receive feedback on a Microsoft Word 2010 document — 259
Creating a list workflow using SharePoint Designer 2010 — 267
Using Microsoft Visio 2010 to model a SharePoint workflow — 277

Appendix: Joining the Dots—Creating Composite Applications — 283
Introduction — 283
Understanding composite applications — 284
How to design and build composite applications — 285
Project Management composite application — 287
CRM composite application — 296
Human Resources composite application — 306
Closing thoughts — 322

Index — 323

Preface

This book is for people who want to "*get things done*" in Microsoft SharePoint Server 2010. You won't find a long and detailed history of the SharePoint product or a comprehensive explanation of every SharePoint feature. Rather, this book is a collection of recipes designed to quickly show you how to achieve common SharePoint tasks. Each recipe has a set of easy-to-follow instructions that first show you "how to do it", followed by an explanation of "why it works".

This is not a "*tell me everything about SharePoint*" book. You can read that for free on the Microsoft websites. Much like driving a car, you don't need to know how the engine works to be able to take the kids to school. This book is not "*SharePoint explained*"; rather this book is "*SharePoint applied*".

Taken individually, each recipe will make you more productive when using SharePoint 2010. The recipes are intended to be read "stand-alone". Feel free to dip in and out of the book as and when you need to know how to perform a particular task.

However, if you read this book as a whole, the simple, intermediate, and advanced recipes that it contains will walk you through a range of collaboration, data integration, business intelligence, electronic form, and workflow scenarios. The recipes will build your SharePoint knowledge to a point where you can "*think SharePoint*", applying the skills you have learnt to solve complex business problems. At the end of the book, I present three "no code" SharePoint applications that show you how to approach this.

This book is written from the perspective of the end user, not the SharePoint product. In creating its recipes, I haven't restricted them along product boundaries. Along with the standard SharePoint recipes that you would expect, you will also find recipes that show you how to use SharePoint Designer and InfoPath Forms Designer when they are needed to get the job done. You will also find a number of recipes that focus on integrating SharePoint 2010 with Office 2010. Some authors would have you buy several books to cover all these topics; I ask you to buy only one.

If you want to be more productive with SharePoint, then this book is for you.

What this book covers

This book is presented in eight chapters and an appendix covering the following areas:

Chapter 1: Getting Started—SharePoint Essential focuses on SharePoint 2010 fundamentals, including creating and using your My Site, tracking colleagues, bookmarking sites, registering for alerts, and using themes to change how SharePoint looks and feels. Recipes are provided that show you how to create columns, lists, content types, and how to secure information on a SharePoint 2010 site.

Chapter 2: Working Together—Using SharePoint to Collaborate explores the tools that allow you to use SharePoint 2010 to work more effectively. It shows you how to create a Team Site and add users to it. You will learn how to create a shared calendar for important events and a shared task list to keep track of your team's tasks. You will see how to manage the calendar and tasks using Outlook 2010. You will learn how to use the site to gather feedback using a discussion forum and how to share PowerPoint slides using a slide library.

Chapter 3: SharePoint as the Data Hub—Storing and Integrating Data is all about storing and integrating data in SharePoint 2010. It covers storing data directly in SharePoint, using custom lists, and so on. It shows you how to include data from an external database using external content types and how to include common terms in the managed metadata store. Important list concepts are covered including creating list views and columns based on metadata.

Chapter 4: SharePoint Document Management Deep Dive explores document management in SharePoint 2010. You will learn how to upload and download documents and use the document management features such as versioning, "check in/check-out", publishing, and content approval. You will see how to take your documents offline using Outlook 2010. You will see how to use content types to store different types of documents in the same document library. You will learn how the new co-authoring features allow multiple authors to work on the same document at the same time.

Chapter 5: Getting the Message Out—Using SharePoint to Communicate focuses on SharePoint 2010's communication features. It explains how to create a blog on your My Site and how to post to that blog from Word 2010. It shows how to create and publish web pages in a publishing site, how to use announcements to communicate important news, and how to use audiences to target your messages to the right people.

Chapter 6: Where's My Stuff?—Finding Things with SharePoint is all about using SharePoint's search facility. It shows how to use basic and advanced searches to find documents, information, and people. It shows how to save your searches as alerts so that you will automatically be notified if the results change.

Chapter 7: *Gaining Insights—Using SharePoint for Business Intelligence* explains the business intelligence capabilities of SharePoint 2010. It shows you how to create master/detail views of SharePoint data and how to create Key Performance Indicators. The creation of charts is illustrated using the built-in Chart Web Part and the PerformancePoint Dashboard Designer. Reports are created using the Report Builder tool, and Excel Services is used to run spreadsheets directly on the SharePoint server.

Chapter 8: *Automating Business Processes—Recipes for Electronic Forms and Workflows* examines SharePoint's electronic forms and workflow capabilities. Recipes are included that provide a deep dive into InfoPath 2010 and the electronic forms technology included in SharePoint Server. You will learn how to use the Collect Feedback workflow to receive feedback on a document that you have authored. You will see how to create custom workflows using Microsoft Visio 2010 and SharePoint Designer 2010. You will learn how to view a workflow's current execution status, its execution history, and how to start SharePoint 2010 workflows directly from inside a Word 2010 document.

Appendix: *Joining the Dots—Creating Composite Applications* draws together all the recipes presented early in the book to create three "no code" SharePoint 2010 applications. These simple Human Resources, Customer Relationship Management, and Project Management solutions build upon and reinforce the concepts presented earlier in the book. The purpose of this chapter is to teach you how to "*think SharePoint*", applying the knowledge and tools you have gained to solve real business problems in the future.

What you need for this book

To follow all the recipes in this book, you will need the following software:

- SharePoint 2010 Enterprise Edition
- Outlook 2010
- SharePoint Designer 2010
- InfoPath Forms Designer 2010
- Word 2010
- Excel 2010
- Visio Premium 2010
- Internet Explorer 7 or higher

You will need to have access to a "My Site" and will need various SharePoint 2010 permission levels from Reader up to Site Administrator. If you have another version of SharePoint 2010 (Foundation, Standard) or lower access permissions you will still find many of the recipes in the book useful. Details of the software and permissions levels that you require and the SharePoint versions that it will work with are included in each recipe.

SharePoint 2010 is both an application and a development platform. It allows for extensive post-installation customization and development. The recipes in this book have been tested and verified on a vanilla SharePoint 2010 Enterprise Edition installation. It is possible that your installation may look or behave differently depending on the amount of customization that has been applied.

If you don't have access to SharePoint 2010 Enterprise Edition but would like to try all the recipes in this book, Microsoft has a 180-days' evaluation version that you can download and install. However, SharePoint is a heavyweight server product, so make sure your machine can meet the hardware prerequisites before you do. Find the evaluation download at `http://technet.microsoft.com/en-us/evalcenter/ee388573.aspx`.

During the production of this book, Microsoft released Office 365, including the latest version of their SharePoint Online offering. All the recipes in this book have been tested against the Office 365 E4 service plan.

SharePoint Designer is a free download located at `http://www.microsoft.com/downloads/en/details.aspx?FamilyID=d88a1505-849b-4587-b854-a7054ee28d66`.

Who this book is for

This book is for people who want to "*get things done*" in SharePoint 2010. It doesn't matter if you consider yourself a SharePoint user, project manager, business analyst, trainer, administrator, or developer; if you need to work with SharePoint 2010, then this book is for you.

Unfortunately, many SharePoint "experts" never take the time to learn SharePoint 2010 as the user sees it. They simply fail to understand what the product can do, and end up either constantly selling their customers short or reinventing the wheel.

Conventions

In this book, you will find a number of styles of text that distinguish between different kinds of information. Here are some examples of these styles, and an explanation of their meaning.

New terms and **important words** are shown in bold. Words that you see on the screen, in menus, or dialog boxes for example, appear in the text like this: "Open the **Site Actions** menu and select the **More Options** menu option".

 Warnings or important notes appear in a box like this.

Tips and tricks appear like this.

Reader feedback

Feedback from our readers is always welcome. Let us know what you think about this book—what you liked or may have disliked. Reader feedback is important for us to develop titles that you really get the most out of.

To send us general feedback, simply send an e-mail to feedback@packtpub.com, and mention the book title via the subject of your message.

If there is a book that you need and would like to see us publish, please send us a note in the **SUGGEST A TITLE** form on www.packtpub.com or e-mail suggest@packtpub.com.

If there is a topic that you have expertise in and you are interested in either writing or contributing to a book, see our author guide on www.packtpub.com/authors.

Customer support

Now that you are the proud owner of a Packt book, we have a number of things to help you to get the most from your purchase.

Downloading the example code

You can download the example code files for all Packt books you have purchased from your account at http://www.PacktPub.com. If you purchased this book elsewhere, you can visit http://www.PacktPub.com/support and register to have the files e-mailed directly to you.

Errata

Although we have taken every care to ensure the accuracy of our content, mistakes do happen. If you find a mistake in one of our books—maybe a mistake in the text or the code—we would be grateful if you would report this to us. By doing so, you can save other readers from frustration and help us improve subsequent versions of this book. If you find any errata, please report them by visiting http://www.packtpub.com/support, selecting your book, clicking on the **errata submission form** link, and entering the details of your errata. Once your errata are verified, your submission will be accepted and the errata will be uploaded on our website, or added to any list of existing errata, under the Errata section of that title. Any existing errata can be viewed by selecting your title from http://www.packtpub.com/support.

Piracy

Piracy of copyright material on the Internet is an ongoing problem across all media. At Packt, we take the protection of our copyright and licenses very seriously. If you come across any illegal copies of our works, in any form, on the Internet, please provide us with the location address or website name immediately so that we can pursue a remedy.

Please contact us at `copyright@packtpub.com` with a link to the suspected pirated material.

We appreciate your help in protecting our authors, and our ability to bring you valuable content.

Questions

You can contact us at `questions@packtpub.com` if you are having a problem with any aspect of the book, and we will do our best to address it.

1
Getting Started—
SharePoint Essentials

In this chapter, we will cover:

- ▶ Creating a SharePoint list
- ▶ Creating a site column
- ▶ Creating a content type
- ▶ Creating and accessing my My Site
- ▶ Updating my user profile
- ▶ Tracking colleagues using my My Site
- ▶ Viewing the SharePoint sites I am a member of
- ▶ Tagging a SharePoint page so I can find it again later
- ▶ Reviewing the tags and notes other users have posted on a SharePoint page
- ▶ Adding an alert to a SharePoint page
- ▶ Managing my alerts in SharePoint
- ▶ Determining my permissions in a SharePoint site
- ▶ Checking another user's permissions in a SharePoint site
- ▶ Applying unique permissions to a SharePoint list

Introduction

The recipes in this chapter cover SharePoint fundamentals essential for every SharePoint user.

The first three recipes of this chapter will introduce you to some of the fundamental building blocks of SharePoint: **lists**, **site columns**, and **content types**. Pay particular attention to content types. As your knowledge of SharePoint grows, you will come to realize that these are key to unlocking all the magic that SharePoint has to offer.

SharePoint 2010 Server provides the ability to give each user his/her own individual **My Site**. This site contains a wealth of tools for sharing information, tagging content, and tracking other users. Think of your My Site as the hub of your workings within SharePoint, it is your LinkedIn or Facebook site in the enterprise. The next six recipes in this chapter will show you how use your My Site effectively.

SharePoint makes it very easy to create websites where you can collaborate and share information. But keeping track of changes across hundreds of sites can be a challenge. Thankfully SharePoint allows you to register for **alerts** so that you can be notified when there is something new or updated that you should look at. Recipes are included that show you how to create new alerts and how to manage the alerts you already have.

The final three recipes tackle SharePoint 2010 security, introducing **permissions**, **permission levels**, and the **security trimmed user interface** from a practical business perspective.

We will learn how to create more building blocks, such as **sites** and **document libraries**, in later chapters. But enough of the introductory waffle. Let's get started!

Creating a SharePoint list

SharePoint is built around lists. If you want to store things in SharePoint, then you will need to know how to create the different types of list. This recipe shows you how.

Getting ready

This recipe works for:

- ► SharePoint 2010 Foundation
- ► SharePoint 2010 Standard Edition
- ► SharePoint 2010 Enterprise Edition
- ► SharePoint 2010 Online (Office 365 Edition)

You require either the **Design** or the **Full Control** permission level to create a new SharePoint list.

The choice of lists that you have available is determined by the SharePoint version you have. SharePoint 2010 Standard and Enterprise editions add more lists to those already available in SharePoint 2010 Foundation.

How to do it...

1. Open the **Site Actions** menu and select the **More Options** menu option.

2. SharePoint will now show all the different types of content you can create. Filter your view by clicking on **List** on the left side of the window.

3. Choose the type of list that you want to create. Enter the name of the list and then click on the **Create** button.

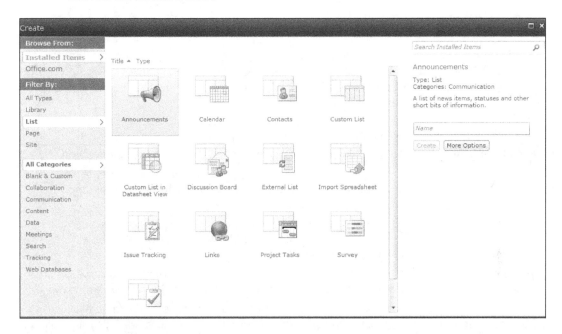

4. The new list will be created and displayed. You can now add items to your list, continue to customize it, or connect it to your office applications as you wish.

How it works...

SharePoint stores information in lists, in fact almost everything in SharePoint is stored in lists. Document libraries (for storing documents), media libraries (for audio and video files), and form libraries (for storing InfoPath forms) are all just special types of lists. Lists are a fundamental building block in SharePoint.

This recipe shows you how to create a list. You need to tell SharePoint the template (meaning the type of list) that you want to create and provide some basic properties (such as the name of the list). SharePoint will then do the rest, adding the columns, views, and configuring the list as required.

Once your list has been created, you can start adding data or customize it further. There are many options and variations for doing this, which are covered in later recipes throughout this book.

There are many different list templates available. Each template provides different columns, views, and other functionality designed to support its particular function. I have listed some of the common ones in the next section.

There's more...

SharePoint Foundation provides a core set of list templates, and the Standard and Enterprise versions of SharePoint add a whole lot more. The choice of lists that you will be able to create depends on which site you are in and which features have been activated. However, some of the more commonly encountered lists are as follows:

List	Description
Announcements	A list of news items, statuses, and other short bits of information.
Calendar	A calendar of upcoming meetings, deadlines, or other events. Calendar information can be synchronized with Microsoft Outlook or other compatible programs.
Contacts	A list of people your team works with, like customers or partners. Contacts lists can synchronize with Microsoft Outlook or other compatible programs.
Custom List	A blank list to which you can add your own columns and views. Use this if none of the built-in list types are similar to the list you want to make.
Custom List in Datasheet View	A blank list which is displayed as a spreadsheet in order to allow easy data entry. You can add your own columns and views. This list requires a compatible datasheet ActiveX control such as the one provided in Microsoft Office.
Discussion Board	A place to have newsgroup-style discussions. Discussion boards make it easy to manage discussion threads and can be configured to require approval for all posts.
External List	An external list to view the data in an External Content Type.
Import Spreadsheet	A list which duplicates the columns and data of an existing Spreadsheet. Importing a spreadsheet requires Microsoft Excel or another compatible program.
Issue Tracking	A list of issues or problems associated with a project or item. You can assign, prioritize, and track the status of issues.

List	Description
Links	A list of web pages or other resources.
Project Tasks	A place for team or personal tasks. Project tasks lists provide a Gantt Chart view and can be opened by Microsoft Project or other compatible programs.
Survey	A list of questions that you would like to have people answer. Surveys allow you to quickly create questions and view graphical summaries of the responses.
Tasks	A place for team or personal tasks.

You can use this recipe to experiment with the different types of lists that you can create and get to know their functionality.

"Roll your own"—creating custom lists

If none of the SharePoint lists described earlier meets your needs, you are more than welcome to create your own. SharePoint gives you the custom list template as a basic starting point. Once you have created a custom list, you can add whatever columns, views, and custom settings you need to achieve the purpose that you have in mind. Refer to *Creating a custom list* in *Chapter 3* for more details.

Lists to show external data

Before SharePoint 2010, SharePoint lists were limited to just displaying and updating data found within SharePoint. However, SharePoint 2010 introduced the concept of **External Lists**. SharePoint 2010 can now take data from an external source (such as database) and show it to users as a SharePoint list. The users can edit that information and the update will get written back to the database, all without a single line of code or a developer in site. The recipe *Creating an external list* in *Chapter 3* shows you how to do so.

How much data can your store in a list

One of the problems with earlier versions of SharePoint was that it was easy to store too much data in a list, making the whole thing slow down. In IT speak, SharePoint lists "didn't scale well". Thankfully, SharePoint 2010 has resolved those issues and you can now store far more information in a SharePoint list than you ever really should.

The magic numbers for reference are:

- ▶ Up to 30,000,000 items in a list (or documents in a document library)
- ▶ Up to 400,000 major versions of a document
- ▶ Up to 1,000 different security scopes (custom permissions)
- ▶ 8K bytes per list item (7,744 bytes reserved for custom columns)

The number of columns that you can add to a list depends on the type of columns that you add, as different columns take up different amounts of space. Column widths range from 4 to 40 bytes, and there are rules about how many of the same kind of columns you can add to a list. You can find a full list of these rules at `http://technet.microsoft.com/en-us/library/cc262787.aspx#Column`.

For all practical scenarios, if your SharePoint list usage is anywhere approaching these limits, then you are probably doing something wrong and I suggest you give a good SharePoint architect a call for help!

See also

▸ *Adding a slide library to share PowerPoint slides, Chapter 2*

▸ *Creating a SharePoint contact list and connecting it to Outlook 2010, Chapter 2*

▸ *Creating a custom list, Chapter 3*

▸ *Creating an external list, Chapter 3*

Creating a site column

We can add custom columns to our SharePoint lists. However, having to recreate the same column over and over again quickly becomes a pain. Site columns, which are shared between all the sites in your site collection, are the answer.

Getting ready

This recipe works for:

▸ SharePoint 2010 Foundation

▸ SharePoint 2010 Standard Edition

▸ SharePoint 2010 Enterprise Edition

▸ SharePoint 2010 Online (Office 365 Edition)

You require either the **Design** or **Full Control** permission level to create a site column.

How to do it...

1. In the top-level site of your site collection, open the **Site Actions** menu and select the **Site Settings** option.
2. From the **Site Settings** page, select the **Site Columns** link from the **Galleries** heading.
3. The **Site Columns** page is displayed. Existing site columns are listed on this page. To create a new site column, click on the **Create** link at the top of the page.

4. Enter a name for your site column, select its data type, and click on **OK**.

5. Your new column is created and added to the list of site columns.

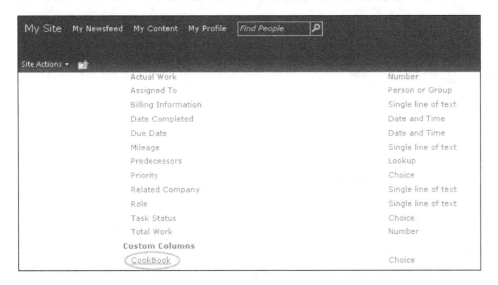

How it works...

SharePoint lists are made up of different columns. These columns can be defined locally (on each list as they are needed) or as site columns, which can be shared by lists throughout the site collection.

If you think that you will need a column more than once, then you should once consider creating it as a site column rather than just adding it to your list directly.

Site columns are particularly useful for columns that contain lookup data or a set of choices (for example, your company's departments or its locations). Using site columns helps you get more consistency in the information that you store within SharePoint.

Site columns are a necessary first step to creating content types, as described in the next recipe.

See also

▸ *Creating a content type*

▸ *Creating a list column based on a term set, Chapter 3*

▸ *Creating an external content type, Chapter 3*

Creating a content type

This recipe shows you how to create a content type. Content types are a powerful way to model real world objects in SharePoint.

Getting ready

This recipe works for:

- ► SharePoint 2010 Foundation
- ► SharePoint 2010 Standard Edition
- ► SharePoint 2010 Enterprise Edition
- ► SharePoint 2010 Online (Office 365 Edition)

You require either the **Design** or **Full Control** permission level to create a content type.

You will need one or more site columns to add to your content type as you create it. If you need instructions on how to create a site column, then please refer to *Creating a site column* recipe.

How to do it...

1. In the top-level site of your site collection, open the **Site Actions** menu and select the **Site Settings** option.

2. From the **Site Settings** page, select **Site content types** link from the **Galleries** heading.

3. The **Site Content Types** page is displayed. To create a new content type, click on the **Create** link.

4. Give the content type a **Name**, **Description**, and **Parent Content Type** (to inherit from). You can add the content type to an existing group or create a new group for this content type as you wish.

5. Click on the **OK** button to create the content type.

Name:

Description:

Parent Content Type:

Select parent content type from:

Document Content Types ▼

Parent Content Type:

Basic Page ▼

Description:
Create a new basic page.

Put this site content type into:

◉ Existing group:

Custom Content Types ▼

○ New group:

6. Your new content type will be created and displayed in the list of available content types.

How it works...

SharePoint lists and libraries have a fairly major shortcoming: every item must have the same columns applied. Imagine a real-world scenario, such as the account department of your organization. They might want to store many different types of documents, such as invoices, purchase orders, bills received, credit notes, and so on. The different documents need different columns (or **metadata**) associated with them. For an invoice, customer amount and due date might be important. A purchase order might record a purchase order number, supplier name, expected delivery date, and payment terms. How can we store all these different types of documents in the same document library? Content types are the answer.

Content types allow us to define the document template and metadata columns for a particular type of document. In our accounts department scenario, we would create a content type for "invoice" and another content type (with different columns and template) for "purchase order". Once we have created the content types, we could add them to our accounts department document library. Now rather than creating a new document, SharePoint will provide us with the ability to create a new invoice or new purchase order in the library. The recipe *Using content types to store different types of documents in the same document library* in *Chapter 4* describes how to do this.

Content types are built up in a hierarchy. The content types you create must extend either a built-in type (such as document) or a custom type that you have previously created.

Content types can be defined centrally and shared throughout all the SharePoint sites within the organization. They can have "business rules" information management policies and workflows attached. Wherever the content type is used, a consistent template, metadata, and rules can be applied.

Content types can be used to bring order to the "information chaos" that most organizations experience. Defining and sharing content types for real-world business objects is the key to unlocking all the power of SharePoint. Use them!

See also

> ▸ *Creating a site column*

> ▸ *Using content types to store different types of documents in the same document library, Chapter 4*

> ▸ *Creating an external content type, Chapter 3*

Creating and accessing my My Site

This recipe shows you how to access your My Site. The content of your My Site is created the first time you access it.

Getting ready

This recipe works for:

> ▸ SharePoint 2010 Standard Edition

> ▸ SharePoint 2010 Enterprise Edition

> ▸ SharePoint 2010 Online (Office 365 Edition)

My Sites must be configured and active in the SharePoint installation. You can run this recipe from any SharePoint 2010 site that you have access to.

How to do it...

1. From within any SharePoint site. Click on your name (top right of the page). Select the **My Site** link from the menu that is displayed.

2. You are presented with the generic **My Newsfeed**. Once you have created your My Site and started tracking colleagues, this is the page where you will see their updates.

3. To actually create your own individual My Site (or access it again if you created it earlier), click on the **My Content** link at the top of the page.

 There may be a short delay while your My Site is created.

4. Your My Site is created and the **My Content** page is displayed.

How it works...

Your My Site is a special SharePoint site designed especially for you. It is the site where you can store private documents, videos, and other SharePoint content, or where you add content that you want to share with others. You can use your My Site to access and update your **User Profile** (information about yourself), track your colleagues, reference the information that you have tagged on other SharePoint sites, and so on. Think of your My Site as your LinkedIn or Facebook site in the enterprise. Your My Site is the hub of your interaction with the many SharePoint 2010 sites that you will eventually be granted access to. It is also the site where you are likely to have the highest permission levels, so it makes it a great place to try out the other recipes presented in this book.

 Some organizations shy away from implementing My Sites because they worry that the functionality might be abused by their staff. To my mind, this is a bit like owning a Ferrari and then leaving it parked in the garage. My Sites are central to SharePoint 2010's communities and collaboration functionality—I strongly recommend that you make use of them.

There's more...

If you know the URL where the My Sites have been created in your SharePoint installation, then you can access your My Site directly without needing to first visit another SharePoint site. The address might be something similar to `http://my.sp2010cookbook/default.aspx`. Access your My Site using this recipe and then have a look at the address displayed in your web browser to see what format has been used in your system.

See also

- ▶ *Updating my user profile*
- ▶ *Tracking colleagues using my My Site*
- ▶ *Viewing the SharePoint sites I am a member of*
- ▶ *Tagging a SharePoint page so I can find it again later*
- ▶ *Creating a blog in my My Site, Chapter 5*

Updating my user profile

This recipe shows you how to update your user profile using your My Site.

Getting ready

This recipe works for:

- SharePoint 2010 Standard Edition
- SharePoint 2010 Enterprise Edition
- SharePoint 2010 Online (Office 365 Edition)

My Sites must be configured and active in your SharePoint installation.

How to do it...

1. Open your My Site (refer to *Creating and accessing my My Site* recipe for instructions).
2. Select the **My Profile** link.
3. Select the **Edit My Profile** link.

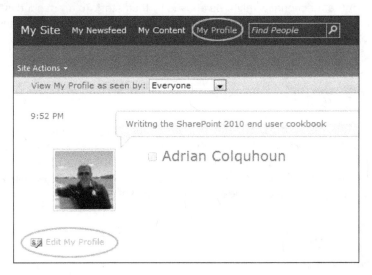

4. Make the changes you require in your profile.
5. Click on the **Save & Close** button to save your changes.

How it works...

SharePoint 2010 stores information about users in their user profiles. It uses this information in news feeds, people searches, and audiences (to target information to particular groups of SharePoint users).

Your user profile is shown in your My Site. This is the place where you can view your profile as others would see it and make changes to the values stored in your user profile properties.

Depending on how your administrator has configured SharePoint, you won't be able to change all the properties that you see. Some information will be read only and may show information that has been imported from other external systems, such as your organization's Active Directory (where organizations commonly store user information). The properties you can see and change will have been preconfigured by your administrator and you may have different properties depending on your role in the organization (SharePoint allows administrators to create different "types" of profiles).

There's more...

One of the first things that you should do after you have created your My Site is to complete your user profile. This will allow co-workers to locate your skills, connect to you, and start to call on your (I have no doubt undervalued) experience. As soon as your profile is complete, you will start showing up in SharePoint's people search.

Who knows, you may get invited to work on the exciting new "Project X" or requested to meet a client or attend a conference in some beautiful exotic location. Keep your profile up-to-date if you want to maximize your opportunities.

 Resist the temptation to upload inappropriate pictures or comments in your profile. Your colleagues (particularly your superiors) are unlikely to see the funny side. Remember that SharePoint is a set of tools to help you *work* better together. Save all the other stuff for your Facebook site.

See also

- *Creating and accessing my My Site*
- *Reviewing the tags and notes other users have posted on a SharePoint page*
- *Tagging a SharePoint page so I can find it again later*
- *Viewing the SharePoint sites I am a member of*
- *Tracking colleagues using my My Site*
- *Creating a new document in your My Site, Chapter 4*
- *Finding experts using a people search, Chapter 6*

Tracking colleagues using my My Site

Before SharePoint, knowing who was doing what in an organization was really difficult. Now SharePoint can keep track of your colleagues automatically. This recipe shows you how.

Getting ready

This recipe requires your My Site. The recipe works for:

- ▸ SharePoint 2010 Standard Edition
- ▸ SharePoint 2010 Enterprise Edition
- ▸ SharePoint 2010 Online (Office 365 Edition)

My Site must be configured and active in the SharePoint installation.

How to do it...

1. Open your My Site and navigate to the **My Profile** page.
2. Select the **Colleagues** tab.
3. Click on the **Add Colleagues** link.

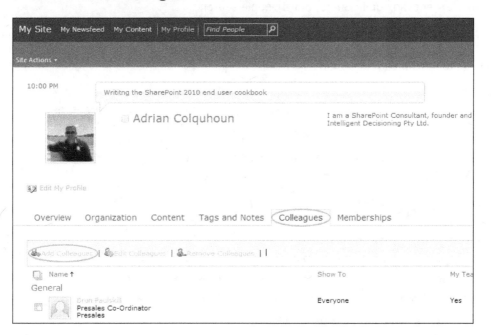

4. In the dialog displayed, enter the names of the colleagues you wish to add. You can choose if you want to add them to **My Team** and organize them into different groups. Adding colleagues to your team allows them to see more information from your user profile.

5. When you have added all the colleagues that you need, click on the **OK** button.

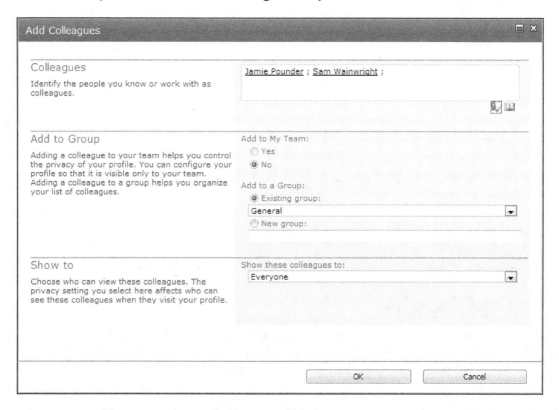

6. Your new colleague is now shown on your **Colleagues** tab and you can view their My Site by clicking on their name.

How it works...

SharePoint 2010 allows you to track your team members, colleagues, and subject matter experts through your My Site. When you add a colleague, you can add them to different groups such as **My Team**. Adding colleagues to your team will allow them to access more information from your user profile.

Once you have added a colleague, SharePoint will automatically keep you up-to-date with their activity. This includes the changes that they make to their user profiles, the content that they author, the pages that they tag, and their status message updates. All this information will be displayed on your **My Newsfeed** page when you again access your My Site. SharePoint will also send you e-mails to tell you about important changes and will even suggest colleagues to you based on its analysis of the colleagues you already have, and the people that they have added to their networks.

By tracking colleagues in this way, SharePoint helps you build up strong and effective networks within your organization. You can then leverage these networks to get your work done more effectively.

The track colleagues functionality wasn't invented by Microsoft to help you stalk "that pretty little thing from accounts". Using it for that purpose will almost certainly land you in a lot of trouble. Don't do it!

See also

▸ *Creating and accessing my My Site*

▸ *Updating my user profile*

▸ *Viewing the SharePoint sites I am a member of*

▸ *Tagging a SharePoint page so I can find it again later*

▸ *Creating a blog in my My Site, Chapter 5*

Viewing the SharePoint sites I am a member of

As the number of SharePoint sites grow, it can be easy to lose track of them. Fortunately, SharePoint keeps tracks of the sites, which you are a member of, automatically. This recipe shows you how to see that list of sites.

Getting ready

This recipe requires your My Site. The recipe works for:

▸ SharePoint 2010 Standard Edition

▸ SharePoint 2010 Enterprise Edition

▸ SharePoint 2010 Online (Office 365 Edition)

My Site must be configured and active in the SharePoint installation.

How to do it...

1. Go to your My Site.

2. Select **My Profile** and then click on the **My Memberships** tab. A link to each site that you have been added to as a member is displayed.

3. You can click on any link to navigate to that site.

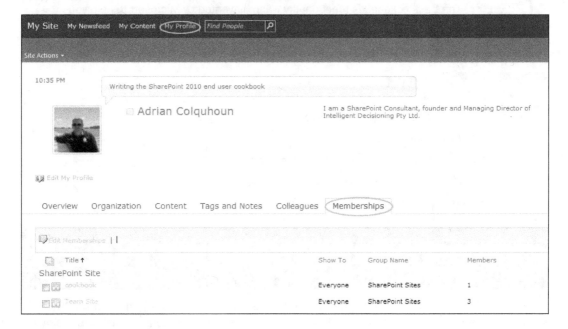

How it works...

SharePoint 2010 automatically keeps track of the all the sites that you have been explicitly added to as a member (such as the sites that you can contribute to) and gives you a link to them on your membership tab in your My Site. You can use your My Site as your personal navigation hub. From any SharePoint sites, jump into your My Site, check your memberships, and jump back out to where you want to go. You need never be lost in SharePoint again!

Importantly, the memberships tab doesn't show the sites that you only have a read-only access to. If you want to save links to these sites, then tag them as described in the *Tagging a SharePoint page so I can find it again later* recipe. Confusingly, it also doesn't show the sites that you have or the ones which you have full control of. To see those sites, add yourself to the member group of the site.

SharePoint recalculates your memberships using a background timer job, so expect a delay between being added to the site and it showing up in your memberships tab.

See also

▸ *Creating and accessing my My Site*

▸ *Updating my user profile*

▸ *Tracking colleagues using my My Site*

> ▸ *Tagging a SharePoint page so I can find it again later*

> ▸ *Creating a blog in my My Site, Chapter 5*

Tagging a SharePoint page so I can find it again later

This recipe shows you how to use SharePoint 2010's tags to bookmark information that you want to find again later.

Getting ready

This recipe works for:

> ▸ SharePoint 2010 Standard Edition

> ▸ SharePoint 2010 Enterprise Edition

> ▸ SharePoint 2010 Online (Office 365 Edition)

It requires you to be logged in and have read access but no other privileges are necessary.

You will need a My Site to be able to review and make use of the tags that you have created.

How to do it...

1. Navigate to the page you wish to tag.

2. Click on the **Tags and Notes** icon on the top-right of the screen.

3. Enter the text for the tag you wish to apply into the dialog box. If you don't want anyone to know you added the tag, then check on the **Private** checkbox (other users will still see the tag's text).

4. Click on the **Save** button.

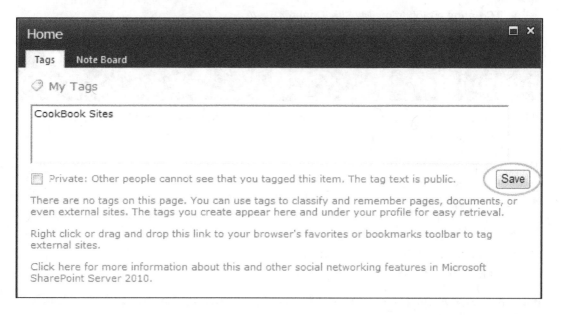

5. Navigate back to your My Site. Select the **My Profile** page and click on the **Tags and Notes** tab; your new tag will be displayed under **Activities for** heading.

6. You can filter the activity view to a particular tag by clicking on it under the **Refine by tag** heading.

How it works...

SharePoint 2010 allows you to apply keyword tags to the information that you find. Once you tag an item, you will be able to find it gain from your My Site (just click on the tag).

Good tags to use might be the name of a project (for example, "Project X"), a department, or a technical term. By allowing users to tag content, the information in SharePoint is progressively classified and refined.

As you tag, SharePoint learns. It adds the tags you create into its own keyword set. As you type a tag, SharePoint will suggest tags based on the ones it already knows about. In this way SharePoint helps to build up a consistent tagging system through the enterprise.

The data tagged in SharePoint represents a powerful information set. SharePoint makes use of this everywhere, but particularly in its search results. When you search for "Project X", the pages that were tagged should appear higher than those that were not. Tags are like signposts, pointing users to relevant information. Tags can be used to refine your searches, getting you to the information that you really need with just a few clicks.

So tags don't just help you find information again, they help your colleagues find it too. So go on—get tagging!

There's more...

If you want to quickly tag pages that you approve of, SharePoint gives you a pre-created tag—"**I Like It**". Simply click on the **I Like It** icon on the top right side of the page and you are done.

See also

- ▶ _Creating and accessing my My Site_
- ▶ _Performing a basic search, Chapter 6_
- ▶ _Reviewing the tags and notes other users have posted on a SharePoint page_

Reviewing the tags and notes other users have posted on a SharePoint page

Tags and notes bring SharePoint pages to life. You can start to access the collective intelligence and opinions of your co-workers by reviewing the tags and notes they leave for you.

Getting ready

This recipe works for:

▶ SharePoint 2010 Standard Edition

▶ SharePoint 2010 Enterprise Edition

▶ SharePoint 2010 Online (Office 365 Edition)

It requires you to be logged in and have read access but no other privileges are necessary.

How to do it...

1. If there are tags or notes on a page, the **Tags and Notes** icon on the top right-hand corner of the page turns red. To review the information, click on the icon.

2. The **Tags** and **NoteBoard** dialog is displayed. You can review the tags that other users have left on the page.

3. To switch to the notes view, click on the **Note Board**.

How it works...

Tags help you find pages again or classify the information that they contain. Notes are public comments that you leave on the pages for others to see. Use notes to add to the content, to correct any obvious mistakes, or explain information that is unclear. Don't use notes for observations such as "*the author of this page is obviously a blithering idiot*" unless you are confident that you can defend your viewpoint to the Managing Director without getting fired.

See also

  ▶ *Creating and accessing my My Site*

  ▶ *Tagging a SharePoint page so I can find it again later*

  ▶ *Performing a basic search, Chapter 6*

Adding an alert to a SharePoint page

SharePoint is a great place for people to share useful information. However, no doubt you are far too busy to keep checking your SharePoint sites on the off chance that someone posted something new. Alerts allow SharePoint to e-mail you when something interesting happens. This recipe shows you how to create them.

Getting ready

This recipe works for:

▸ SharePoint 2010 Foundation

▸ SharePoint 2010 Standard Edition

▸ SharePoint 2010 Enterprise Edition

▸ SharePoint 2010 Online (Office 365 Edition)

It requires you to be logged in and have read access but no other privileges are necessary.

To create an alert, your SharePoint administrator will need to have configured your SharePoint server to send e-mail (or SMS messages). The **Alert Me** icon will not be displayed if the e-mail function is not enabled.

How to do it...

1. Navigate to the page you wish to set an alert for. Select the **Page** tab from the ribbon and click on the **Alert Me** icon.

2. From the drop-down list, click on **Set an alert on this page**.

3. In the **New Alert** dialog box, enter an alert title, what you would like to be notified of, and the delivery method. You can also select what will trigger the alert.

4. Once finished click on **OK** and your new alert will be saved.

 If you are logged into the site as an administrator, then you will be able to set alerts for other users. Otherwise you will only be able to set your own alerts.

How it works...

Think of SharePoint as a machine. There are lots of processes continually running in SharePoint that are just waiting to do useful work for you. One of these processes is SharePoint's alert system. It can send you e-mails when something changes in a SharePoint site. All you need to do is tell it what you want to know and how often you want to be told. The SharePoint alert system will do the rest.

You can register for alerts on all sorts of different SharePoint objects, such as sites, pages, documents libraries, shared calendars, blogs, and documents. Just select the object you are interested in and check the ribbon. If you see the **Alert Me** icon, then you will be able to set an alert. Alerts can be sent instantly or rolled up into daily or weekly summaries of changes. You can even opt to receive your alerts as an SMS too, assuming that your SharePoint administrators have configured this service.

There's more...

Users new to SharePoint often go "wow!" when they discover alerts. Pretty soon they are setting up alerts anywhere and everywhere. Then the e-mails start coming from SharePoint. On a busy SharePoint site, perhaps, tens or hundreds of alert e-mails are received every day. What started out as a good idea soon turns into information overload.

Think hard before setting up alerts. Only add them where you really need to know if something changes. Use the daily or weekly rollups where you can.

See also

▸ *Managing my alerts in SharePoint*

▸ *Creating an alert on a document to be notified when it is updated, Chapter 4*

▸ *Saving a search as an alert and being notified when the results change, Chapter 6*

Managing my alerts in SharePoint

Alerts are a powerful way to let SharePoint keep you informed of important changes and updates. However, you will soon need to manage your alerts, removing the ones you don't really need and reducing the frequency of others so that you don't slip into alert overload. This recipe shows you how to manage your alerts and stay in control.

Getting ready

This recipe works for:

▸ SharePoint 2010 Foundation

▸ SharePoint 2010 Standard Edition

▸ SharePoint 2010 Enterprise Edition

▸ SharePoint 2010 Online (Office 365 Edition)

It requires you to be logged in and have read access but no other privileges are necessary.

If you want to manage your alerts, then you will need to have created at least one alert before going through this recipe. The recipe *Adding an alert to a SharePoint page* shows you how.

How to do it...

1. Open the SharePoint site that you wish to manage alerts for.
2. Select the **Page** tab from the ribbon and click on the **Alert Me** icon.
3. From the drop-down menu select the **Manage My Alerts** option.

4. You will then be shown a list of all the alerts you have set for the site; from here you can create, edit, and delete alerts.

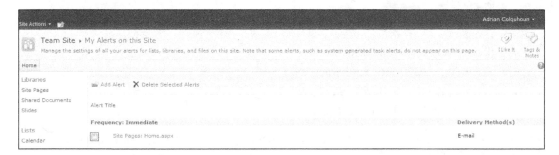

5. You can add new alerts by clicking on the **Add Alert** link.

6. To delete one or more alerts, select the checkbox and then click on the **Delete Selected Alerts** link.

7. To change settings for an alert (for example, to change its frequency), click on the alert's title. This will take you into the alert's settings dialog where you can make any necessary changes.

How it works...

SharePoint offers you tremendous flexibility to create alerts and to specify why and how often you receive them. It provides built-in functionality to allow you to manage those alerts, create new alerts, and adjust or remove existing alerts for a single administration page. You can use this page to adjust your alerts, ensuring that you don't get overwhelmed by SharePoint alert e-mails.

See also

▶ *Adding an alert to a SharePoint page*

▶ *Creating an alert on a document to be notified when it is updated, Chapter 4*

▶ *Saving a search as an alert and being notified when the results change, Chapter 6*

Determining my permissions in a SharePoint site

This recipe shows you how to work out the permission levels you have been granted in a SharePoint Team Site.

Getting ready

This recipe works for:

▶ SharePoint 2010 Foundation

▶ SharePoint 2010 Standard Edition

▶ SharePoint 2010 Enterprise Edition

▶ SharePoint 2010 Online (Office 365 Edition)

You will need a SharePoint site that you want to check your permissions on. This recipe uses a Team Site for illustration.

You do not require any particular permission level to use this recipe. However, the outcome of this recipe is directly determined by the permission levels that you have been granted.

 You will only be able to follow this recipe as far as your permission levels will allow. If you have not been granted any access to the site, an error message will be displayed when you attempt to access it. Once you are unable to proceed, the recipe is complete. Check the *How it works* section for a detailed explanation of the permission levels that you have.

How to do it...

1. Open Internet Explorer and navigate to the SharePoint Team Site that you want to check your permissions in.

2. If the Team Site is displayed, then you have been granted **Read** permission level or higher (an **Access Denied** error means you have not been granted any access to the site).

3. Access the **Page** ribbon on the home page. Confirm that you can see the **Edit** icon.

4. Access any document library (for example, **Shared documents**), confirm that you can you can see the **Add document** link.

5. If either item is present, then you have been granted at least the **Contribute** permission level in the Team Site.

6. Access the **Site Actions** menu. The options displayed should match those in the following screenshot. If all these options are present, then you have been granted the **Full Control** permission level to the site. If the **Site Permissions** and **New Site** options are missing, then you only have the **Design** permission level.

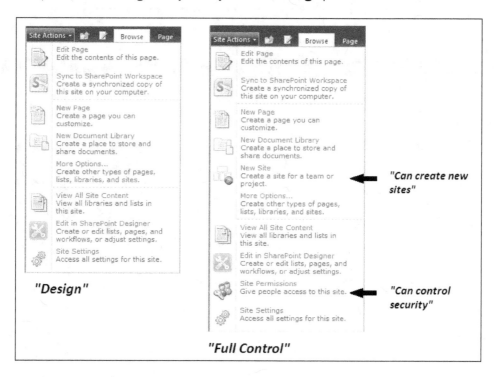

How it works...

Everything that you can or can't do in SharePoint is determined by the **permissions** that you have been granted. SharePoint doesn't tell you the permissions that you have, it only stops you doing or seeing the things that require permissions that you do not have. SharePoint employs a "*security trimmed user interface*". This means that SharePoint doesn't let you see or do the things you don't have permissions for. It only shows you the content, menus, and commands that you are allowed to access.

Unfortunately, as a user, there is no built-in way to determine your permission levels. This recipe uses a systematic approach to work out the permission levels by testing for the functionality that is granted at each level. If we find the functionality we expect, then we can infer that you have been granted that permission level. As permission levels build up in a hierarchy, we start from the lowest level (that is, no access) and work upwards until we find all the permissions levels that apply to you.

Individual SharePoint permissions are collected together into permission levels. A SharePoint Team Site creates six permission levels by default: **Limited Access**, **View Only**, **Read**, **Contribute**, **Design**, and **Full Control**. You may have been allocated one or more permission levels in the site. The total permissions you have are the sum of all the permissions from the permission levels that you have been allocated.

 If you receive an **Access Denied** message when you try to open the site, then you have not been granted any permission levels at all.

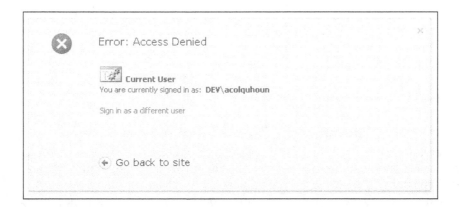

The **limited access** permission does not give any direct access to the site. It is designed to be combined with the fine-grained permissions to give access to just particular items within a site (for example, it is possible that you would have access to just a single document library in a site but nothing else). You will not normally encounter this except in highly customized sites.

If you can see the Team Site in your browser, then you have at least **View Only** or **Read** permissions level. For all practical purposes, these permissions levels are identical so we do not try to differentiate them any further in this recipe.

If you have the ability to change things in the Team Site (for example, edit pages or upload documents) then you have been granted at least the **Contribute** permission level, that is, you have the ability to contribute things to the site.

If you have access to the advanced commands located on the **Site Actions** menu, then you have been granted **Design** or **Full Control** permission level in the site. You will probably encounter the **Full Control** permission level in Team Sites that you are responsible for administering or within your My Site. **Full Control** means that you can access all the power of SharePoint within the bounds of the current collection of sites that you are working in. You will have the ability to create new sites, add users, set permission levels, and do all sorts of wonderful stuff. However, with power comes responsibility—there is also the potential to mess things up when you have full control! Don't worry, there are plenty of recipes in this book that will help you and make sure that doesn't happen.

There's more...

Checking your permission levels in other SharePoint sites

SharePoint provides the ability to create many different types of site, such as, Team Sites, My Sites, Document Workspaces, and Publishing Sites. Some of these sites introduce extra permission levels such as **Manage Hierarchy** or **Approve**. The same principles used to determine the permission levels in a Team Site can be applied to the other sites.

SharePoint users and groups

SharePoint permissions levels can be directly assigned to individual SharePoint users. However, administrators do not usually do this as it quickly becomes very complex and difficult to manage. Instead, SharePoint sites can contain **groups**. These groups are used to hold collections of users who all require the same permissions levels (that is, need to be able to play the same roles) in the site. Multiple permission levels are assigned to the SharePoint groups, and then the users, who require those permissions levels, are added to the group.

Understanding "securable objects" and inheritance

SharePoint has a hierarchy of securable objects that is things that can be secured by permissions in SharePoint. Normally, permission levels are inherited from their parent objects (as this keeps things simple and easy to manage). Site collections define the security to be applied and these settings are inherited down through all the sub sites, pages, document libraries, lists, documents, and list items that they contain.

However, this inheritance can be broken and permission levels can then be applied at any level in the hierarchy. We might want to do this in a number of scenarios—for example, to create a document library that contains sensitive document that only selected employees are allowed to see. If you encounter odd permissions or access errors within a SharePoint site, consider that the site administrator may have chosen to break the security inheritance and applied unique permissions to the item you are trying to access.

See also

- ▶ *Checking another user's permissions in a SharePoint site*
- ▶ *Applying unique permissions to a SharePoint list*
- ▶ *Adding users to a Team Site, Chapter 2*

Checking another user's permissions in a SharePoint site

This recipe shows you how check another user's permissions in a SharePoint site.

Getting ready

This recipe works for:

- SharePoint 2010 Foundation
- SharePoint 2010 Standard Edition
- SharePoint 2010 Enterprise Edition
- SharePoint Online (Office 365 Edition)

You will need the URL of the SharePoint site you want to check your permissions on.

You will need the **Full Control** permission level to run this recipe. Normally, this will mean that you are a member of the site owner's group.

How to do it...

1. Open Internet Explorer and navigate to the SharePoint site that you want to check you permissions for.
2. Access the **Site Actions** menu and select the **Site Permissions** menu option.
3. Select the **Check Permissions** icon on the **Permission Tools** ribbon.

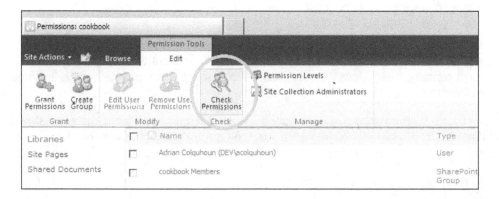

4. Enter the name of the user or group that you want to check the permissions for in the displayed dialog box. Click on the book icon to browse for the user if you are not sure of their name.
5. Click on the **Check Now** button.

6. The permission levels granted to the user (and the details of how those permission levels have been assigned) are displayed.

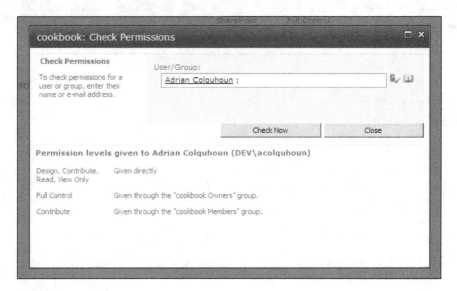

How it works...

As a user, everything that you can or can't to in SharePoint is determined by the permissions that you have been granted. Individual SharePoint permissions are collected together into permission levels. SharePoint 2010 provides built-in functionality that gives site owners the ability to check the permission of any user in a site.

There's more...

In SharePoint, security permissions are normally inherited with pages, lists, document libraries, and the items that they contain all inheriting their security permissions from the site which contains them. However, it is possible to break this inheritance and apply unique permissions to any of these items.

Where custom permissions have been applied, SharePoint 2010 provides the same **Check Permissions** functionality for each object. Just look for the **Check Permissions** icon on the ribbon for the list, document library, or page that you want to check the permissions for.

See also

 ▶ *Determining my permissions in a SharePoint site*

 ▶ *Applying unique permissions to a SharePoint list*

 ▶ *Adding users to a Team Site, Chapter 2*

Applying unique permissions to a SharePoint list

Sometimes you will want to apply custom security settings to a SharePoint list to control who has access to it. This recipe shows you how.

Getting ready

This recipe works for:

- SharePoint 2010 Foundation
- SharePoint 2010 Standard Edition
- SharePoint 2010 Enterprise Edition
- SharePoint Online (Office 365 Edition)

You require either the **Design** or **Full Control** permission level to edit the permission settings of the list.

How to do it...

1. Select the list that you wish to apply the custom permissions to by clicking on the link to your list in the **Quick Launch** navigation on the left side of the page.

2. Select the **List** tab in the **List Tools** ribbon.

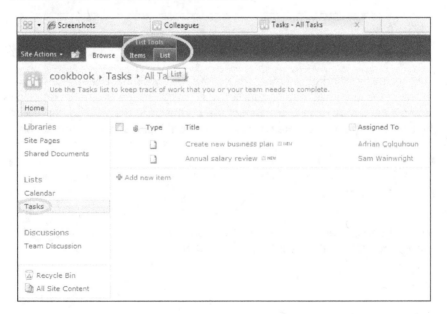

3. Select the **List Permissions** icon in the **List** ribbon as shown in the following screenshot:

4. The current permissions are displayed. You will see that the list is currently inheriting its permissions from the parent site. Select the **Stop Inheriting Permissions** icon.

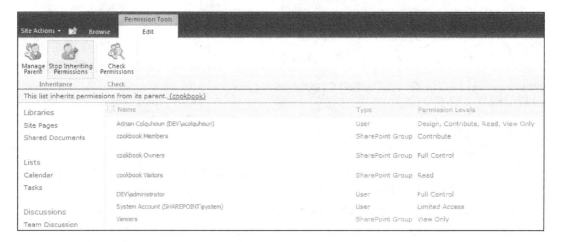

5. You will be prompted to confirm whether you want to create unique permissions on this list. Click on the **OK** button to continue.

6. The previously inherited permissions still apply to your list, but any new permission added at the site level will not apply. If you don't want the original permissions, then you now need to remove them. Select the permissions that you do not require (using the tick box) and click on the **Remove User Permissions** icon on the ribbon.

 Don't remove all your permissions from the list—you may lock yourself out from it!

7. You will be prompted to confirm whether you want to remove the selected permissions. Click on the **OK** button to continue.

8. Now add any new permissions that you want to apply just for this list. Click on the **Grant Permissions** button on the ribbon. In the dialog box displayed, add the users and permissions that you need.

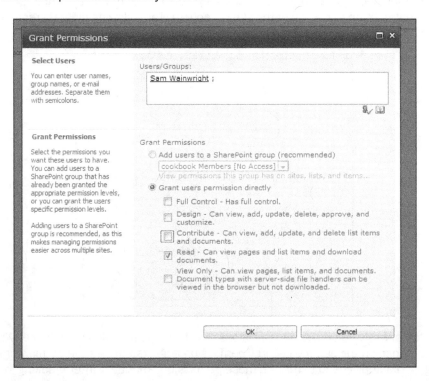

9. The unique permissions that you have assigned to your list are displayed. Review this information carefully to ensure that it is correct.

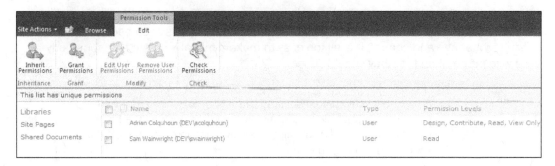

How it works...

Lists inherit their security settings from their parent site (which may in turn inherit its settings from its parent right up to the top of the site collection). The following diagram represents the inheritance hierarchy:

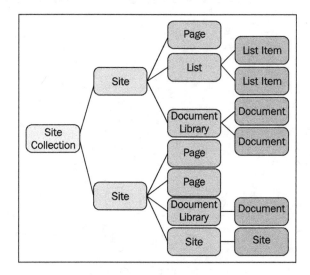

The first step of assigning custom permissions to a list is to break this inheritance. When you break inheritance on the list, the security permission it starts with are the permissions it was inheriting—you actually need to remove these permissions manually after breaking inheritance if you don't want them!

Once you have broken inheritance, you are free to add and remove permissions as you wish.

Use this functionality sparingly. It's generally considered bad practice to use custom SharePoint permissions extensively in your SharePoint sites, as this soon becomes very difficult to manage and control. It is all too easy to make a mistake and to give somebody access to information that they shouldn't see.

 Always test your custom security settings by logging in as different users before you upload sensitive information such as the boards' new salaries. SharePoint will do exactly what you tell it to—get this wrong and you are on your own!

There's more...

Securing individual pages, document libraries, documents, and list items

Exactly the same principles can be used to break inheritance and apply custom permissions to individual pages, document libraries, documents, or list items. Just make sure that you really need to do this before applying custom security throughout your SharePoint sites and always test the changes that you have made.

Alternative ways to secure your sensitive content

There are other approaches you can take to secure sensitive information that might be more appropriate for your needs. One common way to do this is to create a completely separate site (of site collection) for your site collection and only add the users who really need access. That way you can still rely on permission inheritance and you don't have to mess around applying custom permissions further down the hierarchy.

If you want to store your own private documents in a library that only you can see, then your My Site has a specially configured document library, called **Personal Documents**, already set up and configured specifically for that purpose.

See also

- ▸ *Determining my permissions in a SharePoint site*
- ▸ *Checking another user's permissions in a SharePoint site*
- ▸ *Adding users to a Team Site, Chapter 2*

2
Working Together— Using SharePoint to Collaborate

In this chapter, we will cover:

- ▶ Creating a Team Site
- ▶ Adding users to a Team Site
- ▶ Adding a new page to a Team Site
- ▶ Adding a link to the Top link bar in a Team Site
- ▶ Adding a slide library to share PowerPoint slides
- ▶ Adding a slide to a presentation from a SharePoint slide library
- ▶ Creating and tracking a discussion item
- ▶ Managing a Team Site Calendar with Outlook 2010
- ▶ Creating a task and assigning it to another user
- ▶ Using the datasheet to bulk-edit tasks in a task list
- ▶ Managing a SharePoint task list in Outlook 2010
- ▶ Creating a SharePoint contact list and connecting it to Outlook 2010

Introduction

This chapter focuses on using SharePoint to collaborate, working together to create and share documents, ideas, presentations, calendars, tasks, and so on. Central to this collaboration is the SharePoint 2010 SharePoint **Team Site**. Early recipes cover how to create a Team Site, add users to it, add pages, and adjust the navigation links.

The remaining recipes show how you can use a Team Site to work more effectively together. You will see how to use a **Shared Calendar** for important events and how to use the **Discussion Board** to canvass the opinions of you colleagues. Further recipes show how to share lists of **Contacts**, how to create and assign **Tasks,** and how to reuse PowerPoint 2010 slides within your team. Though the Team Site has been used for illustration, the information is these recipes can be applied to any site provided the required list or library has been added.

Throughout this chapter, the integration between SharePoint 2010 and Outlook 2010 is highlighted, illustrating how you can make effective use of SharePoint information without having to leave your familiar Office 2010 applications.

Creating a Team Site

SharePoint 2010 provides a set of templates to allow you to rapidly create websites to perform different functions. The most commonly used collaboration site is the Team Site. This recipe shows you how to create one.

Getting ready

This recipe works for:

- ▸ SharePoint 2010 Foundation
- ▸ SharePoint 2010 Standard Edition
- ▸ SharePoint 2010 Enterprise Edition
- ▸ Office 365 (SharePoint Online)

You will need a SharePoint site where you want to create your Team Site.

You will need the **Full Control** permission level to run this recipe. Normally this will mean that you are a member of the site owner's group.

How to do it...

1. Open the SharePoint site where you want to create the Team Site.

2. Open the **Site Actions** menu and click on **New Site**.

3. SharePoint now shows all the available site templates. Click on the **Team Site** icon. Give the Team Site a name and specify the URL you wish to use.

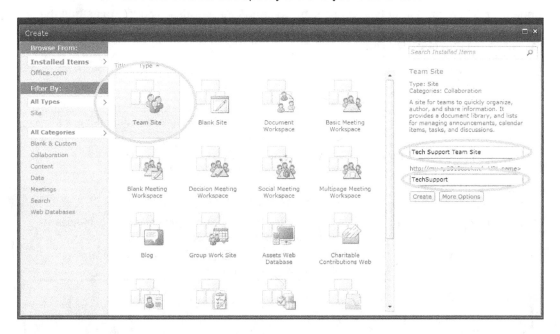

4. After a brief delay your new Team Site is created.

How it works...

One of the key capabilities of SharePoint 2010 is that it allows you to quickly and easily create websites without needing input from the IT department or knowledge of website programming. Each version of the product ships with a set of reusable site templates. These templates can be used to create sites that contain different combinations of pre-created lists, libraries, web parts, and pages designed to perform specific business functions. SharePoint provides site templates for collaboration, communication, web publishing, managing meetings, search, blogs, wikis, business intelligence dashboards, My Sites, and more. These templates can then be augmented with custom site templates developed by SharePoint developers and by your own SharePoint power users.

To create a site, simply select the template that you want to use, provide some basic information, click on **Create**, and let SharePoint do the rest.

As you get more familiar with creating sites, you may want to have a look at the **More Options** button in the create dialog. This simply allows you to provide a few more settings specific to your site template as you create it. It is just a timesaver; anything you set here can be adjusted and changed later if you need to.

There's more...

Understanding the different types of sites that SharePoint provides is critical to getting the most value out of the product. Too often I see customers wasting time and money trying to reinvent sites that already exist!

Some of the more commonly used site templates are listed as follows:

Template name	Used for
Team Site	Collaboration—Sharing calendars, documents, tasks, and discussions.
Basic Meeting Workspace	Meetings—managing agenda, attendees, and supporting documents.
Document Workspace	Collaboration—Provides tools to work together to produce or update a single document.
Document Centre	Documents—Tools for managing and sharing important documents and sets of documents.
Blog	Communication—Broadcasting information form an individual, team, or project.

Test drive the site templates

When it comes to understanding site templates, no amount of reading can substitute for hands-on experience. Take some time to create a site from each site template and have a look at what it can do for you. You will find many of these templates reused throughout the recipes in the remainder of this book. Microsoft provides video previews of key site templates at http://office.microsoft.com/en-us/sharepoint-server-help/a-preview-of-the-sharepoint-server-2010-site-templates-HA101907564.aspx.

Sites versus Site Collections

As you learn more about SharePoint, you will hear people talk about **Sites** and **Site Collections**. For the user it can often be confusing to try and understand the difference between the two. That is because everything you see and interact with is a site—there is nothing to see for a Site Collection. It is just a "collection of sites" that SharePoint can treat as a single unit, applying specific settings, security, databases, backup, administration rights, and so on. Some templates (for example, Publishing Portal and Business Intelligence centre) can only be used at the Site Collection level.

Each Site Collection has a single **Root Site** and as many **Sub Sites** as are required. As a user, you don't have permission to create Site Collections. This is done by your SharePoint administrators using a special website called **Central Administration**. Just bear in mind that sometimes when you are setting properties in SharePoint, the changes that you make will apply to the complete Site Collection, and not just to the Site that you are working in. The following diagram shows the relationship between Sites and Site Collections. The mix of Sites and Site Collections in your particular environment is arbitrary, and is determined by what your SharePoint architect has defined. Unfortunately, there is no way of knowing from the address of a site whether it is a Sub Site or the Root Site of a Site Collection.

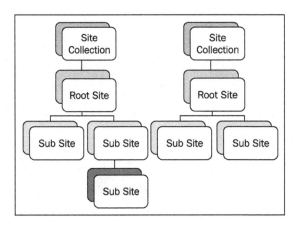

See also

 ▸ *Adding users to a Team Site*
 ▸ *Creating and accessing my My Site, Chapter 1*
 ▸ *Creating a blog in my My Site, Chapter 5*

Adding users to a Team Site

Your Team Site won't be much use for collaboration unless people have access to it. This recipe shows you how to add users and assign them the right **Permission levels**.

Getting ready

This recipe works for:

 ▸ SharePoint 2010 Foundation
 ▸ SharePoint 2010 Standard Edition
 ▸ SharePoint 2010 Enterprise Edition
 ▸ Office 365 (SharePoint Online)

You will need the **Full Control** permission level to run this recipe. Normally this will mean that you are a member of the site owner's group.

How to do it...

1. Open the SharePoint Team Site that you want to add users to.

2. Open the **Site Actions** menu and select the **Site Permissions** option.

3. The current user permissions for the site are displayed. Click on the **Grant Permissions** icon on the ribbon.

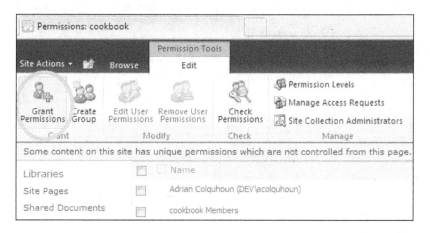

4. The **Grant Permissions** dialog box is displayed. Add the users that you want to give access to this Team Site. Enter the user in the textbox or click on the book icon to browse to the users you need.

5. Assign the users to one of the site groups (**Viewers, Owners, Visitors,** and **Members**) depending on what level of access they require.

6. Check the **Send welcome e-mail to the new users** checkbox selected if you want the users to receive an e-mail notifying them that they have been granted access to the site. You may also type a personal message if you wish in the **Personal Message** field.

7. Click on the **OK** button to add the users to the site.

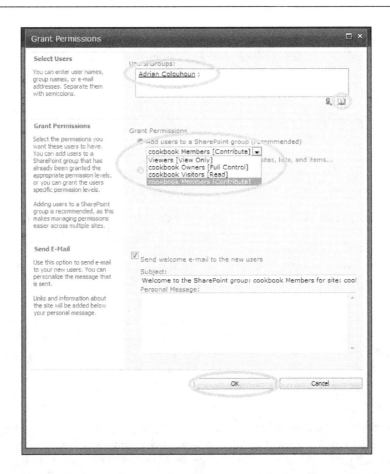

8. The current groups and individual user permissions (for users who are not in groups) for the site are displayed. Click on the link for the group that you added your users to and confirm that your changes have been applied correctly.

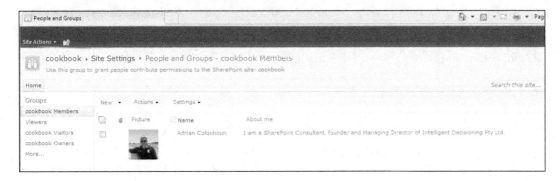

Always check your work when you are dealing with
SharePoint security.

How it works...

SharePoint provides the ability to add users to a SharePoint site and to control what they
can do in the site by granting them different permission levels. These permission levels are
covered in depth in the recipe *Determining my permissions in a SharePoint site, Chapter 1*.

The recommended way to add users to a site is to add them to a **group** rather than
adding them to the site directly. Team Sites have a number of groups already created and
preconfigured with the appropriate permissions levels (for example, Reader, Member, and
Owner). Adding a user to a group ensures they get the permission levels you intended and
reduces the risk that you will make an embarrassing mistake.

Remember that groups are defined at the Site Collection level. Adding
a user to a group gives that user access to every site for which that
group has permissions assigned.

There's more...

Many organizations use **Active Directory** (**AD**) to manage their users and to collect users
together into AD Groups: for example, All Managers, Marketing Department, City Campus
Staff, and so on. If your organizations has AD groups and they are being kept up-to-date, then
you can simplify the task of adding users to your sites by instead adding the appropriate AD
group to one of your SharePoint groups. For example, if you add the Marketing Department's
AD group to your Team Site's Readers group, everyone in the Marketing Department will be
able to read your site (assuming they are in the correct AD group). When a new member joins
the Marketing team, then they can be added to the AD group centrally and will automatically
have access to your site, without requiring any changes at all on your site. This is by-far the
simplest way to manage SharePoint users. Unfortunately, many organizations don't keep their
AD groups up-to-date. Also, SharePoint groups can't contain other SharePoint groups.

See also

- ▶ *Determining my permissions in a SharePoint site, Chapter 1*
- ▶ *Checking another user's permissions in a SharePoint site, Chapter 1*

Adding a new page to a Team Site

SharePoint 2010 makes it very easy to add new pages to your Team Site. This recipe shows you how to do so.

Getting ready

This recipe works for:

- SharePoint 2010 Foundation
- SharePoint 2010 Standard Edition
- SharePoint 2010 Enterprise Edition
- Office 365 (SharePoint Online)

You will need the **Designer** or **Full Control** permission level to run this recipe.

How to do it...

1. Open the SharePoint Team Site where you want to add a new page.
2. Open the **Site Actions** menu and select the **New Page** option.
3. The **New Page** dialog box is displayed. Enter the name **demopage** for the page and click on the **Create** button.
4. The new page is created. You can start entering text immediately by typing directly into the page. Click on **Save & Close** when you are done. Your new page will be displayed on the Team Site.

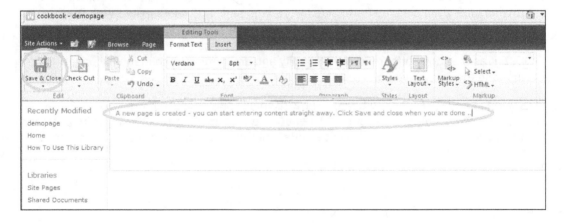

How it works...

This recipe shows you how to create a new page. The page you created was automatically added to the site page's library. The page you created is a **Wiki page**. These pages are really easy to use, and they are the default page type in SharePoint 2010.

Once your page is created, you can just start typing and place your content anywhere you like. The **Editing Tools** ribbon provides access to all sorts of commands for styling your pages, inserting pictures, video, web parts, and more. The whole experience is designed to be very much like editing a Word 2010 document, making it easy and intuitive for you add information that others need to see. If you want more editing and layout power, you can open the page in SharePoint Designer 2010.

Wiki pages are borrowed from the Internet. You may have come across sites such as Wikipedia (http://en.wikipedia.org/wiki/Main_Page). If you have ever contributed to any of those sites, you will know that they have a special editing syntax designed to allow you to enter information quickly and to save you from some of the complexities of HTML. SharePoint Wiki pages support these concepts too. To insert a link into your page simply type [[. SharePoint will display a list of all the pages you can link to. If the page you want isn't there, then just type a name for the new page. SharePoint will create the page for you automatically when you click on the link. Another great feature is that these links won't break if you rename your page or move them around.

There's more...

SharePoint supports a number of different types of pages. You will also encounter **Web Part** pages, **Publishing** pages, and **Application** pages.

Web Part pages were the way pages got created in SharePoint 2007. You can't enter information directly into a Web Part page. Instead the page is divided up into **Web Part Zones**. You add Web Parts to those zones to build up the page's contents. You can achieve different page layouts by rearranging the zones. Web Part pages are still there in SharePoint 2010, but as they don't offer much functionality and are harder to use than Wiki pages, I don't recommend that you use them.

Publishing pages are specific to SharePoint 2010 publishing sites. They offer extra functionality to capture and layout the content of the page making it much easier for users to create pages based on standard **Page Layouts**. Publishing pages are explored in *Chapter 5*.

All the pages mentioned earlier are known as site pages, because they exist within the context of a particular site. However, SharePoint has another type of page, known as an Application page. These pages can be shared between many SharePoint sites, run custom code, and provide complex functionality. Much of SharePoint's built-in functionality is delivered through Application pages. As a user you can't create or edit an Application page. These pages are created by developers, so we won't spend any more time on them here. However, it is useful to know that they exist (and that you can access them directly if you need to). If the page you are looking at has `/_layouts/` in its address, then you can assume that it is an Application page.

See also

▶ *Creating a new page on a publishing site, Chapter 5*

Adding a link to the Top link bar of a Team Site

People need to be able to find their way around your Team Site. Adding links to the **Top link bar** can help. This recipe shows you how to do so.

Getting ready

This recipe works for:

▶ SharePoint 2010 Foundation

▶ SharePoint 2010 Standard Edition

▶ SharePoint 2010 Enterprise Edition

▶ Office 365 (SharePoint Online)

You will need the **Designer** or **Full Control** permission level to run this recipe.

How to do it...

1. From your Team Site, open the **Site Actions** menu and click on the **Site Settings** option.

2. The **Site Settings** page is displayed. Under the **Look and Feel** category, select the **Top link bar** link.

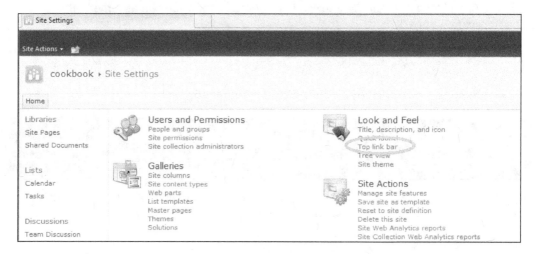

3. The **Top Link Bar** page is displayed. Click on the **New Navigation Link**.

4. Enter the web address and description for the new link as shown in the following screenshot. Click on the **OK** button to create the link.

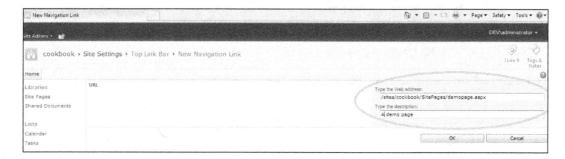

5. The new link now appears on the Top link bar. Click on the link to test whether it works correctly.

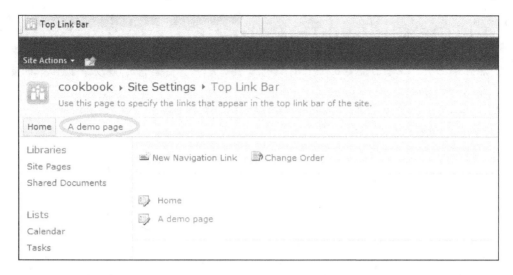

How it works...

SharePoint 2010 Team Sites provide basic navigation controls. The Top link bar allows you to add links that are visible across the Top of your site. When you create a sub site, SharePoint will automatically add it to the top link bar.

Don't type links; copy them

The easiest way to add a link is to open the page that you want to link to in Internet Explorer and then copy its web address from your web browser's address bar. When you create your new top link, just paste the address in the **Type the Web Address** textbox. Use the keyboard shortcuts: *Ctrl + C* to copy and *Ctrl + V* to paste.

You can also add links to the quick-launch navigation (on the left-hand side of the page) in a similar way (using the **Site Actions** and **Site Settings** menu combination). There is also a **Tree View** navigation control which you can enable. The Tree View automatically shows all the content of your site (and sub sites) without you having to manually add it.

There's more...

SharePoint 2010 Publishing Sites offer more sophisticated navigation controls and are covered in *Chapter 5*.

Adding a slide library to share PowerPoint slides

SharePoint 2010 makes it easy to add information, documents, videos, and more. In this recipe, you will learn how to add a **slide library** to your Team Site so that you can share PowerPoint 2010 slides with your colleagues.

Getting ready

This recipe works for:

- ▶ SharePoint 2010 Standard Edition
- ▶ SharePoint 2010 Enterprise Edition
- ▶ Office 365 (SharePoint Online)

You will need the **Designer** or **Full Control** permission level to run this recipe.

You will need PowerPoint 2010 to be able to publish your slides to the slide library.

How to do it...

1. From your Team Site, open the **Site Actions** menu and click on **More Options**.
2. The **Create** dialog box is displayed. Click on the **Library** filter and select the **Slide Library** icon.
3. Click on the **Create** button.

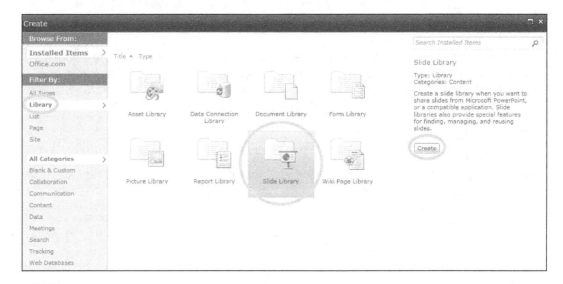

4. A second page is then displayed which prompts for more information about the slide library that you wish to create. Enter a **Name** for the library, if you want to display a link to the library on the **Quick Launch**, and if you want to save a version of the slides in the library each time they are edited.

5. Click on the **Create** button to create the slide library.

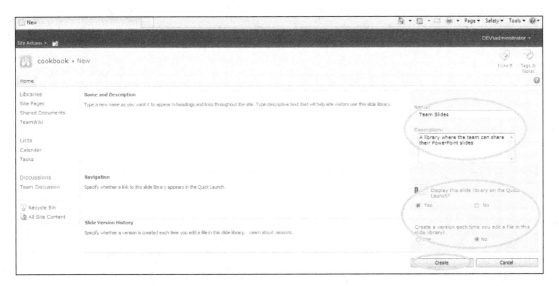

After a short delay the slide library is created and ready to use.

6. To upload a presentation to the slide library, click on the **Upload** icon in the ribbon.

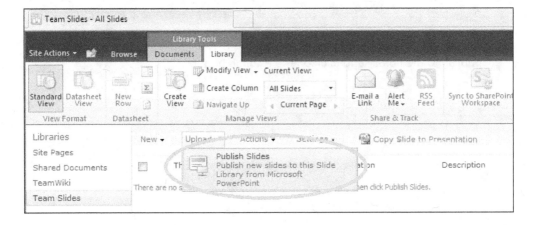

7. PowerPoint 2010 will open and prompt you to browse to a presentation. Select the presentation that you wish to upload.

8. The **Publish Slides** dialog box is now displayed. Select the slides that you want to publish to the library and click on the **Publish** button.

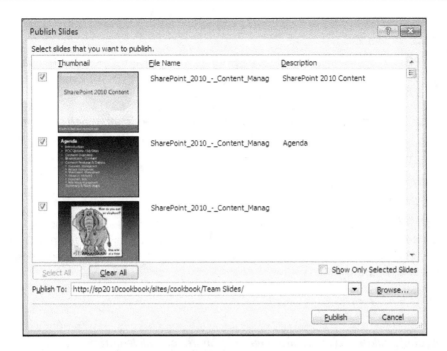

After a short delay, your slides are published to the library.

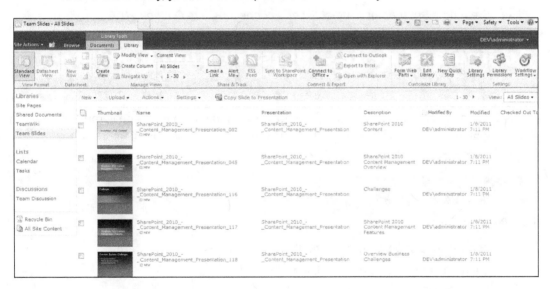

How it works...

SharePoint 2010 provides a whole range of different lists and libraries (lists that can store files) to perform particular functions. Even things that you might not expect, such as the Shared Calendar, is just a SharePoint list under the covers.

The slide library is a special type of document library designed to store and share PowerPoint 2010 slides. Microsoft has provided tight integration with PowerPoint 2010 out of the box. Just add a slide library to your site and start sharing!

There's more...

We will encounter many other lists and libraries through the recipes in this book. Most notable is the **Document Library**, which is used to store, manage, and share documents. Document management is such an important part of SharePoint that I have devoted a whole chapter of recipes to it later in the book.

See also

- ▸ *Adding a slide to a presentation from a SharePoint slide library*
- ▸ *Creating a SharePoint list, Chapter 1*
- ▸ *Creating a SharePoint contact list and connecting it to Outlook 2010*

Adding a slide to a presentation from a SharePoint slide library

Colleagues can share PowerPoint 2010 slides by publishing them to a slide library. You can then reuse those slides in your own presentation, without having to recreate them from scratch.

Getting ready

This recipe works for:

- ▸ SharePoint 2010 Standard Edition
- ▸ SharePoint 2010 Enterprise Edition
- ▸ Office 365 (SharePoint Online)

You will need the **Read** permission level to run this recipe.

You will need a slide library containing slides that you wish to add to your presentation. The recipe *Adding a slide library to share PowerPoint slides* shows you how to do this.

You will need PowerPoint 2010 to be able to add slides from the slide library.

How to do it...

1. Open the slide library. Check the slides that you want to add to your presentation and click on the **Copy Slide to Presentation** link.

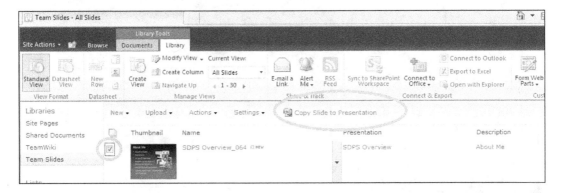

2. PowerPoint 2010 opens and prompts you for more information on how you want the slides you have selected to be copied. Select the options that meet your needs and then click on the **OK** button.

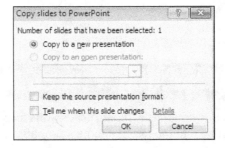

The slides you selected are added to your presentation.

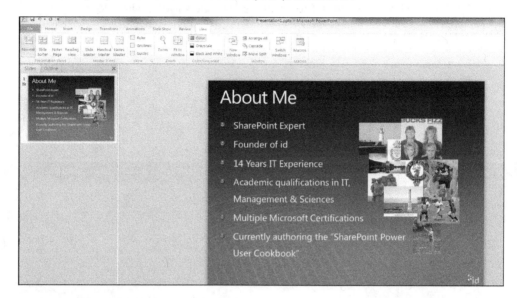

How it works...

Microsoft has ensured integration between SharePoint 2010 and PowerPoint 2010 so that this just works out of the box. Use it!

See also

▶ *Adding a slide library to share PowerPoint slides*

Creating and tracking a discussion item

The SharePoint 2010 Team Site contains a **Team Discussions** forum. This recipe shows you how to add a discussion item to the forum and be automatically notified when your colleagues reply.

Getting ready

This recipe works for:

▶ SharePoint 2010 Foundation

▶ SharePoint 2010 Standard Edition

▶ SharePoint 2010 Enterprise Edition

▶ Office 365 (SharePoint Online)

You will need the **Contribute** permission level to run this recipe. Normally this will mean that you are a member of the site member's group.

You will need a SharePoint 2010 Team Site or any other SharePoint site to which a Discussion Board has been added.

How to do it...

1. Open your Team Site. Select the **Team Discussion** link from the quick-launch menu.

2. The list of current discussions is displayed. Click on the **Add new discussion** link.

3. In the **Team Discussions—New Item** dialog box, enter the **Subject** and the **Body** for the discussion item that you want to create.

4. Click on **Save**.

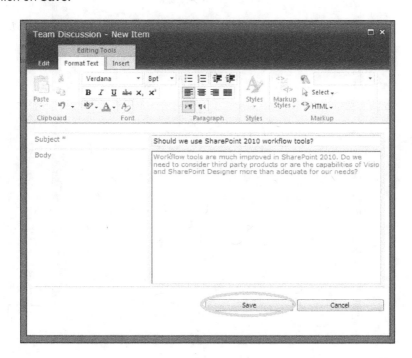

The new discussion item will appear in the current discussions list.

5. Select the checkbox next to the new discussion item and click on the **Alert Me** icon in the ribbon.

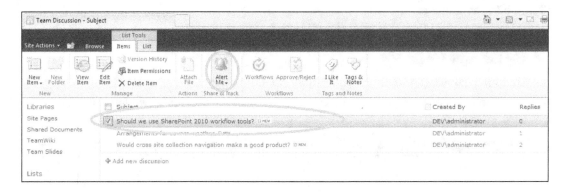

6. The **Alert Me** dialog box is displayed. You can set an alert to be notified when someone responds to the discussion. Select the alert settings you prefer and then click on the **OK** button to set the alert.

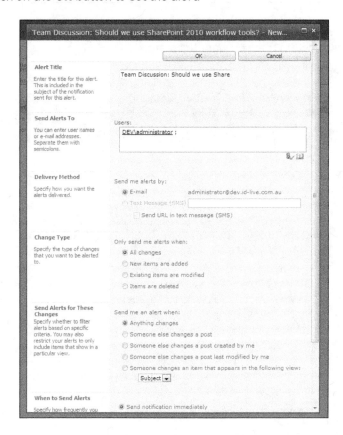

How it works...

The SharePoint Discussion Board is just a special type of SharePoint list. It is designed to give your team a forum where you can discuss important items in the same way as you may have previously encountered on the Internet.

The Team Discussion list is included in your Team Site when you create it, but you can add more discussion boards if you wish. You might want to do this to if you need to change the security settings that control who can post or respond to discussion items.

There's more...

As with the contacts and tasks lists discussed in this chapter, Discussion Boards can be synchronized to Outlook 2010 by using the **Connect to Outlook** icon on the **List Tools** ribbon. Once connected you will be able to track and respond to discussions directly without having to visit the SharePoint site.

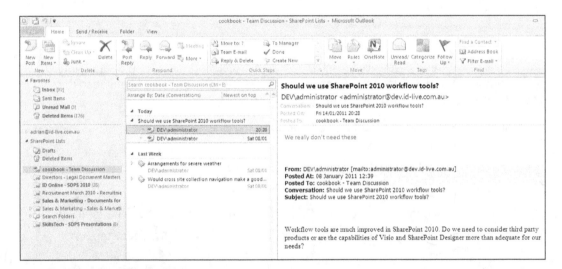

See also

- ▶ *Creating a SharePoint list, Chapter 1*
- ▶ *Creating a SharePoint contact list and connecting it to Outlook 2010*
- ▶ *Managing a SharePoint task list in Outlook 2010*
- ▶ *Applying unique permissions to a SharePoint list, Chapter 1*

Managing a Team Site Calendar with Outlook 2010

The SharePoint Team Site contains a Shared Calendar that is great for managing appointments, meetings, and important events within your team. Additionally, you can connect your calendar to Outlook 2010 and manage all your events straight from there.

Getting ready

This recipe works for:

- ▶ SharePoint 2010 Foundation
- ▶ SharePoint 2010 Standard Edition
- ▶ SharePoint 2010 Enterprise Edition
- ▶ Office 365 (SharePoint Online)

You will need Outlook 2010 installed on your PC.

You will need the **Read** permission level to synchronize calendar data from SharePoint 2010 to Outlook 2010. You will need the **Contribute** permission level to make changes to the calendar in Outlook and save those changes back to SharePoint.

You will need a SharePoint 2010 Team Site or any other SharePoint site to which a calendar has been added.

How to do it...

1. Open your Team Site. Select the **Calendar** link from the quick-launch menu.
2. The Team Site's Shared Calendar is displayed. Click on the **Calendar** tab on the ribbon.
3. Click on the **Connect to Outlook** icon on the ribbon. Click on the **Allow** button on the security prompt (if displayed).

4. Outlook will be opened and the SharePoint calendar will be displayed (Click on **Yes** if you are prompted by Outlook security).

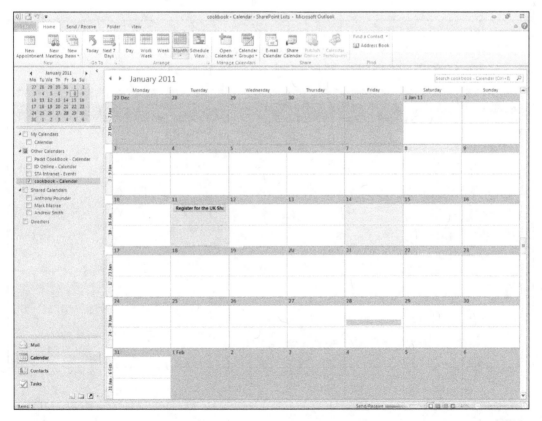

5. You can now add events to your Shared Calendar through Outlook 2010 and they will synchronize back to SharePoint. Double-click on the calendar to add an event.

6. Enter the event details and click on **Save & Close**.

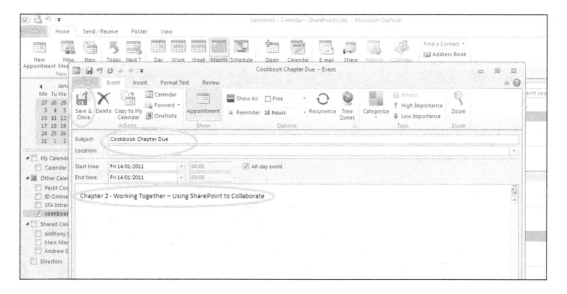

7. Switch back to SharePoint and refresh the **Calendar** page. Your event will be displayed for your colleagues to see.

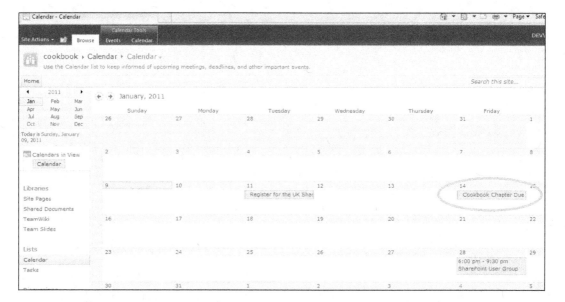

How it works...

A SharePoint calendar is just a special type of SharePoint list, with functionality and views optimized for managing events.

SharePoint 2010 has great "two-way" integration with Outlook 2010. Once you connect your calendar, Outlook 2010 knows how to retrieve the latest events from SharePoint and how to update SharePoint with any changes that you make.

You can synchronize as many SharePoint calendars as you like and have Outlook 2010 display those calendars side by side. You can even "drag-and-drop" between your calendars to rapidly reorganize your events if you need to.

Caution: Always check you are working in the right calendar

If you have multiple calendars open in Outlook, always double-check that you are working in the right one; otherwise you might inadvertently broadcast your private appointments to the rest of your team.

See also

- ▶ *Managing a SharePoint task list in Outlook 2010*
- ▶ *Creating a SharePoint contact list and connecting it to Outlook 2010*

Creating a task and assigning it to another user

Your SharePoint 2010 Team Site contains a **tasks list**, where you can create, assign, and track the shared tasks that your team needs to complete.

Getting ready

This recipe works for:

- ▶ SharePoint 2010 Foundation
- ▶ SharePoint 2010 Standard Edition
- ▶ SharePoint 2010 Enterprise Edition
- ▶ Office 365 (SharePoint Online)

You will need the **Contribute** permission level to create tasks. This normally means that you will be a member of the site member's group.

You will need a SharePoint 2010 Team Site or any other SharePoint site to which a tasks list has been added.

How to do it...

1. Open your Team Site. Select the **Tasks** link from the quick-launch menu.
2. A list of the current tasks for the Team Site is displayed.
3. Click on the **Add new Item** link.

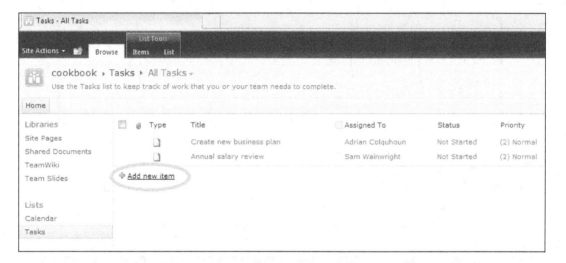

4. In the **Tasks—New Item** dialog box, enter the details for the task. To assign the task to another user, type their name in the **Assigned To** field or click on the book icon to browse to and select them.
5. Click on **Save** to create the task.

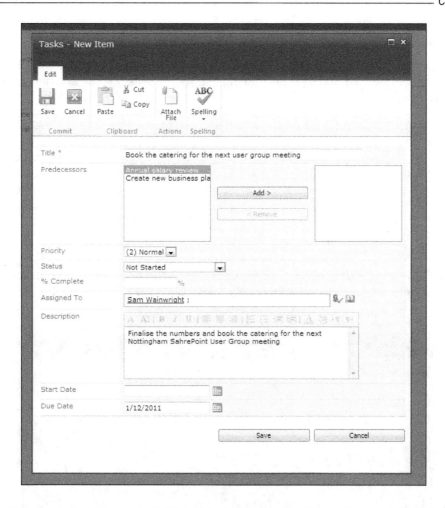

6. The new task is shown in the list of tasks for the site. Depending on the configuration of your task list, the user that the task is assigned to may also receive an e-mail notifying them of the task.

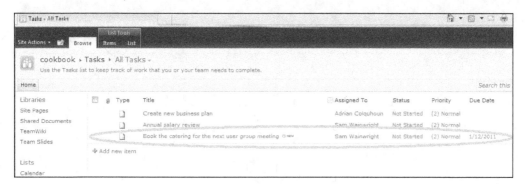

How it works...

A SharePoint tasks list is a special type of SharePoint list, optimized for the creation and management of tasks. By adding tasks into this list, you can easily share and track those tasks within your team.

"Assigning a task" to a user doesn't work in the way that most people expect. Regardless to who the task is assigned to, any user with Contribute permissions (or higher) will be able to view and edit the task. That is just the way SharePoint's security works. Tasks are just items in a list, so they can be changed by anyone who has sufficient permissions. If you need to make sure that only the person to whom a task is assigned can view or edit their tasks, then you will need to apply item level permissions to that task.

There's more...

Tasks lists have a number of pre-defined views that allow you to quickly toggle between to see tasks in different states such as **All Tasks**, **My Tasks**, **Due Today**, and so on.

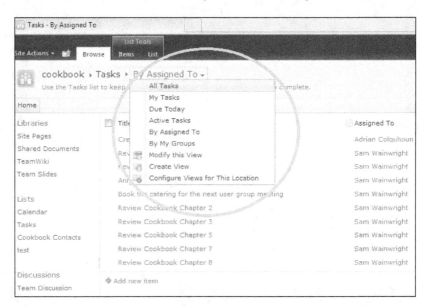

See also

▸ *Using the datasheet to bulk-edit tasks in a task list*

▸ *Managing a SharePoint task list in Outlook 2010*

Using the datasheet to bulk-edit tasks in a task list

The datasheet view allows you to quickly make changes to many tasks in one go.

Getting ready

This recipe works for:

▸ SharePoint 2010 Foundation

▸ SharePoint 2010 Standard Edition

▸ SharePoint 2010 Enterprise Edition

▸ Office 365 (SharePoint Online)

To access the datasheet view, you must have a version of Office 2010 installed.

You will need the **Contribute** permission level to edit tasks in the datasheet. This normally means that you will be a member of the site member's group.

You will need a SharePoint 2010 Team Site or any other SharePoint site to which a tasks list has been added.

How to do it...

1. Open your Team Site. Select the **Tasks** link from the quick-launch menu.
2. A list of the current tasks for the Team Site is displayed. Select the **List** tab from the **List Tools** ribbon.

3. Click on the **Datasheet View** icon in the ribbon to open the datasheet view of the Tasks List. You can now perform bulk update operations to quickly update multiple items.

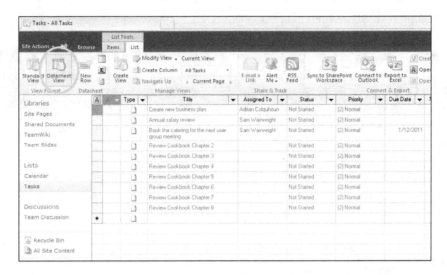

4. The remaining steps illustrate using cut and paste to assign **Sam Wainwright** to the outstanding cookbook review tasks. You can find more information about other bulk-edit operations in the *How it works* section later in this recipe.

5. In the **Assigned To** column, left-click into the cell containing the text **Sam Wainwright**. Right-click to display the context menu and select **Copy**.

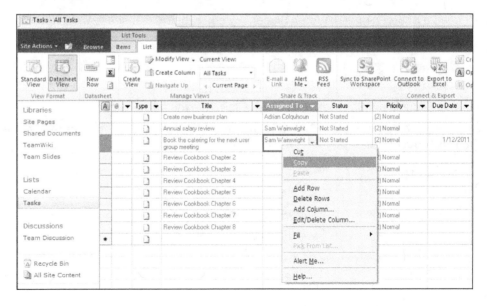

6. Left-click in the empty **Assigned To** cell (next to **Review Cookbook Chapter 2**).

7. Hold the left mouse button and drag down to highlight the empty **Assigned To** cells for the remaining tasks.

8. Right-click to bring up the context menu. Click on **Paste** as shown in the following screenshot:

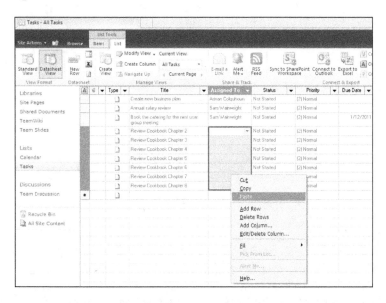

9. Sam Wainwright is assigned to all the previously highlighted tasks. Click on the **Standard View** icon on the **List Tools** ribbon to return to the standard view of the list.

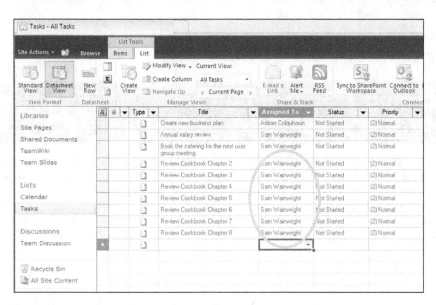

10. All the Review Cookbook tasks have been updated and are assigned to Sam.

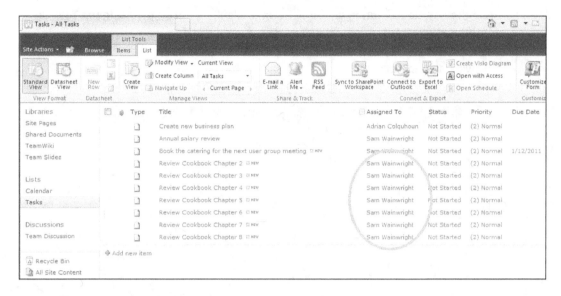

How it works...

SharePoint lists support many different types of views. The datasheet view is a special view which is designed to allow bulk-edit list items. If your list supports the datasheet view, then you will be able to access it from the **Lists** tab of the **List Tools** ribbon.

See also

▸ *Creating a task and assigning it to another user*

▸ *Managing a SharePoint task list in Outlook 2010*

Managing a SharePoint task list in Outlook 2010

Outlook 2010 provides a great location to view and manage your tasks. By connecting your SharePoint tasks lists to Outlook, you can track all the things that you need to do in one place.

Getting ready

This recipe works for:

▸ SharePoint 2010 Foundation

- ► SharePoint 2010 Standard Edition
- ► SharePoint 2010 Enterprise Edition
- ► Office 365 (SharePoint Online)

You will need the **Contribute** permission level to edit tasks in Outlook 2010 and have those changes synchronized back to SharePoint 2010. This normally means that you will be a member of the site member's group.

You will need the **Reader** permission level if you want to synchronize tasks (read-only) to Outlook 2010. You will be able to change the tasks but those changes will not be saved back to SharePoint 2010.

You will need a SharePoint 2010 Team Site or any other SharePoint site to which a tasks list has been added.

You will need Outlook 2010 installed on your client machine.

How to do it...

1. Open your Team Site. Select the **Tasks** link from the quick-launch menu.

2. A list of the current tasks for the Team Site is displayed. Select the **List** tab from the **List Tools** ribbon.

3. The **List Tools** ribbon is displayed. Click on the **Connect to Outlook** icon. A security prompt is displayed. Click on **Allow**.

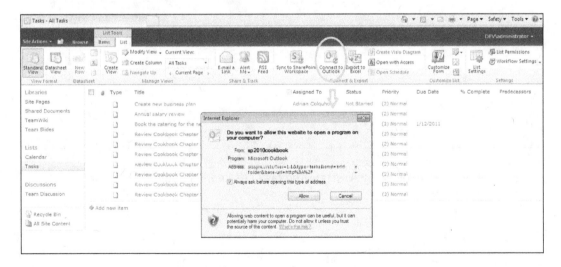

4. Outlook 2010 may also issue a security prompt. Click **Yes** to continue.

5. The SharePoint tasks will now be shown in Outlook.

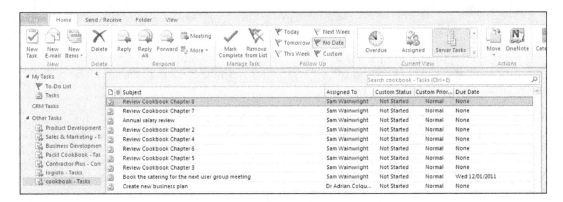

6. You can now work with these tasks in the same way as any other Outlook tasks. Double-click any task to open it.

7. Click on the **Mark Complete** button to mark the task as completed. Perform a **Send & Receive** and then switch back to SharePoint.

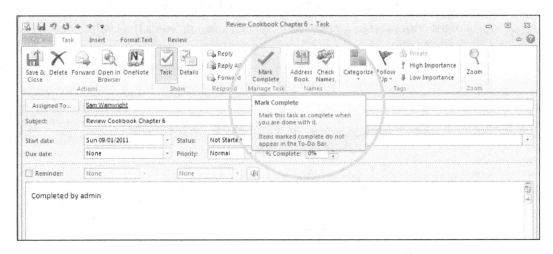

8. Refresh SharePoint's **Tasks** page. The task has been updated and is marked as complete.

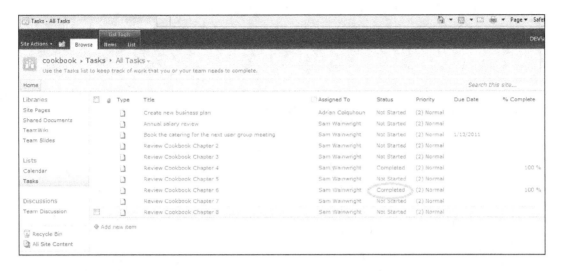

How it works...

Outlook 2010 provides in-depth task-management capabilities. SharePoint 2010 allows you to take advantage of these by providing the functionality to allow you to connect your task lists to Outlook 2010. Once connected, you can view and edit your tasks in Outlook 2010 and have the changes automatically synchronized back to SharePoint 2010. You can track tasks lists from multiple SharePoint sites in the same place and any tasks explicitly assigned to you will appear in your Outlook 2010 **To-Do List**.

There's more...

Observant readers will notice that the task that I completed in this recipe wasn't actually assigned to me. That is just the way SharePoint security works. By default, anyone with **Contributor** permission level or above in the site can edit any task. To change this behavior, you would need to apply item-level permissions to the individual tasks.

See also

- ▸ *Creating a task and assigning it to another user*
- ▸ *Using the datasheet to bulk-edit tasks in a task list*

Creating a SharePoint contact list and connecting it to Outlook 2010

SharePoint 2010 and Outlook 2010 both provide sophisticated contact-management capabilities. By joining the two together you can get the best of both worlds.

Getting ready

This recipe works for:

- ▸ SharePoint 2010 Foundation
- ▸ SharePoint 2010 Standard Edition
- ▸ SharePoint 2010 Enterprise Edition
- ▸ Office 365 (SharePoint Online)

You will need the **Contribute** permission level to edit contacts in Outlook 2010 and have those changes synchronized back to SharePoint. This normally means that you will be a member of the site member's group.

You will need the **Reader** permission level if you want to synchronize contacts (read-only) to Outlook 2010. You will be able to change the contacts but those changes will not be saved back to SharePoint 2010.

You will need Outlook 2010 installed on your client machine.

How to do it...

1. From your Team Site, open the **Site Actions** menu and click on **More Options**.
2. The **Create** dialog box is displayed. Select the **Filter By: List** option. The available lists are displayed. Click on the **Contacts** icon. Give your contacts list a name and click on the **Create** button.

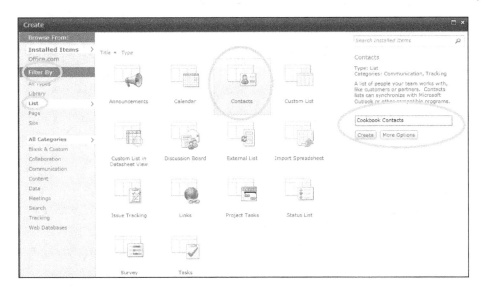

3. The new contacts list is displayed in SharePoint. On the **List Tools** ribbon, click on the **Connect to Outlook** icon. If the Internet Explorer security prompt is displayed, click on the **Allow** button.

4. If you are prompted by Outlook security, click on the **Yes** button.

5. The new contacts list is displayed in SharePoint. Click on the **New Contact** icon.

6. The **Contact** form is displayed. Fill in the details you require and click on the **Save & Close** icon.

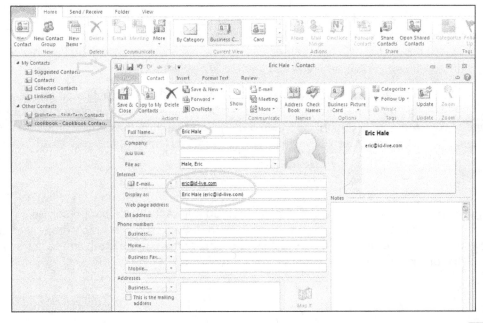

The new contact is displayed in Outlook.

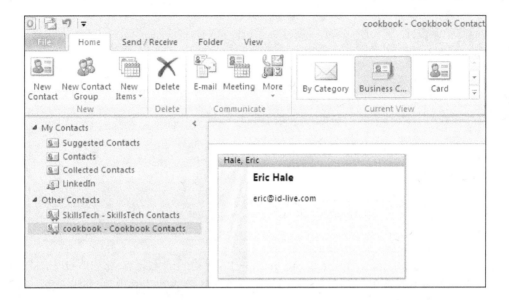

7.   Perform a **Send & Receive** and then switch back to SharePoint.

8.   Refresh the SharePoint contacts page. The new contact is displayed in SharePoint.

How it works...

A SharePoint 2010 **contacts list** is a special type of list designed for managing contacts. SharePoint 2010 provides the functionality that allows you to connect the contact list to Outlook. Once connected, you can create, edit, and delete contacts in Outlook, and have those changes automatically synchronized back to SharePoint.

Outlook 2010's contact-management user interface is much more sophisticated and powerful than that available through SharePoint 2010 alone. As an illustration, complete the address for one of your contacts in Outlook and then click on the **Map It** button. A new browser window will open and you will be shown a Bing map of your contacts location. Powerful stuff!

There's more...

Often, when you receive an e-mail from someone, you will want to add that person as a new contact. Once you have connected your contact list to Outlook, you can simply drag that e-mail from your **Inbox** and drop it on the contact list (hover over the **Contacts** tab first to get the contact list displayed).

Outlook will automatically open a **Contact** dialog box and fill in the details from the e-mail. Just add any further information you need, save the contact, and you are done. Simple!

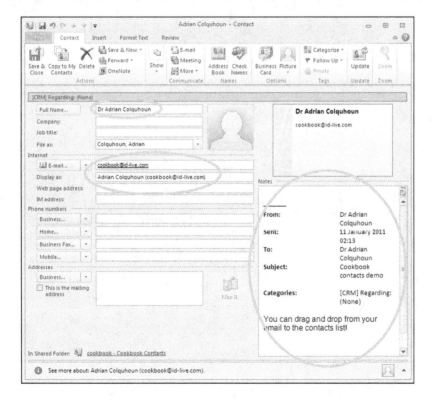

See also

▸ *Managing a Team Site calendar with Outlook 2010*

▸ *Managing a SharePoint task list in Outlook 2010*

3

SharePoint as the Data Hub—Storing and Integrating Data

In this chapter, we will cover:

- ▶ Creating a custom list
- ▶ Creating a custom list view
- ▶ Creating a term set using the managed metadata service
- ▶ Creating a list column based on a term set
- ▶ Creating an external content type
- ▶ Creating an external list

Introduction

The recipes in this chapter explore different ways to store and integrate data into SharePoint. Many of the recipes presented in this chapter make use of SharePoint Designer, an important application in the SharePoint power user's toolbox.

Recipes are included that cover storing and displaying data directly within SharePoint, by creating custom lists and custom list views. We then learn how to use the managed metadata service to first define **Term Sets** and then use them as columns in our SharePoint lists.

SharePoint 2010 is capable of read/write integration with external data stored in databases, web services, and other line-of-business systems. The final recipes in this chapter demonstrate how to create external content types and external lists to exploit this functionality, turning SharePoint into the data hub for your business.

Creating a custom list

SharePoint provides loads of great lists out of the box, but there will still be times when you need to create your own list. This recipe shows you how to use SharePoint Designer to create a custom list to track customer orders.

Getting ready

This recipe works for:

- ▸ SharePoint 2010 Foundation
- ▸ SharePoint 2010 Standard Edition
- ▸ SharePoint 2010 Enterprise Edition
- ▸ Office 365 (SharePoint Online)

You will need a SharePoint site where you want to create your custom list.

You will need the **Design** or **Full Control** permission level to run this recipe.

You will need SharePoint Designer 2010 installed on your machine, and permission to use SharePoint Designer against your site.

How to do it...

1. Open **Site Actions** menu and click on the **Edit in SharePoint Designer** option.
2. SharePoint Designer 2010 will load and open the site ready for editing.
3. Select **List and Libraries** in the **Site Objects** pane.
4. Select the **Custom List** icon in the **List and Libraries** ribbon.

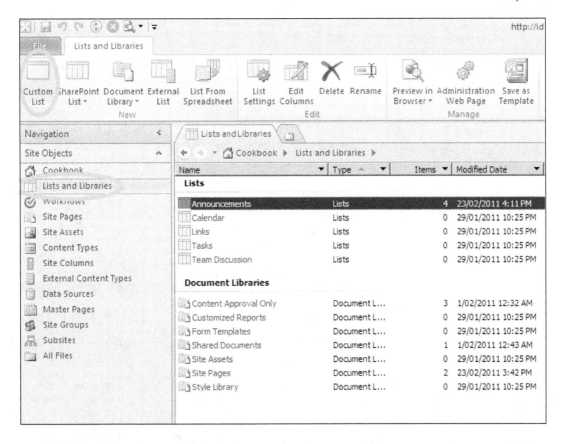

5. The **Create list or document library** dialog box is displayed. Enter the **Name Orders** for your list.

6. Click on the **OK** button to continue.

7. The **Orders** list is created and added to the **Lists and Libraries** shown in SharePoint Designer.

8. Highlight the **Orders** list and click the **Edit Columns** icon in the **Lists and Libraries** ribbon.

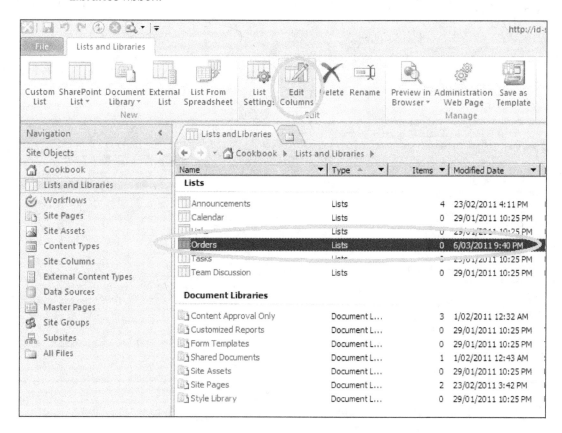

9. The list has a single column, **Title**. Click on the upside-down triangle under the **Add New Column** icon in the **Columns** ribbon. Select **Date & Time** from the column type drop-down menu.

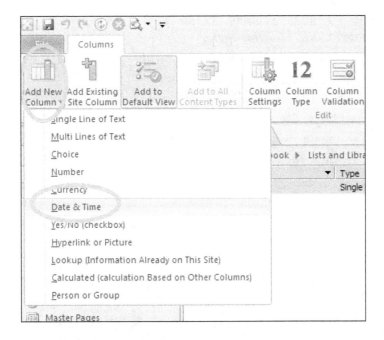

10. Enter **Order Date** in the **Column Name** field.

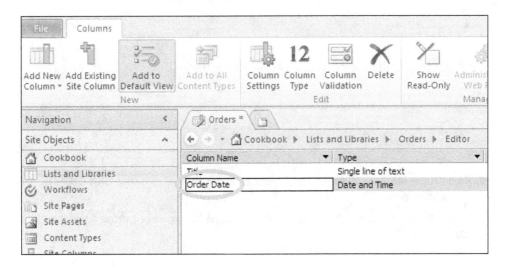

11. Repeat step 9, this time selecting **Currency** from the column type drop-down menu. Enter **Amount** for the **Column Name**.

12. Double-click on the **Amount** column that you have just created. The properties dialog is displayed.

13. Uncheck the **Allow blank values?** checkbox.

14. Set the **Number of decimal places** to **2**.

15. Check the **Minimum value allowed** and set the value to **0**.

16. Click on the **OK** button.

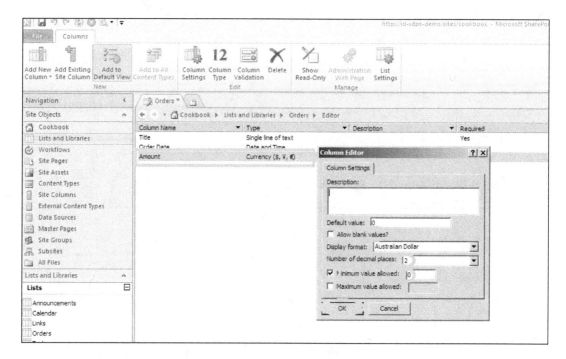

17. The orders list is now complete. Select **List and Libraries** in the **Site Objects** navigation pane.

18. Highlight the **Orders** list and select the **Preview in Browser** button from the **Lists and Libraries** ribbon.

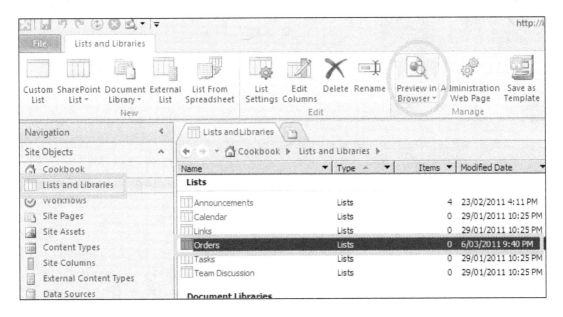

19. The **Orders** list is displayed in Internet Explorer.

How it works...

SharePoint ships with a number of built-in list templates that allow you to create commonly used lists (such as **Tasks**, **Contacts**, **Announcements**, and so on). The types of list that are available to you depends on your SharePoint version. When these lists don't meet your needs, you can simply create your own.

In this recipe we use SharePoint Designer 2010 to first create a custom list and then add the custom columns that we need. We can choose from a range of different data types for our columns and add custom validation to them as required. Once we have finished, our list works just like any other list in SharePoint, and we are ready to start adding data straight away.

It's also possible to declare a custom list using the web browser interface if you don't want (or are unable) to use SharePoint Designer.

> **SharePoint Designer versus the Web Browser Interface**
>
> Many SharePoint 2010 power user tasks can be achieved either through the web browser or SharePoint Designer 2010. Whenever you have a choice, I recommend that you use SharePoint Designer. This is a much more powerful and productive tool. As your knowledge develops you will find that there are a number of advanced tasks that can only be achieved using the SharePoint Designer application.

There's more...

An existing SharePoint list is often a good starting point for your custom-list requirements. The existing lists are designed to be customized so there is no need to reinvent the wheel and create your new custom list from scratch. Start by creating an instance of the SharePoint list that is closest to your needs and then add and remove columns until you achieve exactly the structure you want.

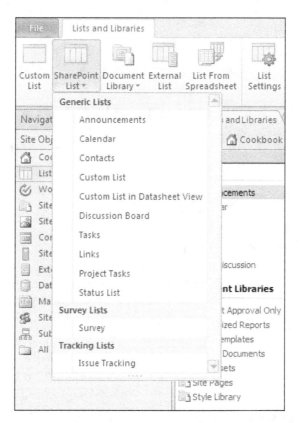

The same approach can be applied to the columns in your lists. First spend some time familiarizing yourself with SharePoint's existing site columns, as you may find something already exists that meets your needs. If you want to use a custom column in more than one list, consider defining it as a custom site column first and then adding it to your lists as required.

Creating a custom list from a spreadsheet

A common scenario is to create a custom list and then import existing data from a spreadsheet. SharePoint 2010 has a great timesaver for this, allowing you to create this list and import the data in a single operation.

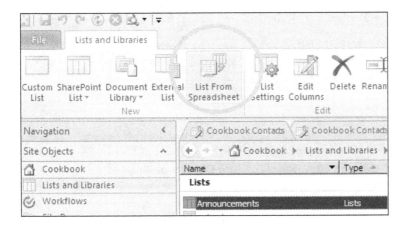

Begin by creating a spreadsheet that contains the list data that you want to import. Ensure that the first row of the spreadsheet has the column names that you require. Browse to the location of your spreadsheet using SharePoint Designer and let SharePoint do the rest. It will create your custom list, read all the rows of data, use the labels in the first row as your column headings, work out the correct data types for your columns, and then add all the data. This is great way to get a lot of data into SharePoint very quickly and do one-off imports from external systems. However, for seamless two-way integration with external systems, take a look at the *Creating an external list* recipe later in this chapter.

See also

> ▸ *Creating a SharePoint list, Chapter 1*
>
> ▸ *Creating a SharePoint contact list and connecting it to Outlook 2010, Chapter 2*
>
> ▸ *Creating an external list*

Creating a custom list view

SharePoint lists support different views, allowing you to see the information they contain in many different ways. This recipe shows you how to create your own custom views on a list.

Getting ready

This recipe works for:

> ▸ SharePoint 2010 Foundation
>
> ▸ SharePoint 2010 Standard Edition
>
> ▸ SharePoint 2010 Enterprise Edition
>
> ▸ Office 365 (SharePoint Online)

You will need the **Design** or **Full Control** permission level to run this recipe.

You will need a SharePoint list where you want to create a custom view. For illustration, the recipe uses the Orders list created in the previous recipe to create a custom view of large orders placed in the previous week.

How to do it...

1. Open the site containing your **Orders** list in SharePoint Designer.
2. Select **List and Libraries** in the **Site Objects** pane.
3. Select the **Orders List** icon in the main window.

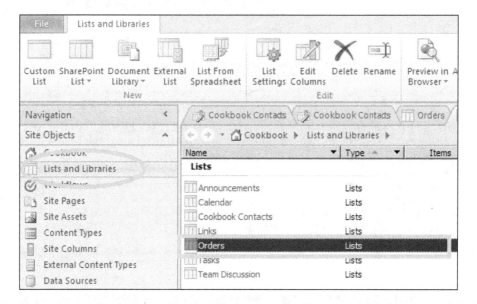

4. The Orders text is a hyperlink. Click on this hyperlink to activate the **List Settings** page.
5. Click on the **List View** icon in the **List Settings** ribbon.

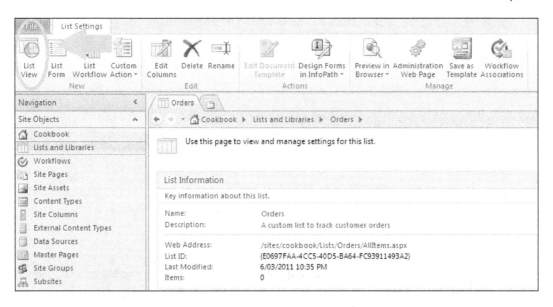

6. The **Create New List View** dialog is displayed. Name the list view **Large Orders in the Last 7 Days**.

7. Click on the **OK** button to continue.

8. The view is created and added to the **Views** pane. Click on the **Large Orders in Last 7 Days** hyperlink to edit the view settings.

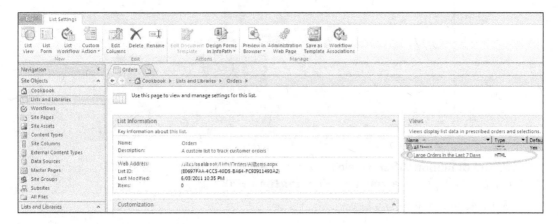

9. The view is created and added to the **Views** pane. Click on the **Large Orders in Last 7 Days** hyperlink to edit the view.

10. After a short delay, the custom view is loaded into SharePoint Designer. Click on the view to activate the **List View Tools** ribbon.

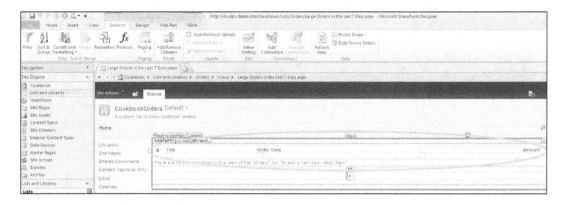

11. Activate the **Conditional Formatting** drop-down menu (click the upside-down black triangle) on the **List View Tools** ribbon. Select **Format Row**.

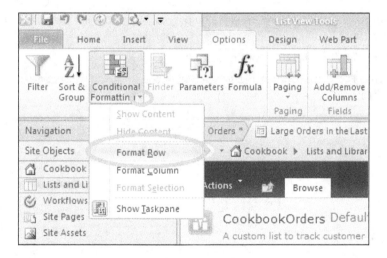

12. The **Condition Criteria** dialog box is displayed. Use the controls in this dialog to specify the criteria **Amount** is **Greater Than 2000**.

13. Click on the **Set Style** button.

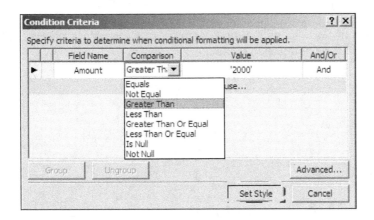

14. The **Modify Style** dialog is displayed. Select **background-color** and set the **color** to light green.

15. Click on the **OK** button.

16. Select the **Home** tab of the **List View Tools** ribbon.

17. Select the **Preview in Browser** icon.

18. You will be prompted to save your changes. Click on the **Yes** button.

19. The custom list view opens in the browser. Select the **List** tab of the **List Tools** ribbon and click on the **Modify View** option.

20. The **Edit View** page is displayed. Scroll down to the **Filter** section. Enter the expression shown to restrict the view to the last seven days' orders (**Order Date is greater than or equal to [Today] − 7**).

21. Scroll down and expand the **Totals** section.

22. Set the **Amount** column to **Sum**.

23. Scroll down and click on the **OK** button

24. The custom view is displayed in the web browser.

How it works...

This recipe creates a custom view of the Orders list using both SharePoint Designer and the web browser interface. The view only shows orders placed in the previous seven days. It conditionally formats all orders over $2,000 with a green background. The total value of the previous seven days orders is calculated and displayed at the top of the view.

The SharePoint Designer **List View Tools** ribbon provides many different options that you can use to create sophisticated custom views. You can apply conditional formatting, control paging, use filters, and add and remove columns to achieve exactly the view that you need. On the **Design** tab you will find some preset **View Styles**. You can easily switch between these styles and see the effects in the designer window. The second half of this recipe illustrates how to modify the custom view using the web browser interface.

Like many SharePoint artifacts, list views can be created through SharePoint designer (my recommend approach) and the web browser. There are some items, such as conditional formatting, that can only be accessed in SharePoint Designer, and others, such as custom date ranges and subtotals, that are much easier to specify using the browser. This recipe illustrates both approaches so that you are able to achieve results beyond what is possible using either tool on its own. Notice the use of the **[Today]-7** expression in the **Filter** section of the view. **[Today]** is a special token that SharePoint automatically replaces with the current date, allowing you to specify dynamic date ranges in your views. **[Me]** is another useful token, allowing you to filter or format views with items that are relevant to the current user.

Custom list views are an extremely powerful and flexible way to display list data. Spend some time exploring all the features that list views have to offer.

See also

▸ *Creating a custom list*

Creating a term set using the managed metadata service

SharePoint 2010 provides the ability to centrally define common terms and reuse those terms in lists and libraries. This saves you time and brings consistency to your SharePoint data.

Getting ready

This recipe works for:

▸ SharePoint 2010 – Standard Edition

▸ SharePoint 2010 – Enterprise Edition

▸ Office 365 (SharePoint Online)

You will need the **Full Control** permission level to run this recipe. You will need to have been added as **Term Store Administrator** to one or more **Groups** in the **Managed Metadata Service** to be able to create a new **Term Set**. This recipe creates a new **Term Set** under the **Cookbook** group for illustration.

How to do it...

1. Open the SharePoint site where you want to create a new term set.

2. Open the **Site Actions** menu and click **Site Settings**.

3. From **Site Settings** click on **Term Store Management** under the **Site Administration** section.

4. The **Term Store Management Tool** is displayed. Right-click on the **Cookbook** group and select **New Term Set** from the context menu displayed.

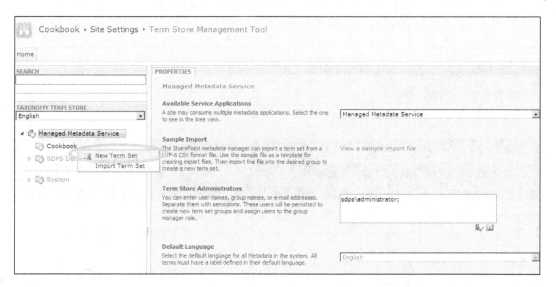

5. A **New Term Set** is added. Rename the term set as **Sales Location**.

6. Right-click on the **Sales Location** term set and select **Create Term** from the context menu displayed.

7. Continue to create terms in a hierarchy until the terms appear as shown in the following screenshot:

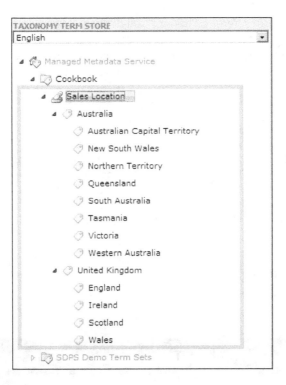

How it works...

SharePoint's managed metadata service provides the ability to define term sets (collections of useful terms or reference data) and then reuse these term sets throughout your SharePoint sites. You can define hierarchical terms (such as the sales locations in this recipe) and then reuse those values in columns attached to your lists or libraries. The next recipe shows you how to do this.

There's more...

The term set is an extremely powerful and a sophisticated new feature in SharePoint 2010.

SharePoint provides all the tools and user interfaces required to create, manage, and consume term sets. Term sets support features such as synonyms (different labels for terms that mean the same thing). Term sets can be closed (with a fixed set of values) or open (allowing users to add values to the term set as they require).

Wherever you have a set of reference data or well-defined set of terms you should consider placing them in a term set. This saves you time and helps enforce consistency in your SharePoint data. Values of terms can be updated centrally and those changes are automatically rippled out to where the affected terms are used.

If you have existing terms you can import them as CSV files to get started.

> Whenever you find yourself creating a lookup column in SharePoint, ask yourself "should this be a term set?" The more you make use of term sets, the more consistent and structured data you put into SharePoint. *Putability* is the key concept which underpins successful SharePoint information architectures. The better you put data in, the easier it is for users to get useful information out.

See also

▸ *Creating a list column based on a term set*

Creating a list column based on a term set

Once defined, term sets can be used to create list columns that allow users to quickly select term-set values rather than trying to type in data from scratch.

Getting ready

This recipe works for:

▸ SharePoint 2010 – Standard Edition

▸ SharePoint 2010 – Enterprise Edition

▸ Office 365 (SharePoint Online)

You will need a list where you wish to define your column and a term set that you want to use in the column definition. This recipe uses the **Orders** list created earlier in this chapter and the **Sales Location** term set defined in the previous recipe for illustration.

How to do it...

1. Open the **Orders** list.

2. Select the **List** tab in the **List Tools** ribbon.

3. Click on the **Create Column** icon.

4. The **Create Column** dialog is displayed. Name the column **Order Location** and select **Managed Metadata** for the column type.

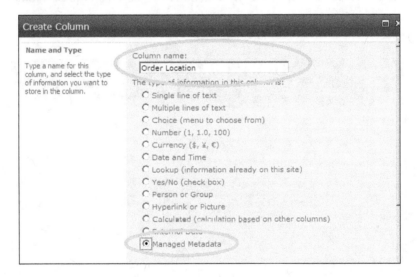

5. Scroll down through the **Create Column** dialog until the **Term Set Settings** are displayed.

6. Select the **Sales Location** term set.

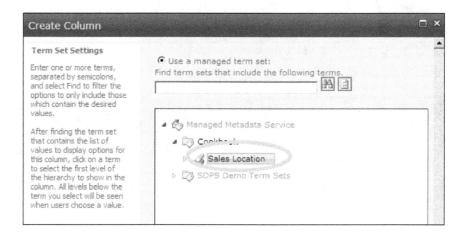

7. Scroll to the bottom of the **Create Column** dialog and click on the **OK** button.

8. The **Order Location** column is added to the list.

9. Select the first item in the list.

10. Select the **Items** tab from the **List Tools** ribbon and click on the **Edit Item** icon.

11. The Edit Item dialog is displayed with the **Order Location** column added. Click on the **tags** icon to select an order location.

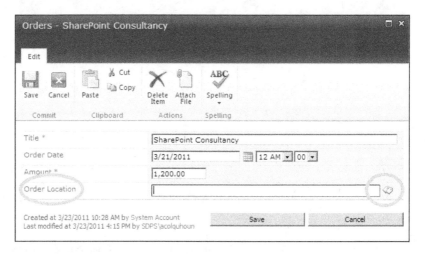

12. The term set selection dialog is displayed. Navigate to the term set required and click on the **Select** button.

13. Click on the **OK** button.

14. The selected value is added to the **Order Location** column. Click on the **Save** button.

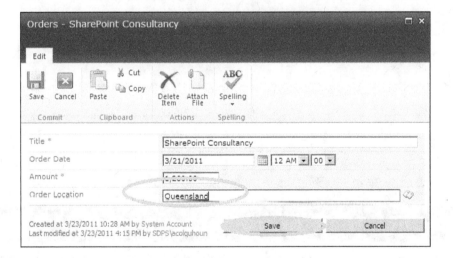

15. The selected value is shown in the list.

How it works...

The first half of this recipe demonstrates how to add a new managed metadata column, based on the **Sales Location** term set, to the existing **Orders** list. It then illustrates how to use that column to enter sales locations for existing list items. SharePoint provides the necessary user interface that allows sales locations to be quickly selected from the existing term-set values. In this case, you are only able to select a single, pre-existing value, ensuring control and consistency of the data entered.

There's more...

When you have one or more-term set columns defined on a list you can enable metadata navigation. You will find this option under **List Settings | Metadata Navigation**. The next screenshot shows metadata navigation enabled for the **Order Location** column. SharePoint adds a term store navigator control that allows the list to be filtered by any value in the term set. For example, you could first view all the orders for the **Australia** region and then drill down to only see orders for **Queensland**.

See also

> ► *Creating a term set using the managed metadata service*

Creating an external content type

An external content type is used to connect SharePoint columns and external lists to external data stored in databases, web services, and other systems. Creating external content types is the key to turning SharePoint into your organization's data hub.

Getting ready

This recipe works for:

- ► SharePoint 2010 Foundation
- ► SharePoint 2010 Standard Edition
- ► SharePoint 2010 Enterprise Edition
- ► Office 365 (SharePoint Online)

You will need the **Full Control** permission level to run this recipe.

You will need connection details for an external data source that you wish to connect to. This recipe uses the Adventures sample database for illustration. You can download the AdventureWorks database from – `http://msftdbprodsamples.codeplex.com/releases/view/37109`

You will need a SharePoint site where you wish to define the external content type.

How to do it...

1. Open your site using SharePoint Designer. From the Navigation pane click on **External Content Types**.

2. The **External Content Types** ribbon is displayed. Click on the **External Content Type** icon.

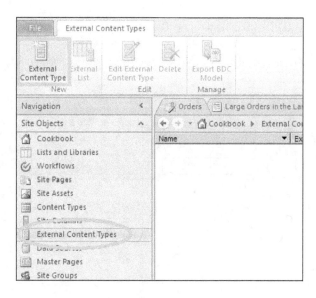

3. Set the **Name** and **Display Name** to **Contacts**.

4. Click on the **Operations Design View** icon from the **External Content Types** ribbon.

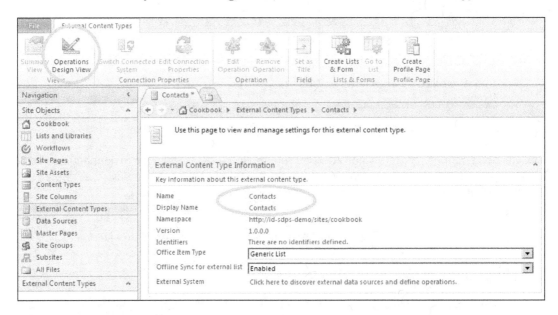

5. The **Operations Designer** is displayed. Click on the **Add Connection** button.

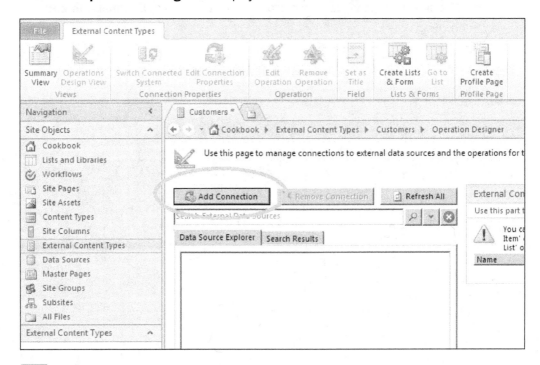

6. The **External Data Source Type Selection** dialog is displayed. Set the **Data Source Type** to **SQL Server**.

7. Click on the **OK** button.

8. Set the connection properties required to access your database.

9. Click on the **OK** button.

10. In the **Data Source Explorer**, right-click on the **Contacts** table to activate the content menu. Select the **Create All Operations** option.

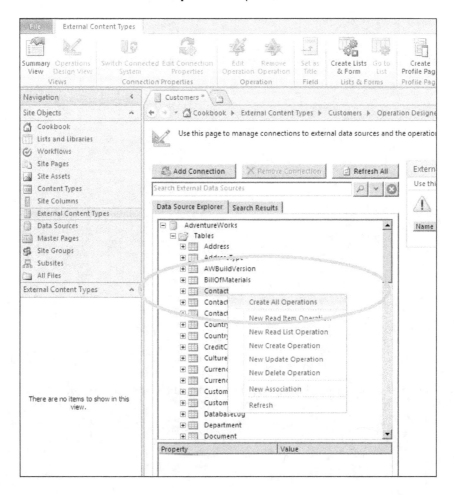

11. The **All operations** wizard is displayed.

12. Click on the **Next** button.

13. Set the **Parameters Configuration** as shown.

14. Click on the **Next** button.

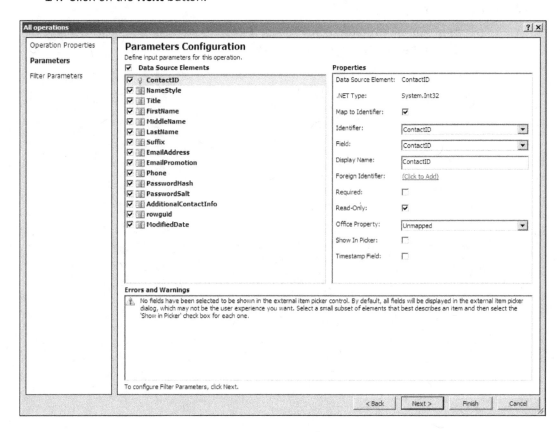

15. Click on the **Add Filter Parameter** button to add the **ContactID** filter.

16. Click on the **Click to Add** hyperlink next to **Filter:** in the **Properties** window.

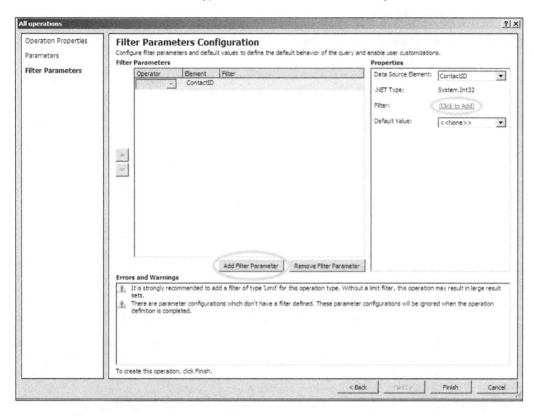

17. The **Filter Configuration** dialog is displayed. Change the **Filter Type** to **Limit**.
18. Click on the **OK** button.

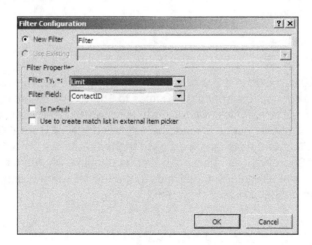

19. Enter **100** for the **Default Value**.

20. Click on the **Finish** button.

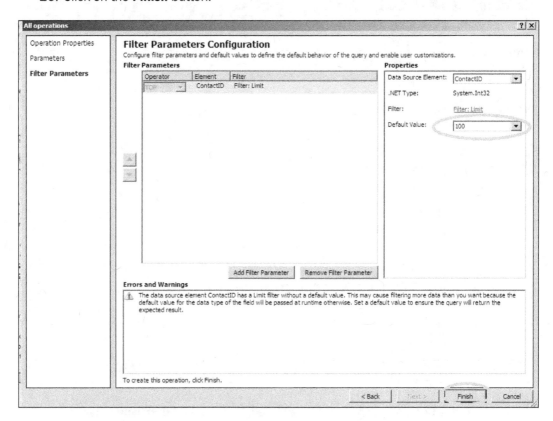

21. The **Contacts** external content type has now been created and is displayed in SharePoint Designer.

How it works...

SharePoint Server 2010 includes the Business Connectivity Service. This provides the plumbing required to connect external data sources to SharePoint. SharePoint Designer 2010 contains tools and wizards that allow you to create read/write connections to external data without writing code. The connection is made by first creating an **External Content Type**. Once created, this external content type can be exposed in SharePoint as an external list or as a column on a regular SharePoint list. Users can then manipulate and update the data in the same way as they update a regular list, oblivious to the fact the data is actually being fed from an external database or line-of-business system.

This recipe creates an external content type, which describes a read/write connection to the Contacts table in the AdventureWorks database. The next recipe shows you how to use this external content type to create an external list.

This recipe illustrates how to define a **Limit Filter** that restricts the data retrieved from the external database to 100 rows. Defining filters is important to prevent huge amounts of data being retrieved that can bring your SharePoint installation to a grinding halt.

This recipe merely scratches the surface of external content types. Despite the no-code tools provided by SharePoint Designer, external content types will stretch your dealings with SharePoint to the limit. There are many different options available for the authentication, configuration, and use of external content types. Whole books have been written on the Business Connectivity Service and the subject becomes very complicated quite quickly. Nevertheless, the external content type presented here, together with the external list described in the next recipe, is a working example with real business benefit.

 I strongly recommend that you call upon professional SharePoint developers, architects, and administrators to help when working with external content types.

There's more...

Creating the external content type is only half the story. You won't be able to use it to display data in external lists or columns until your SharePoint administrator grants the necessary security permissions on it. This operation can only be performed through Central Administration and is beyond the scope of this book. You will need to ask your SharePoint administrator to do this for you. You will receive an **Access denied by Business Data Connectivity** error each time you try and use the external content type until this is done.

See also

▶ _Creating an external list_

Creating an external list

SharePoint can expose data from a database, web service, or custom line-of-business system in the same way as a regular SharePoint list. What's more, users can update that data in SharePoint and their changes can be written back to the source data without requiring a custom user interface or code.

Getting ready

This recipe works for:

- SharePoint 2010 Foundation
- SharePoint 2010 Standard Edition
- SharePoint 2010 Enterprise Edition
- Office 365 (SharePoint Online)

You will need the **Full Control** permission level to run this recipe.

You will need an **External Content Type** to create your external list from. This recipe uses the **Contacts** external content type from the previous recipe for illustration.

You will need a SharePoint site where you want to create your external list.

How to do it...

1. Open your site in SharePoint Designer.
2. Select **External Content Types** in the **Site Objects** pane.
3. Highlight the **Contacts** external **content** type.
4. Select **Edit External Content Type** from the **External Content Types** ribbon.

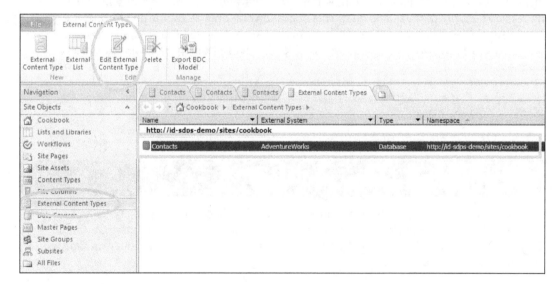

5. Select the **Create Lists & Form** icon from the **External Content Types** ribbon.

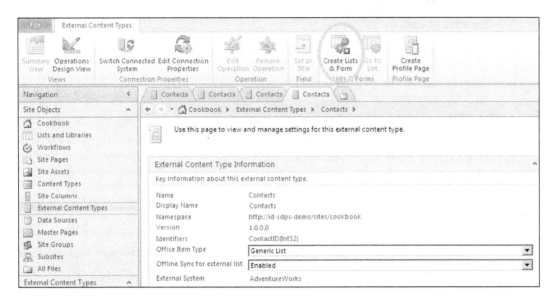

6. The **Create List and Form for Contacts** dialog is displayed. Set the dialog properties as shown in the screenshot and click on the **OK** button.

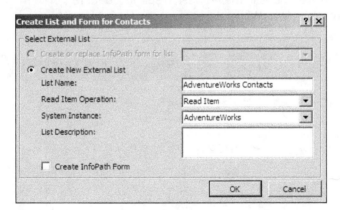

7. The **AdventureWorks Contacts** external list is created. Highlight the external list in SharePoint Designer. Click on the **Preview in Browser** icon from the **Lists & Libraries** ribbon.

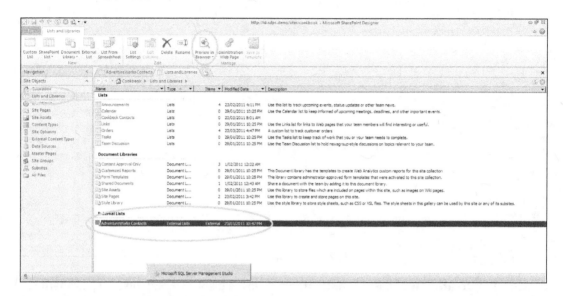

8. The external list opens in the browser, displaying data retrieved from the Contacts table of the AdventureWorks database.

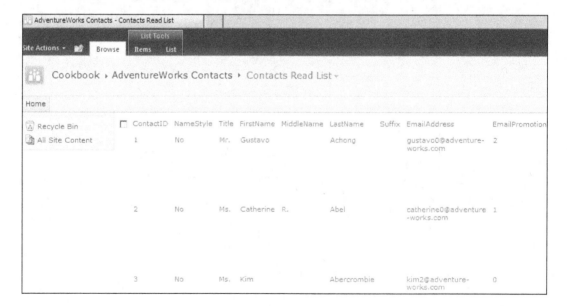

How it works...

This recipe shows how to use a previously defined external content type to create an external list. Once created, the external list appears just like any other list in SharePoint. You can use SharePoint's familiar list user interface to view data, filter, sort, and so on. You can even change data values in the list and have those changes automatically saved back to the database.

External lists represent a powerful way to show external data in SharePoint. That data can be read/write (as illustrated here) or read-only if you prefer. As mentioned in the previous recipe, there are many subtleties and nuances with external lists, so I strongly recommend getting SharePoint professionals to help before using external lists in anger.

 Some features of regular lists, such as alerts, versioning, datasheet view, and workflows are not available on external lists.

There's more...

External lists are just one way of surfacing external data in SharePoint. You can also use external content types to define list columns, allowing you to attach external data to your regular SharePoint lists, with the viewer unaware that the data is being derived from two different data sources.

See also

- ► *Creating an external content type*
- ► *Creating a custom list*
- ► *Creating a SharePoint list, Chapter 1*

4
SharePoint Document Management Deep Dive

In this chapter, we will cover:

- ▶ Uploading an existing document to a document library
- ▶ Uploading multiple documents to a document library
- ▶ Creating a new document in your My Site
- ▶ E-mailing a link to a document in SharePoint
- ▶ Downloading a copy of a document
- ▶ Creating an alert on a document to be notified when it is updated
- ▶ Requiring users to check out a document before they can edit it
- ▶ Enabling versioning on a document library
- ▶ Publishing a major version of a document
- ▶ Restoring a previous version of a document
- ▶ Enabling content approval on a document library
- ▶ Taking SharePoint documents offline using Outlook 2010
- ▶ Co-authoring an important document
- ▶ Using content types to store different types of document in the same document library

Introduction

Document management is probably the most well-known and widely used SharePoint feature. This chapter provides a deep dive into SharePoint 2010's document management capabilities and shows you how to make best use of them.

The recipes guide you through common document management operations such as uploading documents, versioning, e-mailing links to documents, downloading document copies, and setting alerts to be notified when a document changes.

Recipes are included that deal with more advanced functionality, such as publishing major versions of a document, restoring previous versions, taking document libraries offline with Outlook 2010, and using content types to store different types of document in the same document library.

There will be times when you will need exclusive access to a document while you update it. A recipe is included that shows how to require the checkout of a document so that others cannot change it while you work on it.

However, often the reverse is true. You may need to work collaboratively with other authors to quickly produce an important document. Office 2010 and SharePoint 2010 offer the ability to co-author documents in real time. It's really powerful stuff, and there is a recipe included that shows you exactly how to do it.

Uploading an existing document to a document library

Document libraries are used to store and manage documents in SharePoint. This recipe shows you how to upload a document that you have already created.

Getting ready

This recipe works for:

- SharePoint 2010 Foundation
- SharePoint 2010 Standard Edition
- SharePoint 2010 Enterprise Edition
- Office 365 (SharePoint Online)

You will need a SharePoint site with a document library where you want to upload your document. This recipe uses a SharePoint 2010 Team Site for illustration.

You will need the **Contribute** permission level to run this recipe.

How to do it...

1. Open the SharePoint Team Site that you want to upload your document to.
2. Select the **Shared Documents** link in the **Quick Launch** menu.
3. Select the **Add Document** link.
4. The **Upload Document** dialog is displayed. Click on the **Browse...** button to locate the document you want to upload.

5. The **Choose File to Upload** dialog is displayed showing documents on your computer. Browse to the document that you want to upload, select the document and click on the **Open** button.

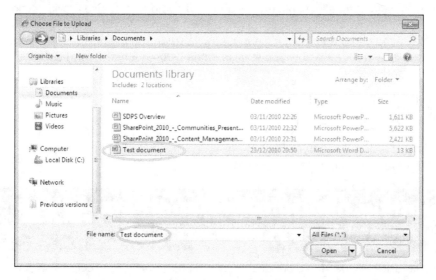

6. The name of the file that you want to upload is copied into the **Upload Document** dialog. Click the **OK** button to upload the file to SharePoint.
7. There may be a short delay while your file is uploaded. Once the processing is complete your document appears in the **Shared Documents** library.

How it works...

Everything in SharePoint is ultimately stored in lists. However, SharePoint has a special type of list for storing documents – the **Document Library**. This is designed to allow you to upload documents that you have previously created. Document libraries provide loads of built-in document management functionality, such as versioning, content approval, check in, check out, and so on. You can add extra columns to your document library to store other information (metadata) related to the document. SharePoint will index your document's contents (Office documents only), its metadata, and it will add this information to its search index. You can restrict who gets access to your documents by applying document library or item level permissions and you can use SharePoint's built-in review and approval workflows to get feedback or authorization of your document from your co-workers. Document libraries offer many advantages over file shares, e-mail inboxes, and your local computer and so you should consider using them for storing your documents wherever possible.

There's more...

SharePoint document libraries don't just store Word documents. You can add spreadsheets, presentations, PDF documents, pictures, videos, audio, text files, and so on. In fact virtually any type of file can be added to a document library unless your administrators have explicitly blocked it or it is too big (50 MB is the default maximum size limit). That's not to say that you should store everything in your document libraries. SharePoint provides other libraries that are specially designed for slides, pictures, video, and audio files. It also provides content types and document sets (not available in SharePoint Foundation 2010) to help classify you documents. Spend some time thinking about how you want to organize your documents and other content in SharePoint before you start uploading documents. This will save you a lot of time and frustration later on.

See also

▶ *Uploading multiple documents to a document library*

▶ *Creating a new document in your My Site*

Uploading multiple documents to a document library

Document libraries are used to store documents in SharePoint. This recipe shows you how to quickly upload multiple documents that you have previously created.

Getting ready

This recipe works for:

- ▸ SharePoint 2010 Foundation
- ▸ SharePoint 2010 Standard Edition
- ▸ SharePoint 2010 Enterprise Edition
- ▸ Office 365 (SharePoint Online)

You will need a SharePoint site with a document library where you want to upload your document. This recipe uses a SharePoint 2010 Team Site for illustration.

You will need Office 2010 installed on your client machine.

You will need the **Contribute** permission level to run this recipe.

How to do it...

1. Open the SharePoint Team Site that you want to upload you documents to.
2. Select the **Shared Documents** link in the **Quick Launch** menu.
3. Select the **Documents** tab in the **Library Tools** ribbon.
4. Click on the small black triangle at the right of the **Upload Document** icon.
5. A drop-down menu is displayed. Click on the **Upload Multiple Documents** menu option.

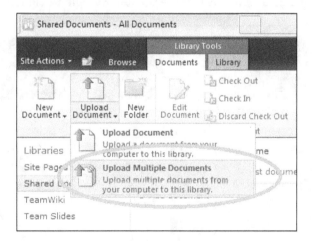

6. The **Upload Multiple Documents** dialog box is displayed.

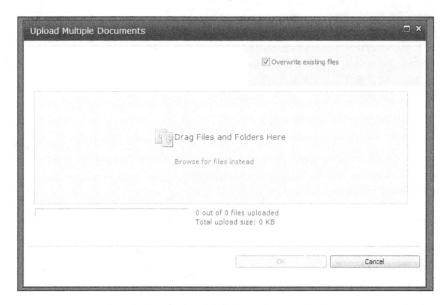

7. Open Windows Explorer on your computer. Navigate to the folder containing the documents that you want to upload.

8. Select the documents that you wish to upload. Hold down the *Ctrl* key and select multiple documents by clicking the mouse.

9. Drag the selected documents into the **Upload Multiple Documents** dialog.

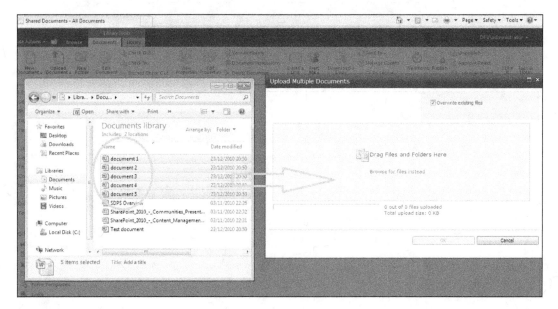

10. The names of the documents to be uploaded are copied into the dialog. Click on the **OK** button to start the upload.

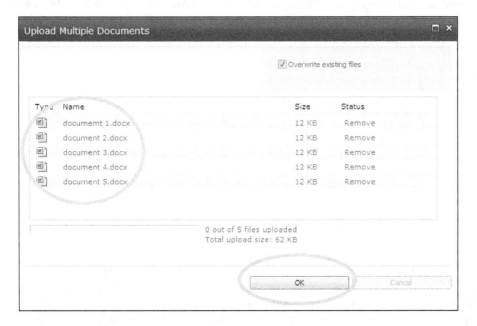

11. The progress of the upload is displayed. When all the files are uploaded, click on the **Done** button.

12. The uploaded documents are added to the **Shared Documents** document library.

How it works...

SharePoint document libraries are a great place to store your important documents. However, uploading your documents one by one isn't much fun. Thankfully, SharePoint 2010 provides a drag-and-drop control that allows you to quickly upload multiple documents to a document library. You can upload up to 100 documents at once using this approach. You may find it easier to collect together all the documents that you want to upload into a single folder on your local computer first, and then drag-and-drop all your documents in one go from there.

See also

▸ *Uploading an existing document in a document library*

▸ *Creating a new document in your My Site*

Creating a new document in your My Site

Your My Site is a great place to create your personal documents, particularly if you're not quite ready to share them with the rest of the world. This recipe shows you how to do it.

Getting ready

This recipe works for:

▶ SharePoint 2010 Standard Edition

▶ SharePoint 2010 Enterprise Edition

▶ Office 365 (SharePoint Online)

You will need a SharePoint My Site. If you are not sure how to access your My Site, see the *Creating and accessing my My Site* recipe in *Chapter 1*.

 If you don't have a My Site or only have SharePoint Foundation available, you can substitute any SharePoint site into the recipe provided that it contains a document library. Be aware that whoever has access to read that document library will be able to then read the document that you create.

How to do it...

1. From within any SharePoint site, click on your name (top right of the page). Select the **My Site** link from the menu that is displayed.

2. Select the **My Content** link.

3. Click on the **Personal Documents** link on the **Quick Launch** menu.

4. Click on the **New Document** icon on **Documents** tab of the **Library Tools** ribbon.

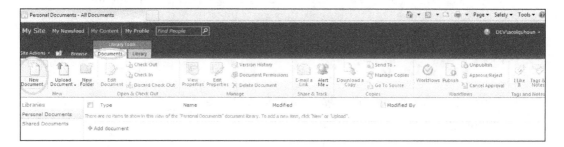

5. Microsoft Word 2010 will open. Enter some content into the document and click on the **Save** icon.

6. You will be prompted for the name and location to save your document. This will already be set to the **Personal Documents** library of your My Site. Enter a suitable file name and click on the **Save** button.

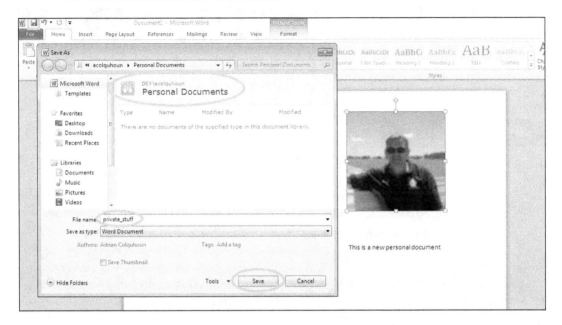

7. Close the document and return to your My Site in the browser.

8. The document you created is now stored in the **Personal Documents** library (If you can't see the document, press *F5* to refresh your web browser).

How it works...

Your **My Site** contains two preconfigured document libraries. The Personal Documents library is designed for storing documents that you want to keep private. You will be able to see any documents that you create here, but other visitors to your My Site will not. By contrast, any documents you create in the Shared document library will be visible to everyone who has access to your My Site.

When you click on the **New Document** icon in the ribbon, Microsoft Word 2010 automatically opens and you can add your content. When you come to save your document, Word is already configured to save the document back to the correct document library—just provide a suitable file name and you are done.

See also

▸ *Uploading an existing document to a document library*

▸ *Uploading multiple documents to a document library*

E-mailing a link to a document in SharePoint

SharePoint document libraries provide a great alternative to e-mailing documents around. If you want someone else to read a document, just e-mail them a link instead. This recipe shows you how.

Getting ready

This recipe works for:

▸ SharePoint 2010 Foundation

▸ SharePoint 2010 Standard Edition

▸ SharePoint 2010 Enterprise Edition

▸ Office 365 (SharePoint Online)

You will need a SharePoint site with a document library containing a document that you wish to e-mail a link to. This recipe uses a SharePoint 2010 Team Site for illustration.

You will need the **Read** permission level to run this recipe.

You will need Outlook 2010 installed on your machine.

How to do it...

1. Open the SharePoint Team Site containing the document you want to send the link to.
2. Open the **Shared Documents** link in the **Quick Launch** menu.
3. Select the **Documents** tab in the **Library Tools** ribbon.
4. Click on the checkbox for the document that you want to e-mail links for.
5. Click on the **E-mail a Link** icon in the **Documents** tab of the **Library Tools** ribbon.

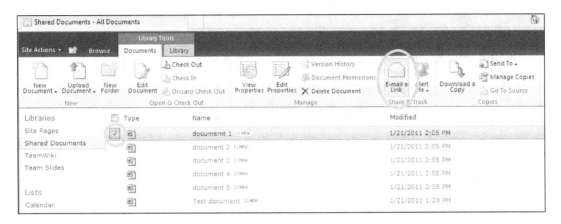

6. If you receive a security prompt, click on **Allow**.

7. Outlook 2010 opens and a new e-mail is created with the link to your document inserted. Add the recipients, subject line and any other text that you require then click on **Send**.

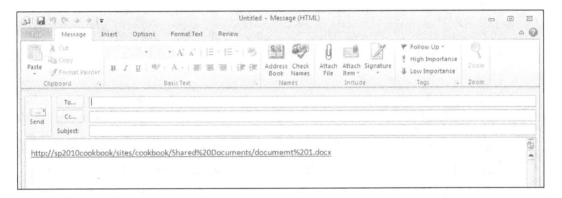

How it works...

Every document in a SharePoint document library can be accessed by its link. SharePoint has a built-in command to get this and place it into an e-mail so that you can send it to your colleagues. Anyone who receives the link can click on it to try to open the document. However, SharePoint's security model still applies. If the other user doesn't have the correct permissions to access the site and open the document then SharePoint won't let them do it, whether they have the link to the document or not.

See also

▶ *Downloading a copy of a document*

Downloading a copy of a document

SharePoint 2010 is a great place to store documents, but there will still be times when you need a document on your local computer. This recipe shows you how to download a copy.

Getting ready

This recipe works for:

▶ SharePoint 2010 Foundation

▶ SharePoint 2010 Standard Edition

▶ SharePoint 2010 Enterprise Edition

▶ Office 365 (SharePoint Online)

You will need a SharePoint site with a document library containing a document that you want to download. This recipe uses a SharePoint 2010 Team Site for illustration.

You will need the **Read** permission level to run this recipe.

How to do it...

1. Open the SharePoint Team Site that you want to download a document from.
2. Open the **Shared Documents** link in the **Quick Launch** menu.
3. Select the **Documents** tab in the **Library Tools** ribbon.
4. Click on the checkbox for the document that you want to download.
5. Click on the **Download a copy** icon in the ribbon.

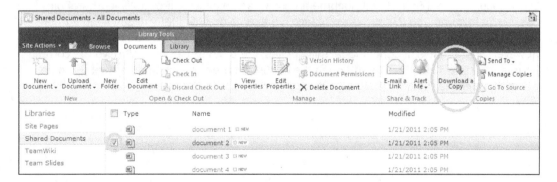

6. The **File Download** dialog is displayed. Click on the **Save** button.

7. Select the folder where you want to save the document.

8. A copy of the document is now saved on your computer.

How it works...

SharePoint provides a built-in command to allow you to download a document from a document library and save it to your local computer. This is a great way to download a few documents. However, if you need to download multiple documents, try opening the document library in windows explorer using the **Library Tab** of the **Library Tools** ribbon or download the whole document library using Outlook 2010 as described later in this chapter.

See also

▶ *E-mailing a link to a document in SharePoint*

▶ *Taking SharePoint documents offline using Outlook 2010*

Creating an alert on a document to be notified when it is updated

SharePoint can automatically alert you when a document is changed. This recipe shows you how.

Getting ready

This recipe works for:

▶ SharePoint 2010 Foundation

▶ SharePoint 2010 Standard Edition

▶ SharePoint 2010 Enterprise Edition

▶ Office 365 (SharePoint Online)

You will need a SharePoint site with a document library containing a document that you want to create an alert on. This recipe uses a SharePoint 2010 Team Site for illustration.

You will need the **Read** permission level to run this recipe.

How to do it...

1. Open the SharePoint Team Site where you want to set your document alert.
2. Open the **Shared Documents** link in the **Quick Launch** menu.
3. Select the **Documents** tab in the **Library Tools** ribbon.
4. Click on the checkbox for the document that you want to set the alert on.
5. Click the **Alert Me** icon in the ribbon.
6. A drop-down menu is then displayed. Click on the **Set alert on this document menu** option.

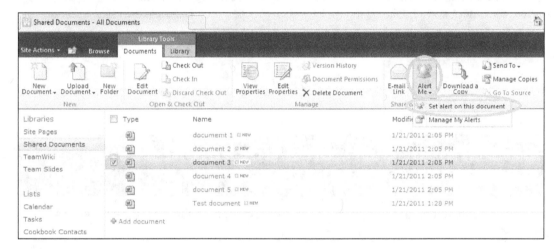

7. In the dialog box displayed, set the options that you require for your alert and then click on **OK**.

How it works...

SharePoint can send alerts when something changes. You can receive alerts by e-mail or SMS (assuming that your administrator has configured these options). This recipe shows you how to set an alert for a single document, but you can set alerts on lots of other SharePoint items too. For more information on setting and managing alerts, refer to the alerts recipes included in *Chapter 1*.

See also

▸ *Adding an alert to a SharePoint page, Chapter 1*

▸ *Managing my alerts in SharePoint, Chapter 1*

Requiring users to check out a document before they can edit it

If you want to prevent multiple people from editing a document at the same time, you can require that documents are checked out first.

Getting ready

This recipe works for:

▸ SharePoint 2010 Foundation

▸ SharePoint 2010 Standard Edition

▸ SharePoint 2010 Enterprise Edition

▸ Office 365 (SharePoint Online)

You will need a SharePoint site with a document library where you want to require check out. This recipe uses a SharePoint 2010 Team Site for illustration.

You will need the **Design** or **Full Control** permission level to run this recipe.

How to do it...

1. Open the SharePoint Team Site where you want to require check out.
2. Open the **Shared Documents** link in the **Quick Launch** menu.
3. Select the **Library** tab in the **Library Tools** ribbon.
4. Click on the **Library Settings** icon.

5. The **Document Library Settings** page is displayed. Click on the **Versioning settings** link.

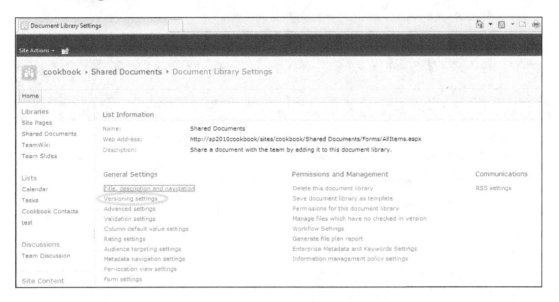

6. Set **Require Checkout** section, and set the **Require documents to be checked out before they can be edited?** radio button to **Yes**.

7. Click on the **OK** button. Users will now be prompted to check out documents before they can edit them.

How it works...

SharePoint document libraries support the concepts of check in and check out. When you check out a document, you effectively place an exclusive lock on it. This is like saying "*I am changing this document so nobody else can work on it*". Other users will still be able to open a read only copy of the document, but they won't be able to edit it. Nor will they see the changes that you make until you check the document back in.

You can check out a document before editing it in any SharePoint document library (regardless of the require checkout setting). If you don't check out a document before you edit it then SharePoint applies the "last save wins" rule. The changes you make could be overridden by the changes made by somebody else to an earlier copy of the document. Setting the require check out option as described in this recipe forces a document to be explicitly checked out before it can be edited and so prevents this from happening.

There's more...

Office 2010 Professional now allows multiple authors to edit the same document at the same time and merge their changes together in real time. See the *co-authoring an important document* recipe later in this chapter for details on how to do this.

See also

▶   *Co-authoring an important document*

Enabling versioning on a document library

SharePoint document libraries can automatically save previous versions of a document. This recipe shows how to enable this.

Getting ready

This recipe works for:

▶   SharePoint 2010 Foundation

▶   SharePoint 2010 Standard Edition

▶   SharePoint 2010 Enterprise Edition

▶   Office 365 (SharePoint Online)

You will need a SharePoint site with a document library where you want to enable versioning. This recipe uses a SharePoint 2010 Team Site for illustration.

You will need the **Design** or **Full Control** permission level to run this recipe.

How to do it...

1.   Open the SharePoint Team Site where you want to enable versioning.

2.   Open the **Shared Documents** link in the **Quick Launch** menu.

3.   Select the **Library** tab In the **Library Tools** ribbon.

4.   Click on the **Library Settings** icon.

5.   The **Document Library Settings** page is displayed. Click on the **Versioning** link.

6. The **Version Settings** page is displayed. Select the **Create major and minor (draft) versions** radio button and click on the **OK** button.

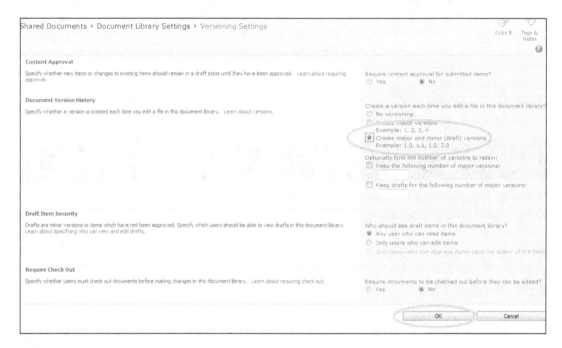

How it works...

Consider the authoring process required for a typical business document. The document will probably have many different versions before it is considered complete, for example, first, second, third drafts, reviewer's comments, legal department checks, and so on. Often the document author tries to keep track of all these different document versions by copying and renaming the document itself using naming conventions such as `doc1_afterlegalreview.docx`. This soon gets very messy, and it's easy to lose track of which version of the document is actually the current one.

Fortunately, SharePoint document libraries can track and store multiple versions of the same document automatically. There is no need to manually manage separate document copies or have different document libraries for draft and published documents. SharePoint can be configured (as in this recipe) to distinguish between minor versions (drafts) and major versions (published documents) automatically.

You can also adjust the versioning settings in the document library so that published and draft versions of documents have different visibility. To do this set the **Draft Item Security** option to **Only users who can edit items**. All users will be able to see the published versions of documents while only those with **Contribute** permission level or above will be able to access more recent draft versions.

All changes made to a document are saved as new draft versions. To create a new published version, the document must be published using the functionality provided by SharePoint (see the publishing a major version of a document recipe later in this chapter for more details).

Document libraries maintain a version history for each document and previous versions of the documents can be viewed or restored if necessary.

See also

▶ *Publishing a major version of a document*

▶ *Restoring a previous version of a document*

Publishing a major version of a document

SharePoint document libraries support the concept of publishing. Documents are created as drafts and can be published (as a major version) to make them visible to others. This recipe shows you how.

Getting ready

This recipe works for:

▶ SharePoint 2010 Foundation

▶ SharePoint 2010 Standard Edition

▶ SharePoint 2010 Enterprise Edition

▶ Office 365 (SharePoint Online)

You will need a SharePoint site with a document library with major and minor versioning enabled (see the previous recipe for instructions how to do this). This recipe uses a SharePoint 2010 Team Site for illustration.

You will need the **Design** or **Full Control** permission level to run this recipe.

How to do it...

1. Open the SharePoint Team Site containing the document you want to publish.
2. Open the **Shared Documents** link in the **Quick Launch** menu.
3. Select the **Documents** tab in the **Library Tools** ribbon.
4. Click on the checkbox for the document that you want to publish.

5.   Click on the **Publish** icon in the ribbon.

6.   The **Publish Major Version** dialog is displayed.

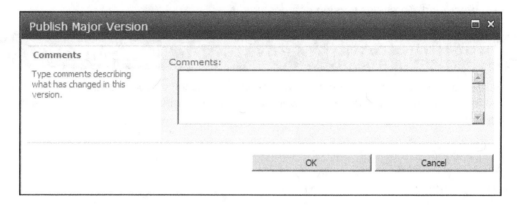

7.   The document is published as a new major version.

How it works...

When major and minor versions are enabled on a SharePoint document library, SharePoint saves all the changes made to a document as new minor (draft) versions. When all the amendments to a document are complete a new major version of the document can be published using the SharePoint functionality described here. Depending on the document library configuration, different users may have different visibility of published and draft documents.

Document publishing is often combined with content approval to give a complete document-management lifecycle, as described in the recipe *enabling content approval* later in this chapter.

See also

►   *Restoring a previous version of a document*

►   *Enabling content approval on a document library*

Restoring a previous version of a document

Sometimes you will need to restore a previous version of a document. This recipe shows you how.

Getting ready

This recipe works for:

- ▸ SharePoint 2010 Foundation
- ▸ SharePoint 2010 Standard Edition
- ▸ SharePoint 2010 Enterprise Edition
- ▸ Office 365 (SharePoint Online)

You will need a SharePoint site with a document library with versioning enabled and a document with a previous version that you wish to restore. This recipe uses the **Shared Documents** library in a SharePoint 2010 Team Site for illustration.

You will need the **Contribute** permission level to run this recipe.

How to do it...

1. Open the SharePoint Team Site with the document library containing the document that you want to restore.
2. Open the **Shared Documents** link in the **Quick Launch** menu.
3. Click on the checkbox to select the document that you want to restore.
4. In the **Library Tools** ribbon, select the **Documents** tab.
5. Select the **Version History** icon.

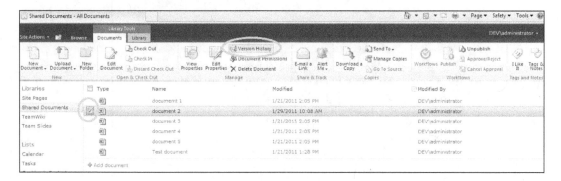

6. The **Version History** dialog is displayed.

7. Use the mouse pointer to hover over the date and time of the version that you wish to restore.

8. A small black upside-down triangle appears. Click on this triangle to reveal the restore menu.

9. Select **Restore**.

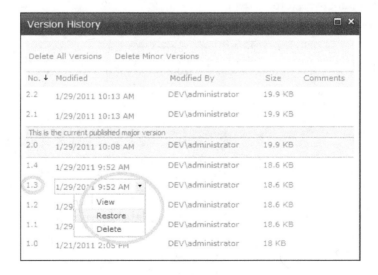

10. You will be prompted to confirm the restore. Click on the **OK** button.

11. The previous version of the document is restored as a new (latest) version of the document in the library.

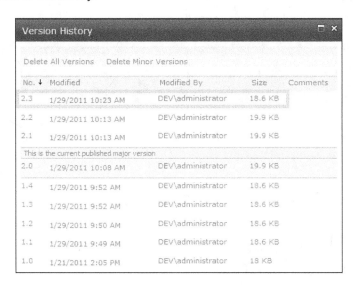

12. Click on **X** (top right-hand corner) to close the **Version History** dialog.

How it works...

When versioning is enabled on a document library, each time the document is changed a new copy of the document is stored in SharePoint's content database. SharePoint allows us to restore any previous version of the document to be the new (latest) version, enabling us to go back in time if we need to.

SharePoint does not roll back the document version numbers, it just creates a new version, which has the contents of the previous document version that you selected.

If check in/check-out is enabled on the document library you will need to check out the document before attempting to restore a previous version.

If you simply want to see what a previous version of the document contained, use the **View** option on the **Restore** menu instead.

See also

▶ *Enabling versioning on a document library*

Enabling content approval on a document library

SharePoint document libraries can be configured to support document approval. Documents stay as drafts (pending) and are not visible to other users until they are approved. This recipe shows you how to turn approvals on.

Getting ready

This recipe works for:

- ▶ SharePoint 2010 Foundation
- ▶ SharePoint 2010 Standard Edition
- ▶ SharePoint 2010 Enterprise Edition
- ▶ Office 365 (SharePoint Online)

You will need a SharePoint site with a document library where you want to enable versioning. This recipe uses a SharePoint 2010 Team Site for illustration.

You will need the **Design** or **Full Control** permission level to run this recipe.

How to do it...

1. Open the SharePoint Team Site that you want to upload your document to.
2. Open the **Shared Documents** link in the **Quick Launch** menu.
3. Select the **Library** tab in the **Library Tools** ribbon.
4. Click on the **Library Settings** icon.

5. The **Document Library Settings** page is displayed. In the **General Settings**, click on the **Versioning settings** link.

6. The **Versioning Settings** page is displayed. Select the **Require content approval for submitted items?** radio button.

7. Click on the **OK** button.

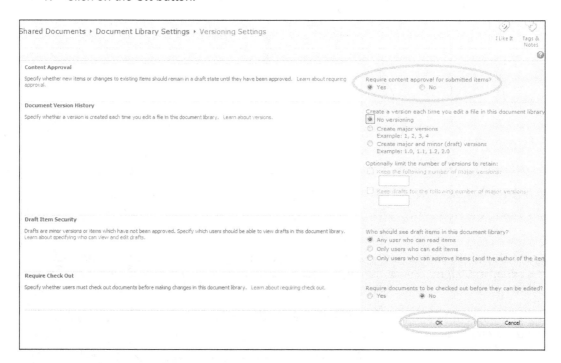

How it works...

SharePoint 2010 document libraries support the concept of content approval. Users may add documents to the library, but those documents will be regarded as draft documents until someone with the necessary permissions approves the document. Each approved version of the document becomes a new major version.

To approve a document, select the document and then click on the **Approve/Reject** icon in the **Documents** tab of the **Library Tools** ribbon. The **Approve/Reject** dialog will be displayed allowing you to approve to document.

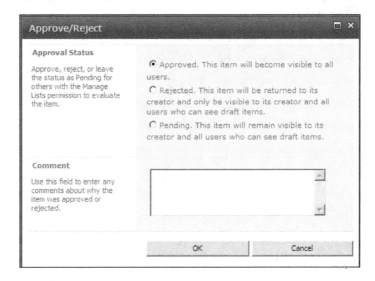

Alternatively, documents can be approved using the SharePoint 2010 approval workflow, described in *Chapter 8, Automating Business Processes—Recipes for Electronic Forms and Workflows*.

Content approval is often combined with major and minor versioning to provide a complete document management life cycle.

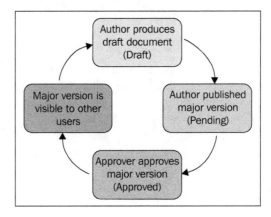

There's more...

Using content approval in a document library means that you don't need to use a separate document library to store your documents that are "works in progress". You can control who gets to see draft documents in the document library by setting the **Draft Item Security** on the **Versioning Settings** page.

When content approval is enabled on a document library this setting defaults to **Only users who can approve items (and the author of the item).** Using this setting, draft (pending or rejected) items are not visible other users unless they have approve permissions or are the document author (in SharePoint terms this actually means the last user to update it).

To understand how this works, consider the following screenshots, where the system administrator has created three documents in the **Content Approval Only** document library. Document two is approved, document one is rejected and the document three is still awaiting approval (pending). When another user (Adrian Colquhoun) visits the document library (with only the **Contribute** permission level), only document two, the approved document, is visible.

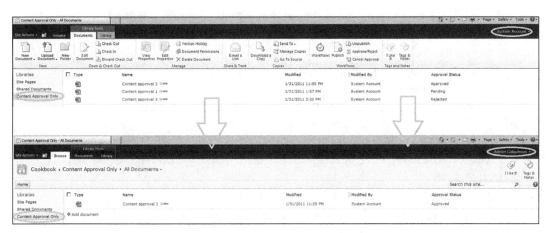

If you want multiple people to work on editing draft items then set the **Draft Item Security** to **Only users who can edit items**.

If you want everyone to be able to see all the documents regardless of their approval status, set the **Draft Item Security** to **Any user who can read items**.

See also

- ▶ *Requiring users to check out a document before they can edit it*
- ▶ *Publishing Add a document*
- ▶ *Enabling versioning on a document library*

Take SharePoint documents offline using Outlook 2010

Outlook 2010 has great two-way integration with SharePoint document libraries. This recipe shows you how to use it to take your document libraries offline.

Getting ready

This recipe works for:

- ▶ SharePoint 2010 Foundation
- ▶ SharePoint 2010 Standard Edition
- ▶ SharePoint 2010 Enterprise Edition
- ▶ Office 365 (SharePoint Online)

You will need the **Contribute** permission level to enable the two-way integration between Outlook 2010 and your document library. You will need the **Reader** permission level if you just want to take the document offline, but not make changes or send new documents back.

You will need a SharePoint site with a document library. This recipe uses a SharePoint 2010 Team Site for illustration.

How to do it...

1. Open the SharePoint Team Site with the document that you want to connect to outlook.
2. Open the **Shared Documents** link in the **Quick Launch** menu.
3. In the **Library Tools** ribbon, select the **Library** tab.
4. Select the **Connect to Outlook** icon.

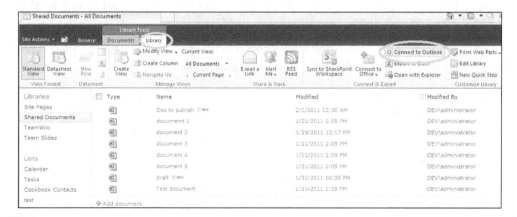

5. If you receive a security prompt click on the **Allow** button.

6. Outlook will prompt you to **Connect this SharePoint Document Library to Outlook**. Click on the **Yes** button.

7. The contents of the document library are synchronized to Outlook.

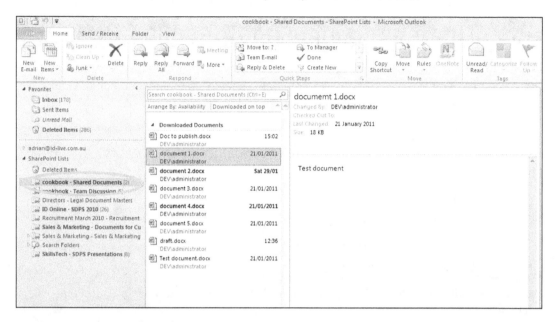

How it works...

Outlook 2010 provides two-way integration with SharePoint 2010 document libraries. This is a great way to take a whole document library offline and automatically receive the latest document versions without having to visit SharePoint. Assuming you have the correct permissions, you can even change documents in Outlook offline and have your changes appear in SharePoint next time you connect.

Outlook-synchronized document libraries are really useful for documents that you frequently send to customers, such as the latest PDF sales-and-marketing flyers for your company. If you add these documents to an Outlook-synchronized document library you can simply drag-and-drop the documents into your customer e-mails as you need them.

The one downside of this approach is that it will copy every document in your document library across the network to your local machine. Check the size of the document library before you do this—use this functionality wisely.

See also

▶ *E-mailing a link to a document in SharePoint*

▶ *Downloading a copy of a document*

Co-authoring an important document

There are times when you need more than one person to product a document. SharePoint 2010 and Microsoft Word 2010 both allow multiple users to simultaneously edit the same document. This recipe shows you how do it.

Getting ready

This recipe works for:

▶ SharePoint 2010 Foundation

▶ SharePoint 2010 Standard Edition

▶ SharePoint 2010 Enterprise Edition

▶ Office 365 (SharePoint Online)

You will need Microsoft Word 2010, and your document must be stored in a SharePoint document library for this to work.

All co-authors will need at least the **Contribute** permission level to edit the document.

How to do it...

1. Open the SharePoint Team Site with the document that you want to co-author.

2. Open the **Shared Documents** link in the **Quick Launch** menu.

3. Select the document that you want to co-author.

4. Click on the **Edit Document** icon in the **Documents** tab of the **Library Tools** ribbon.

5. The document opens in Microsoft Word 2010. Start editing the document.

6. Get one or more co-workers to also edit the same document by repeating steps 1-5 above.

7. A notification icon appears in your Word document informing you that co-workers are also editing the document.

8. Click on the **Notification** icon to see more details of the other authors.

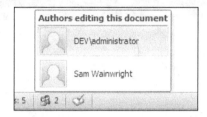

9. Get a co-worker to save their edited document to the server.

10. The **Updates Available** icon appears in your word document. Click on it.

11. The **Info** panel is displayed. Click on the **Save** button to save your changes and merge your co-worker's changes into your document.

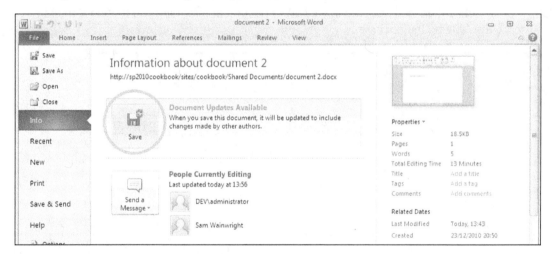

12. Click on the **OK** button to dismiss the Word notification box (if displayed).

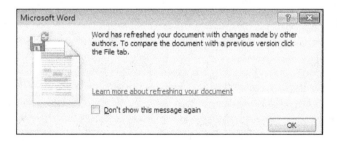

13. Your co-worker's changes are merged into your document. Repeat this process each time updates are available.

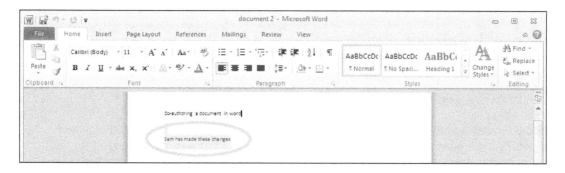

How it works...

Co-authoring is a new MS Office 2010 feature. When a document is stored in a SharePoint document library, each author is kept informed of who else is currently editing the document. When one author makes changes, those changes are notified to the other authors so that they can be automatically merged and their local document copies kept in sync. You are not limited to just two authors and you can collaborate on PowerPoint 2010 presentations in exactly the same way.

This functionality is incredibly powerful and has a huge number of business applications, but the best thing about it is that there is no messing about or complex configuration required, it just works straight out of the box!

See also

▶ *Requiring users to check out a document before they can edit it*

Use content types to store different types of document in the same document library

Document libraries just store documents. But add content types and you can store invoices, quotations, performance reports, or any other type of document you care to define. This recipe shows you how.

Getting ready

This recipe works for:

- ▸ SharePoint 2010 Foundation
- ▸ SharePoint 2010 Standard Edition
- ▸ SharePoint 2010 Enterprise Edition
- ▸ Office 365 (SharePoint Online)

You will need a SharePoint site with a document library where you want to add content types. You will need to pre-create some document content types as described in the *creating a content type* recipe in *Chapter 1, Getting Started—SharePoint Essentials*. This recipe uses a SharePoint 2010 Team Site for illustration with pre-created invoice and quotation content types.

You will need the **Design** or **Full Control** permission level to run this recipe.

How to do it...

1. Open the SharePoint Team Site that you want to enable versioning.
2. Open the **Shared Documents** link in the **Quick Launch** menu.
3. Select the **Library** tab in the **Library Tools** ribbon.
4. Click on the **Library Settings** icon.
5. The **Document Library Settings** page is displayed. Click on the **Advanced Settings** link.
6. The **Advanced Settings** page is displayed. Set the **Allow management of content types?** radio button to **Yes**.
7. The **Document Library Settings** page is displayed. Click on the **Add from existing site content types** link.

8. The **Add Content Types** page is displayed. Select the content types that you have pre-created and click on the **Add** button (I have created Invoice and Quotation content types).

9. Click on the **OK** button.

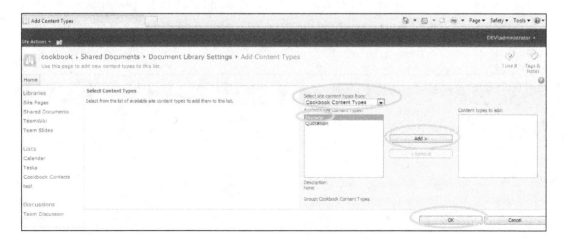

10. The **Document Library Settings** page is displayed. The content types that you added are listed in the **Content Types** section. Click on the **Shared Documents** breadcrumb navigation link to return to the document library.

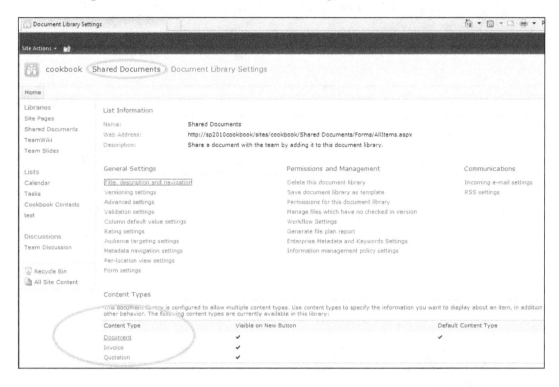

11. Select the **Documents** tab of the **Library Tools** ribbon.

12. Active the **New Document** drop-down menu (Click on the black upside-down triangle).

13. The document library now offers the option to create a new **Invoice** or **Quotation** (or the content types that you have added).

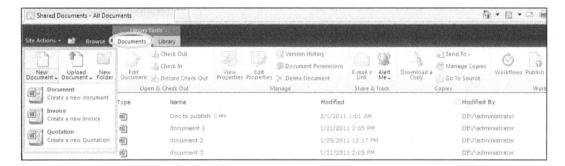

How it works...

Document libraries support the use of content types. When content types are enabled, the document library can store different types of documents in the same library. Only the metadata defined in each content type is captured with its respective document. Different columns are captured for different content types; different document templates can be applied, together with different validation rules, information management policies, and workflows. The combination of features that content types enable provides the foundation for building sophisticated document-management business applications in SharePoint.

See also

▶   *Creating a content type, Chapter 1*

5
Getting the Message Out— Using SharePoint to Communicate

In this chapter, we will cover:

- ▸ Adding an announcement to a Team Site
- ▸ Creating a blog in my My Site
- ▸ Posting to my blog from Microsoft Word 2010
- ▸ Creating a new page on a publishing site
- ▸ Changing the page layout of a publishing site page
- ▸ Publishing a publishing site page
- ▸ Using web analytics to see which are the most popular pages on your site

Introduction

Earlier in the book, we learned how to use SharePoint for collaboration. We have already been introduced to the Wiki page, the default page type in SharePoint 2010. In this chapter we explore how to use SharePoint 2010 sites for communication. The early recipes show you how to use announcements and blogs to get your message out. Then we explore another important SharePoint page type, the publishing page. Through the recipes presented, you will gain an understanding of what publishing pages are and how to use them in your publishing sites. The final recipe in the chapter shows you how to use SharePoint 2010's web analytic reports to understand who is visiting your site so that you can better understand "who's listening" to the messages that you are trying to present.

Adding an announcement to a Team Site

SharePoint includes an announcements list, specially designed to allow you to post announcements and news articles to your site. This recipe shows you how easy it is to make use of it.

Getting ready

This recipe works for:

- ▶ SharePoint 2010 Foundation
- ▶ SharePoint 2010 Standard Edition
- ▶ SharePoint 2010 Enterprise Edition
- ▶ Office 365 (SharePoint Online)

This recipe uses a SharePoint 2010 Team Site for illustration. A Team Site already contains an announcement list, though it is not shown on its pages by default. This recipe first shows you how to add the announcements web part to the Team Site home page and then how to add new announcements to be displayed.

To add the announcements web part to the home page, you will need to have **Design** or **Full Control** permission level. To add an announcement to an existing announcements list you will need the **Contribute** permission level.

How to do it...

1. Open your SharePoint 2010 Team Site. Select the **Edit** icon in the **Page** ribbon to edit the home page.
2. Select the **Insert** tab on the **Editing Tools** ribbon.
3. Select the **Web Part** icon. The **Announcements** web part is displayed in the list of web parts.

4. Click on the **Add** button to insert the announcements web part in the page.

5. Click on the **Save and Close** icon (next to the **Browse** text at the top of the page) to save your changes.

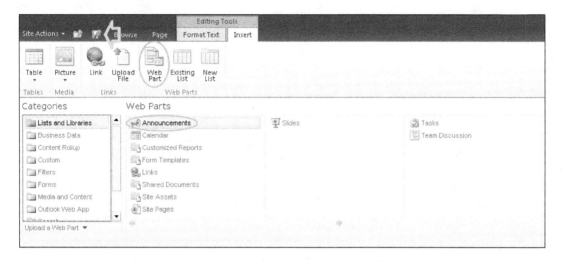

6. The announcements list web part is inserted into the page. Click on the **Add new announcement** link.

7. Enter the details of your new announcement. If the announcement should only be displayed for a set period of time, then set an **Expires** date.

8. Click on the **Save** button.

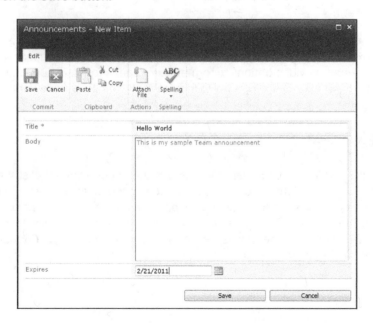

9. Your new announcement is now displayed on the page.

How it works...

The announcements list is used to add announcements or news items to a SharePoint site. You need to first create an instance of the announcements list in your site (if one doesn't exist already) and then add the announcements web part to the page where you want the announcements to be displayed. Then just add your announcements directly to the list and they will automatically show up on your page with no further editing required. You can have the same announcement list being displayed on different pages (and with different **views**) if you wish.

You should aim to keep your announcements short and snappy. Add a short descriptive title and no more than four or five lines of text in the announcement body. You can always insert a link to another page or add a file attachment if you want to present more information.

Your announcement might logically expire at a certain date. In this case, make sure that you set the announcement's expiry date when you create it. That way, you can configure views on the list so that SharePoint will know not to display your announcement when it is no longer relevant.

When you start to type the body of the announcement's text, you will notice that the ribbon in the dialog box will change, and you will see the **Editing Tools** ribbon appear. The **Format Text** tab of this ribbon provides options to format text, change fonts, include bullets, and so on. Switch to the **Insert** tab to see options to include tables, pictures links, or files in your announcement.

There's more...

Beyond the basics, there are a number of features of the announcements list that you may also want to explore. You might need to give some people the ability to post announcements to the list but have others, such as a supervisor, approve those announcements before they become visible to other users. To enable this, turn on content approval for the announcements lists in the same way as we did for document libraries in *Chapter 4, Enabling content approval on a document library* recipe.

Targeting announcements using audiences

SharePoint audiences (SharePoint 2010 Server only) are collections of SharePoint users, pre-compiled on the basis of some common characteristics that they possess for example, all project managers or all users from a particular location. Audiences are created by your SharePoint administrators who define rules against user-profile properties. Audiences are a SharePoint Server-only feature. However, if you do have audiences available, you can enable audience targeting in the list settings of your announcements list. When you create new announcements, you will have the option of selecting which audiences your announcements should be targeted to. SharePoint will then only show those announcements to users in the target audiences, reducing the information overload for everyone else.

> Audiences are a content-targeting mechanism, not a security feature. Users can still find announcements not targeted to them through search or if they know the right links to click. If you really don't want particular users viewing an announcement, then use item-level security, post it on a site that only your target users have access to, or don't post it at all.

See also

▸ *Posting to my blog from Microsoft Word 2010*

Creating a blog in my My Site

A blog is a great way to publish short articles about yourself, the work that you are doing, and the experiences that you have. Your blog posts allow others in the organization to learn from your experiences, replicating the good things that you have done and avoiding the mistakes that you have made.

Getting ready

This recipe works for:

▸ SharePoint 2010 Standard Edition

▸ SharePoint 2010 Enterprise Edition

▸ Office 365 (SharePoint Online)

This recipe uses your My Site to create a blog. However, the blog-site template is available in SharePoint Foundation, so if you don't have a My Site you can still create a blog in another SharePoint site instead.

If you have a My Site, then you will already have the necessary permission to be able to create a blog in it.

How to do it...

1. From within any SharePoint site. Click on your name (top-right of the page). Select the **My Site** link from the menu that is displayed.

2. Select the **My Content** link.

3. Click on the link to **Create Blog** under the **Recent Blog Posts** heading on the right-hand side of the page.

4. Your new blog will be created automatically.

5. To create a new blog post, click on the **Create a post** link under the **Blog Tools** heading.

6. Fill in the details of the blog post and click on the **Publish** button to post to your blog.

How it works...

When your My Site is first created, it contains a link to allow you to create your own blog. All you have to do is click on it. SharePoint will do the rest behind the scenes, creating a new blog and configuring it ready for use. It even adds a **Welcome to Your Blog** post with some useful information. Once you have read it, you will want to delete it and start adding some more interesting content (use the **Manage Posts** link under the **Blog Tools** heading). If you have Microsoft Word 2010 available, then I strongly recommend that you use this to blog from, as the layout and formatting options are much more powerful than you will have available if you create posts through the web browser.

Your My Site blog has content approval enabled by default. This allows you to work on posts and have them automatically saved as drafts (that only you can see) until you are ready to publish them out to the whole organization.

Warning: Put brain in gear before posting to blog

Remember that your blog is intended to be a business tool. Your posts will show up in search and be visible (once published) to the whole organization. Use it to share your knowledge and promote your expertise, not to criticize senior management, post pictures of your favorite pets, or to speculate what might have occurred at the office Christmas party.

See also

▶ *Posting to my blog from* Microsoft *Word 2010*

Posting to my blog from Microsoft Word 2010

Blogs are a great communication tool. However, the experience of posting to a SharePoint blog using a web browser is a bit disappointing. Fortunately, you can post to your SharePoint blog straight from Microsoft Word 2010. You can utilize all the rich editing power that Word can offer than then post text, smart art, graphics, and pictures straight to your blog with a single click.

Getting ready

This recipe works for:

▶ SharePoint 2010 Foundation

▶ SharePoint 2010 Standard Edition

▶ SharePoint 2010 Enterprise Edition

▶ Office 365 (SharePoint Online)

This recipe uses the blog in your My Site for illustration. However, it will work for any SharePoint 2010 blog that you have the rights to post to. You will need Microsoft Word 2010 installed on your PC.

How to do it...

1. Open your **My Site** and navigate to the **My Content** page (Refer to the *Creating a blog in my My Site* recipe in case of doubts).

2. Click on the **Blog** link under the **Sites** heading on the quick-launch menu.

3. Your blog will be displayed.

4. Click on the **Launch blog program to post** link under the **Blog Tools** heading.

5. Microsoft Word 2010 will open. You will be prompted to register your blog. Click on the **OK** button to continue.

6. Word may display a security prompt. Check on the **Don't show me this message again** checkbox and then click on the **Yes** button to continue.

7. Word will register the SharePoint blog account and display a success dialog. Click on the **OK** button to continue.

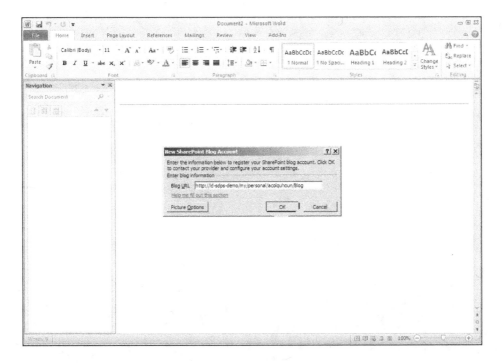

8. Now compose your blog post, adding pictures, text, smart art, and so on as required.
9. When your post is ready, click on the **Publish** icon.

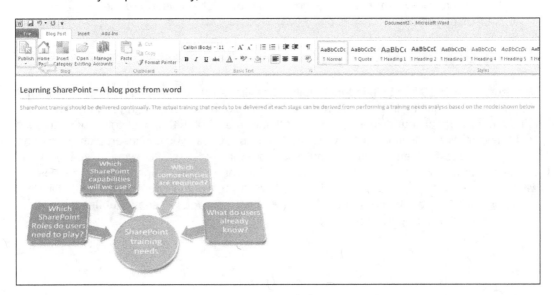

10. Your post will be published on your SharePoint blog. Word will update its status bar to inform you that the post was published successfully.

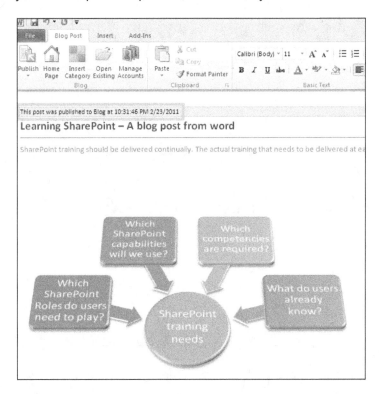

11. Return to your SharePoint blog and refresh your web browser. Your new post will be displayed.

How it works...

Microsoft Word 2010 has built-in functionality that allows you to post to a number of different blog providers, including in this case your SharePoint 2010 blog. Although you won't have the full power of Word at your disposal, you will still have much more than you get working through your browser. Word will first register your SharePoint blog. Then you can insert pictures, charts, smart art, and text. When you click on publish, Word will take care of copying these things up to SharePoint for you and making sure that everything appears in the right place. Your post will automatically be approved and visible to others. If you want to publish a draft version to your blog, then click on the down arrow on the **Publish** icon. You will see a **Publish as Draft** option appear that will let you do this too.

See also

▸   _Creating a blog in my My Site_

Creating a new page on a publishing site

SharePoint Server 2010 provides sophisticated web-content management functionality through its publishing sites. Your organization may use a publishing site on its intranet or for its Internet presence. As a user, you may be required to create a new publishing page and provide its content. This recipe shows you how to do so.

Getting ready

This recipe works for:

▸   SharePoint 2010 Standard Edition

▸   SharePoint 2010 Enterprise Edition

▸   Office 365 (SharePoint Online)

This recipe uses the SharePoint "Adventure Works" example publishing-site template for illustration. The publishing sites you encounter in your own organization may have been branded by professional web designers and look very different from the following screenshot. However, the same basic principles and page creation steps will still apply.

You will need **Design** or **Full Control** permission level to run this recipe. If you have only been granted **Contribute** permission level to your publishing site, then you will only be allowed to create the default page type.

The publishing features need to be enabled (at Site Collection and then Site level) to run this recipe in Office 365.

How to do it...

1.   Go to your publishing site, open the **Site Actions** menu, and select **More Options**.
2.   Filter the **Create** dialog by **Page** and Select **Publishing Page**.
3.   Click on the **Create** button.
4.   The **Create Page** dialog will be shown. Enter a **Title** and **URL** for your page.

5. Select the **Page Layout** that you want to use for your page and click on the **Create** button.

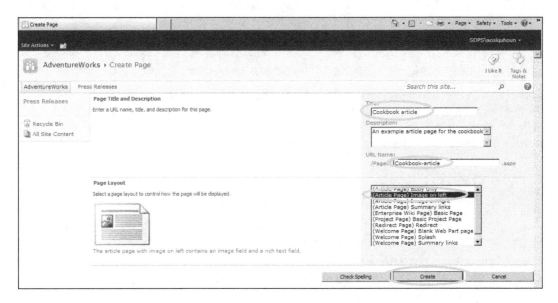

6. The **Page Layout** opens and displays controls that you can enter your data into.

7. In the **Title** control, enter a title for the page.

8. In the **Article Date** control, select the date for this article.

9. In the **ByLine** control, enter by "ByLine" (a sub-heading or short summary of contents) for the page.

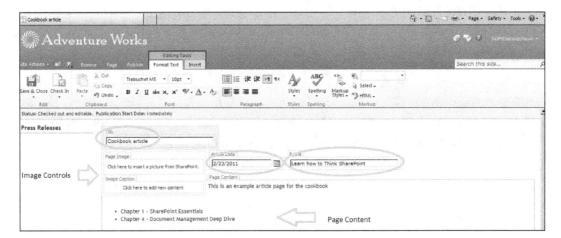

10. In the **Page Image** control, click on the **Click here to insert a picture from SharePoint** link.

11. The **Edit Image** dialog is displayed.

12. To insert an image from SharePoint, click on the first **Browse** button.

13. If Internet Explorer displays a security warning, then click on the **Yes** button to continue.

14. The **Select an Asset** dialog box is displayed.

15. Browse to the **Site Collection Images** library and select the **PR** image.

16. SharePoint will populate the **URL** field. Click on the **OK** button to continue.

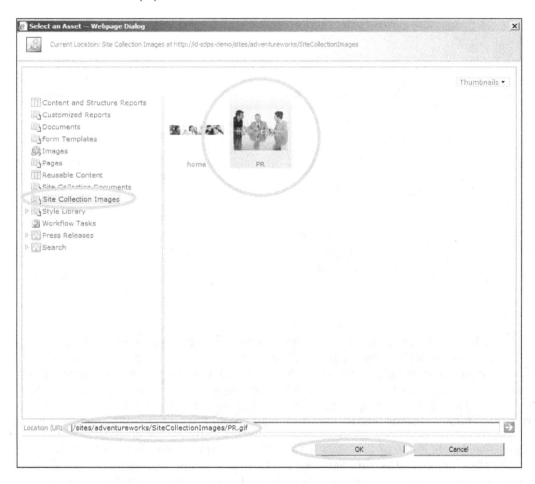

The image is added to the publishing page.

17. Click on the **Save and Close** icon to save the page.

18. The publishing page has now been created; it is still not visible to other users, however (refer to the *Publishing a publishing page* recipe later in this chapter for details on how to do this).

How it works...

SharePoint publishing sites are typically used to create public-facing websites and large-scale intranets. The purpose of these sites is to communicate information. There is often a requirement for such sites to be heavily branded, to the extent that they may not even look like SharePoint at all. This creates a challenge—how can information workers be empowered to create the content for these sites, without needing a detailed knowledge of web design and web authoring techniques? Fortunately, SharePoint publishing page is the answer.

A publishing page works by combining a **content type** and a **page layout**. The content type defines the data to be displayed in (and information about) the page. The page layout determines how the information will be laid out on the page and displayed to the user.

Content types are at the heart of how SharePoint works, so understanding them is critical to become an effective power user. You can find more information on content types in the *creating a content type* recipe presented in *Chapter 1*.

When your web developers create a publishing site, they will define a number of content types which specify the data required for the different publishing pages that you are allowed to create. For example, the data that you need to supply to create an article page (for example, the title, body, and an image to use) might be very different from the data that you will need to create a committee home page (with the name of the committee, objectives, name of the chairman, and so on).

When you create your page, you select the page layout that you want to use. The page layout gives you a template that you type the page data into. Unlike a SharePoint Wiki page, you don't get a blank canvas to work with. The template contains controls that you enter your page data into. The controls are designed to guide you and make your page-editing job easier, with special controls to select dates, insert images, and so on. Behind the scenes, SharePoint takes care of storing the information that you enter in the right content type automatically.

The page layouts, you can select from, may have been pre-created by your web development team. They allow you to create great-looking web pages without knowing a single line of HTML. Simply select the layout you need and you are done. Also, once you have created your page, you can switch between different page layouts at will without having to re-enter your data. The next recipe shows you how to do this.

Not all the data that you are required to enter will be displayed on the page. For example, the publish date is not shown to the users but is instead used by SharePoint to manage the lifecycle of the page, automatically making it available to view on a certain date.

See also

▸ *Changing the page layout of a publishing site page*

▸ *Publishing a publishing site page*

Changing the page layout of a publishing site page

Rearranging the information on your publishing page is as simple as selecting a new page layout. This recipe shows you how to do so.

Getting ready

This recipe works for:

- ▶ SharePoint 2010 Standard Edition
- ▶ SharePoint 2010 Enterprise Edition
- ▶ Office 365 (SharePoint Online)

This recipe uses the SharePoint "Adventure Works" example page created by the earlier *Creating a new page on a publishing site* recipe for illustration. The publishing sites you encounter in your own organizations may have been branded by professional web designers and look very different from the following screenshot. However, the same principles apply.

You will need **Design** or **Full Control** permission level to run this recipe.

How to do it...

1. Navigate to the page you wish to change the layout of.
2. From the **Page** ribbon, click on the **Edit** button.
3. On the **Page** ribbon, select the **Page Layout** icon.
4. From the drop-down list, select the layout you want to apply.

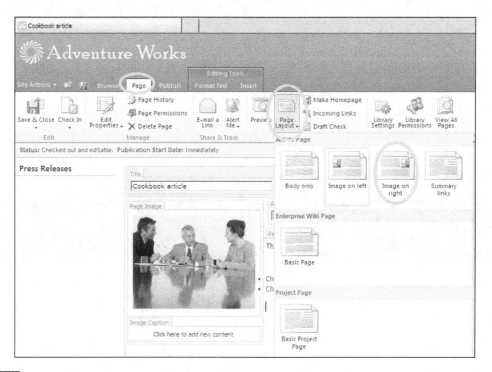

5. The page contents are rearranged automatically to fit the new layout.

How it works...

The data for your publishing page is stored in a content type. The display of that data is controlled by its page layout. You can select any page layout that is compatible with your page's content type and the page will be rearranged accordingly. It is that simple—no web-design skills required!

Your rearranged pages still won't be visible to other users until you publish it. Refer to the next recipe for instructions on how to do this.

See also

▶ *Creating a new page on a publishing site*

▶ *Publishing a publishing site page*

Publishing a publishing site page

Earlier in the chapter, we learned how to create a new publishing page. However, that was only half the story. To make the page visible to a user, the page needs to be published and approved. This recipe walks you through the process.

Getting ready

This recipe works for:

- SharePoint 2010 Standard Edition
- SharePoint 2010 Enterprise Edition
- Office 365 (SharePoint Online)

This recipe uses the SharePoint "Adventure Works" example page created by the earlier *Creating a new page on a publishing site* recipe for illustration. The publishing sites you encounter in your own organizations may have been branded by professional web designers and the pages may look very different from the following screenshot. However, the same concepts still apply.

You will need the **Contribute** permission level to publish your page. You will need the **Approve** permission level to approve the page and make it visible to others.

How to do it...

1. To publish a page you have been working on, open the **Publish** ribbon and click on the **Submit** icon.

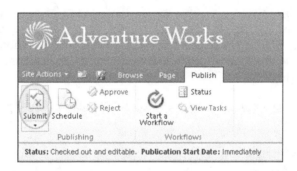

2. The **Submit for Approval** dialog is displayed. You may add a comment if you wish (though this is not required), then click on the **Continue** button.

3. The **Start "Page Approval"** page is displayed. Optionally enter details of the approval, due date, and so on.

4. Click on the **Start** button.

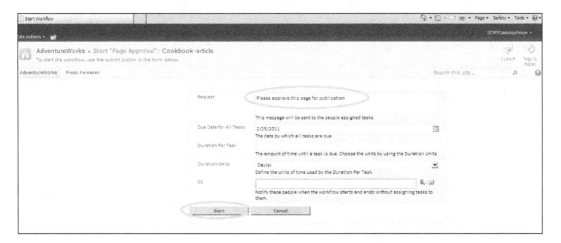

5. SharePoint will update the status of the page.

6. Select the **Publish** ribbon.

7. Click on the **Approve** icon.

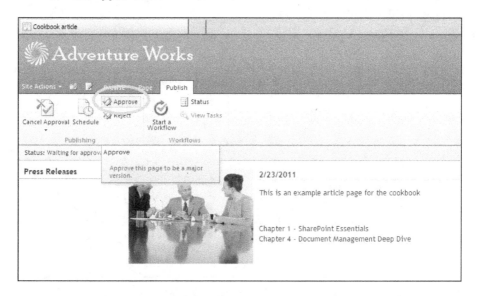

8. The approval workflow task dialog box is displayed.

9. Click on the **Approve** button.

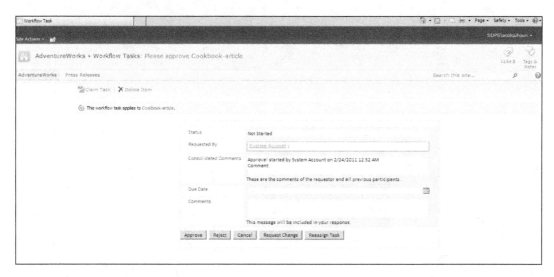

10. The page is now approved and is visible to all authorized users.

How it works...

When you submit your page for approval, SharePoint automatically checks the page in, sets its approval status to **Pending**, and displays the start-up form for its pre-configured page approval workflow. You can supply various pieces of information into this form (such as the nature of your request, due date for tasks, and so on). SharePoint takes the information that you supply and starts its page-approval workflow. This workflow runs in the background to manage the approval process for your page. It creates an approval task in the site's **Workflow Tasks** list and assigns that task to the **Approvers** site group. Assuming outgoing e-mail is enabled, each person in that group will receive an e-mail notifying them of the task.

If you only have **Contribute** permission level, starting the approval workflow is as far as you will be able to proceed. If you have **Approve** permission level, then you will be able to approve your own (and other people's) pages for publication. When you click on the **Approve** icon, the details of the task previously created by the workflow are displayed. (You can also access this dialog directly from the task link that SharePoint e-mails out to you.) SharePoint provides several options in the dialog. As well as approving the page, you may choose to reject it, request a change from its editor, or reassign the task to someone else. Whichever option you choose, the SharePoint workflow will take care of the next steps in the process for you.

When you approve the page, the workflow automatically updates the page's status to **Approved** and the process is complete.

> The data for all the publishing pages that you create, as well as information about their current status and the workflows running against them, is stored in a site collection document library called Pages. Navigate to that document library if you need to see this information.

There's more...

This recipe just scratches the surface of the approval functionality that can be configured on a SharePoint publishing site. Depending on how your SharePoint administrator configures your publishing site, different things may happen when you publish your page. The site might be configured to automatically start a pre-configured publishing workflow for example, to route the publish request around the various departments or people that need to approve the page before it is released. The example site in this recipe starts a workflow that gives an approval task to the approver's SharePoint group.

Conversely, the site may have been configured with no approval workflow, or such that no approval is required. In that scenario, the act of publishing the page will then make it immediately visible to your other users.

See also

▶ *Creating a new page on a publishing site*

▶ *Changing the page layout of a publishing site page*

Using web analytics to see which are the most popular pages on your site

SharePoint can automatically track who visits your sites and what they get up to. This recipe shows you how to access the reports that it creates.

Getting ready

This recipe works for:

▶ SharePoint 2010 Standard Edition

▶ SharePoint 2010 Enterprise Edition

▶ Office 365 (SharePoint Online)

Web analytics must have been enabled by your SharePoint administrator.

You will need the **Full Control** permission to run this recipe.

How to do it...

1. Open the **Site Settings** menu and select the **Site Actions** option.
2. Click on the **Site Collection Web Analytics reports** link.

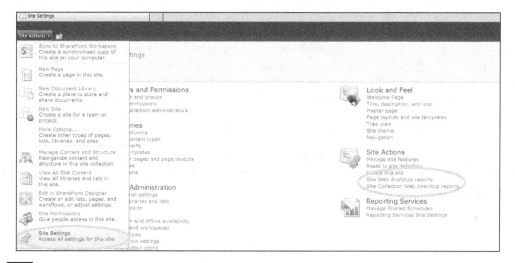

3.   Select the **Top Destinations** link.

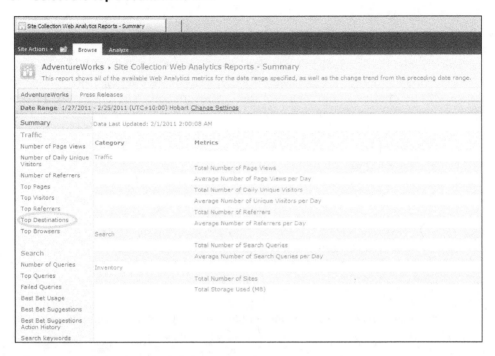

4.   The **Top Destinations** report is displayed.

How it works...

SharePoint Server 2010 has a web analytics service that continually gathers information about what is happening across its SharePoint sites. Your administrator configures the analytics service and the information that it collects. Once it is enabled, you can view reports at the Site Collection or individual Site level. There are lots of pre-built reports you can use, such as top visitors, browsers, and referrers. The top destinations report featured in the recipe shows which pages are most popular in the site collection. Spend some time exploring the other reports to see which ones are most useful for you.

There's more...

Notice the **Analyze** ribbon. This is your gateway to all sorts of useful functionality. From here you can customize the reports, change the date ranges used, export data to Excel, and schedule reports to be automatically e-mailed. You can even create alerts such as to be notified when more than 100 users visit a particular page.

See also

> ▸ *Using search analytics to see what people are searching for, Chapter 6*

6
Where's My Stuff?— Finding Things with SharePoint

In this chapter, we will cover:

- ▶ Performing a basic search
- ▶ Performing an advanced search
- ▶ Finding experts using a people search
- ▶ Saving a search as an alert and being notified when the results change
- ▶ Using search analytics to see what people are searching for

Introduction

The ability to quickly locate documents, presentations, and critical business information is a key selling point for SharePoint. Using search isn't difficult, but few Power Users know how to get the most out of it. This is a short but important chapter. The recipes it contains walk you through essential search techniques to help make you the "SharePoint search guru" of your team.

Performing a basic search

Performing a search in SharePoint is as simple as entering the keyword you want to search for.

Getting ready

This recipe works for:

- SharePoint 2010 Foundation
- SharePoint 2010 Standard Edition
- SharePoint 2010 Enterprise Edition
- Office 365 (SharePoint Online)

Basic search is available in all versions of SharePoint, however, with SharePoint Foundation your search scope is limited to only search for content in the site that you are in.

You only need the **Read** permission level to run a search. However, the results that you see are **security trimmed** according to the permissions that you have. SharePoint search will not show you items that you do not have permission to see, even if they match your keyword search and exist in SharePoint's search index.

This recipe uses a SharePoint 2010 Team Site for illustration.

How to do it...

1. Navigate to your Team Site.
2. Locate the search box at the top-right side of the page.

3. Enter the keyword that you want to search for.
4. Click on the magnifying glass icon or hit *Enter* to execute the search.

5. The results of the search will be displayed.

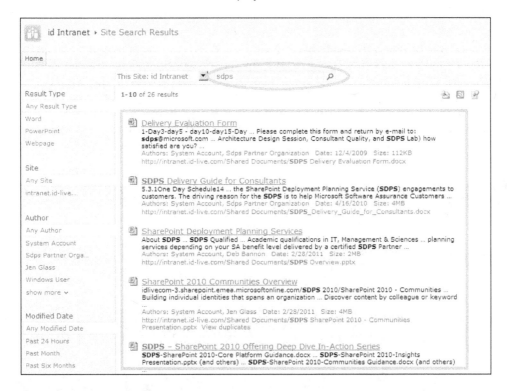

How it works...

Out of the box, SharePoint continually indexes (or crawls) all the content that you place in you SharePoint sites. SharePoint search is clever enough to "read inside" and index the contents of your Office documents, as well as the metadata and tags that have been applied.

When you perform a keyword search, SharePoint will go and find all the results it thinks are relevant to your search in its index. It will apply a number of sophisticated algorithms to try and find the most relevant content for you. SharePoint will security trim the result set, automatically removing results that you don't have permission to see. The results of the search are displayed on the **Site Search Results** page, with the most relevant results at the top of the page.

There's more...

SharePoint keyword searches return all sorts of content in its results, such as documents, presentations, and videos. Depending on the keywords that you use, there may still be too many results for a search to be useful. That is the reason why SharePoint automatically displays a list of refinements on the left side of the search page. Click on the links to automatically filter your results by date, content type, author, and so on, until you only have the results you really need. The following screenshot has a number of search refinements to only show PowerPoint presentations that match the keyword and that are restricted by author, modified date, and site:

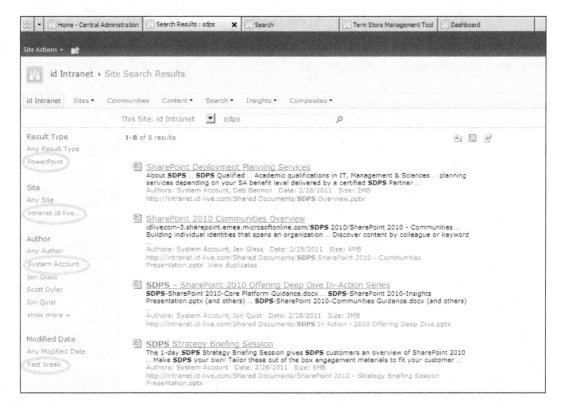

Building better keyword searches

Keyword searches are very powerful, but few users are aware that there is a special syntax that you can use to make you searches better. You can restrict searches to specific authors, look for content in particular sites, join keywords together, exclude keywords, and make all sorts of other adjustments. The better your search request is on the way in, the more useful the information that you will get out.

You can search for multiple keywords and search for phrases by using quotation marks. Use + and – to tell SharePoint how you want the keywords to be defined.

You can also apply property features to restrict the search results to particular authors or file types. Consider the following keyword searches:

- ▶ SharePoint + "User Profile Service"
- ▶ SharePoint - "Document Library"
- ▶ SDPS + filetype:pdf
- ▶ author:"Adrian Colquhoun"

The first search finds items that contain the keyword "SharePoint" and the phrase "User Profile Service". The second search finds items that contain the keyword "SharePoint" but do not contain the phrase "Document Library". The third search finds PDF files that match the keyword search "SDPS", and the fourth search finds content that was authored by "Adrian Colquhoun".

The search in the following screenshot uses the keyword prefix **Skil*** combined with **sharepoint roadmap**, a filetype filter of **docx**, and an author filter **Adrian Colquhoun** to perform a very precise search that returns a single result.

See also

- ▶ *Performing an advanced search*
- ▶ *Finding experts using a people search*

Performing an advanced search

While a keyword search is powerful, SharePoint server offers you even more advanced search options that help focus in on the results that you really need. This recipe shows you how to use them.

Getting ready

This recipe works for:

- SharePoint 2010 Standard Edition
- SharePoint 2010 Enterprise Edition
- Office 365 (SharePoint Online)

You will need an Enterprise search centre to perform an advanced search. Your SharePoint administrator will need to have configured this in your environment.

How to do it...

1. Navigate to your Search Centre. Click on the **Advanced** link.

2. Use the options displayed to focus your search and limit the amount of results that are to be returned.

3. Add one or more property restrictions to further narrow your result set.

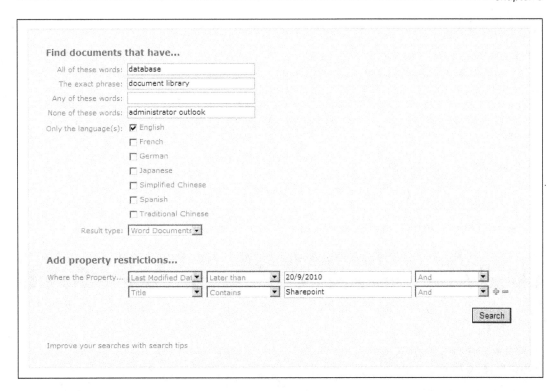

4. Click on the **Search** button to see your results.

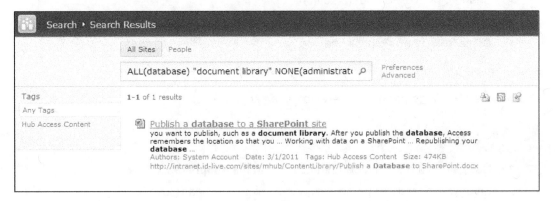

How it works...

Advanced search is designed to make it easy to apply property filters, combinations of keywords, phrases, and other logic to narrow down your search. SharePoint takes the information that you enter and constructs a search string in the correct format for its search engine. The search results that you receive will then be more precise and relevant to your needs. The better the search you construct on the way in, the more useful the results you will get out.

See also

- *Performing a basic search*
- *Finding experts using a people search*

Finding experts using a people search

SharePoint doesn't just index documents, it indexes people too. Use this recipe to find the experts you need.

Getting ready

This recipe works for:

- SharePoint 2010 Standard Edition
- SharePoint 2010 Enterprise Edition
- Office 365 (SharePoint Online)

You will need a SharePoint search centre deployed to run a people search.

You will need the **Read** permission level to run a people search.

How to do it...

1. Navigate to the Search Centre and click on the **People** tab.
2. Enter your search term and click on the magnifying glass icon.
3. The people who match your search term are displayed.

How it works...

People search is only available in SharePoint 2010 Server. It is based on the information stored in the SharePoint 2010 user profiles. SharePoint indexes the user profile data, as entered through My Sites or imported from external systems. You can use SharePoint's people search to quickly find experts within your company, assemble teams for particular projects, or track down people who worked on a particular project. People search is an incredibly powerful tool that allows you to really start to make use of the "human assets" that you have at your disposal.

See also

▸ *Performing a basic search*

▸ *Performing an advanced search*

Saving a search as an alert and being notified when the results change

Imagine you are working on an important project. You need to know when anyone posts some content relating to your project on SharePoint. There is no need to continually visit your SharePoint site to search for new items. Instead you can set an alert on your search results and have SharePoint automatically notify you when new items are added.

Getting ready

This recipe works for:

- ▶ SharePoint 2010 Standard Edition
- ▶ SharePoint 2010 Enterprise Edition
- ▶ Office 365 (SharePoint Online)

You will need the **Read** permission level to create a search alert in SharePoint.

Your administrator will need to have configured e-mail or SMS services on SharePoint to allow you to receive the alerts.

How to do it...

1. Perform a simple or advanced search as explained in the recipes earlier in this chapter.

2. Click on the **Alert me** icon in the top-right corner of the search result's screen.

3. Set the properties that you require for the alert.

4. Click on the **OK** button to set the alert.

5. You will automatically be notified when the search results change.

Alert Title	
Enter the title for this alert. This is included in the subject of the notification sent for this alert.	Search: sdps
Delivery Method	Send me alerts by:
Specify how you want the alerts delivered.	⦿ E-mail
	○ Text Message (SMS)
	☐ Send URL in text message (SMS)
Change Type	Only send me alerts when:
Specify the type of changes that you want to be alerted to.	⦿ New items in search result
	○ Existing items are changed
	○ All changes
When to Send Alerts	⦿ Send a daily summary
Specify how frequently you want to be alerted. (mobile alert is only available for immediately send)	○ Send a weekly summary
	OK Cancel

How it works...

SharePoint has built-in mechanisms to alert you when things change. We have already seen this being used for tracking changes to documents and web pages in earlier chapters. Here, the same principle is applied to search results. By registering an alert on a search, SharePoint automatically notifies you when there are new items that match what you are looking for. Used intelligently, this is a great timesaver!

See also

- ▸ *Performing a basic search*
- ▸ *Performing an advanced search*
- ▸ *Adding an alert to a SharePoint page, Chapter 1*
- ▸ *Creating an alert on a document to be notified when it is updated, Chapter 4*

Using search analytics to see what people are searching for

Understanding what your colleagues are searching for is essential in ensuring that you are presenting the right information on your SharePoint sites. SharePoint's search analytics reports give you this.

Getting ready

This recipe works for:

- ▶ SharePoint 2010 Standard Edition
- ▶ SharePoint 2010 Enterprise Edition
- ▶ Office 365 (SharePoint Online)

Web analytics must have been enabled by your SharePoint administrator. You will need the **Full Control** permission to run this recipe.

How to do it...

1. Open the **Site Settings** menu and select the **Site Actions** option.
2. Click on the **Site Collection Web Analytics reports** link.

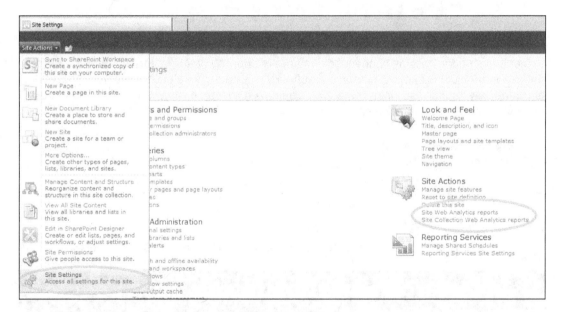

3. The **Site Collection Web Analytics Reports – Summary** screen is displayed.
4. Select **Top Queries** link.

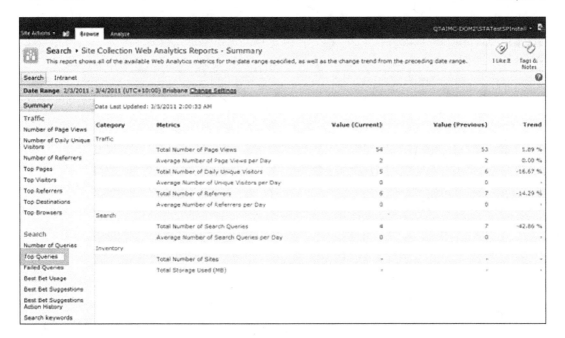

5. The **Top Queries** report is displayed.

How it works...

SharePoint 2010 tracks search information and creates a number of search analytics reports. These contain loads of useful information including the number of search queries, top queries, which queries failed, and so on. You can use this information to track what users are looking for and what they can and can't find on the site. Search analytics information can help ensure that you structure and tag that information correctly so that it can be found more easily. Spend some time exploring the reports that are available to understand which ones will be most useful for you.

See also

▶   *Using web analytics to see which are the most popular pages on your site, Chapter 5*

7
Gaining Insights— Using SharePoint for Business Intelligence

In this chapter, we will cover:

- ▶ Creating a chart using the Chart Web Part
- ▶ Creating a Key Performance Indicator (KPI)
- ▶ Creating an Excel spreadsheet to run on the server
- ▶ Creating a report using Report Builder
- ▶ Creating a chart using the PerformancePoint Dashboard Designer
- ▶ Building a PerformancePoint business intelligence dashboard

Introduction

Business intelligence is the process of turning data into information. Business intelligence tools summarize and visualize information, providing us with insights into problems and allowing us to make sensible decisions based on facts rather than guesswork. The SharePoint design mantra is business intelligence for all, and SharePoint 2010 provides many different Power User business intelligence tools. The recipes in this Chapter explore the options. You will learn how to create graphs and charts using the chart Web Part, build key performance indicators using the status list, publish spreadsheets on the server using Excel services, create traditional tabular reports using reporting services, and building analytical charts and dashboards using PerformancePoint services. The business intelligence tools in SharePoint are powerful and extensive. I recommend you to spend some time and effort exploring them in detail. The recipes in this chapter are more than enough to get you started.

Creating a chart using the Chart Web Part

The Chart Web Part is a great tool for charting a small data set. Your data will need to be already organized to be ready for charting, as the Web Part won't rollup data or calculate totals. This recipe shows you how to chart data from a SharePoint list to display sales figures.

Getting ready

This recipe works for:

- ▶ SharePoint 2010 Enterprise Edition
- ▶ SharePoint 2010 Online (Office 365 Edition)

You will need a SharePoint site with a page where you will insert the chart and a list called **Sales** containing the following columns:

Column Name	Data Type
Title	(Built In)
Region	Choice:
	North
	South
	East
	West
Net Sales	Number

If you need help creating the list, refer to the *Creating a custom list recipe* in *Chapter 3*. Once you have created the list, add rows of data as shown in the following table:

Title	Region	Net Sales
Sales North	North	10000
Sales South	South	34000
Sales East	East	5000
Sales West	West	12000

You will need the **Design** or **Full Control** permission level to run this recipe.

How to do it...

1. Open your SharePoint site and navigate to the page where you will insert the Chart Web Part. Click on the **Edit** button in the **Page** ribbon to edit the page.

2. Open the **Insert** tab of the **Editing Tools** ribbon and click on the **Web Part** button.

3. Filter the list of available Web Parts by the **Business Data** category and then select the **Chart Web Part**.

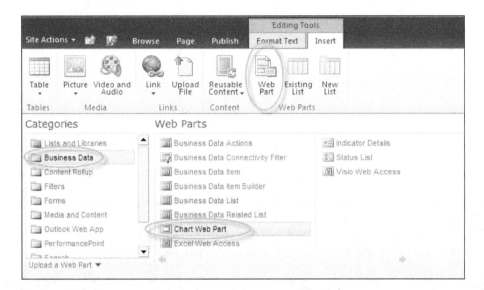

4. A default chart with sample data is inserted into your page. To start customizing the chart with your own data, click on the **Data & Appearance** link.

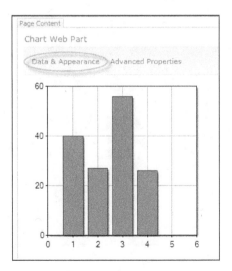

5. The **Data Connections & Chart Appearance Wizards** page is displayed. Click on the **Connect Chart to Data** link.

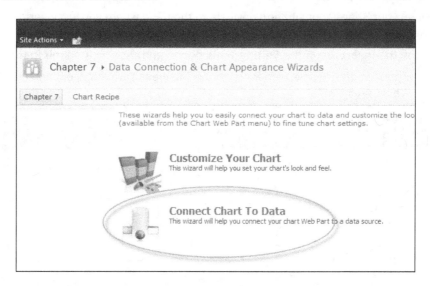

6. The **Data Connection Wizard Step 1: Choose a Data Source** is displayed. Select the **Connect to a List** option and then click on the **Next** button.

7. In **Step 2: Connect to a List**, select the SharePoint **Site** and **List** that contain the sales data for the chart and then click on the **Next** button.

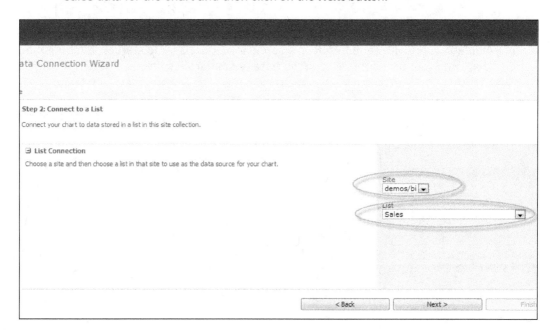

8. In **Step 3: Retrieve and Filter Data**, review the data presented (to check that you have connected to the correct list), and then click on the **Next** button.

9. The final page of the wizard, **Step 4: Bind Chart to Data**, is displayed. Expand the **Series Properties** and enter **Net Sales** for the **Series Name**.

   ❏ Set the **Series Type** to **Pie**

   ❏ Set the **Y Field** to **Net Sales**

   ❏ Set the **X Field** to **Region**.

10. Click on the **Finish** button.

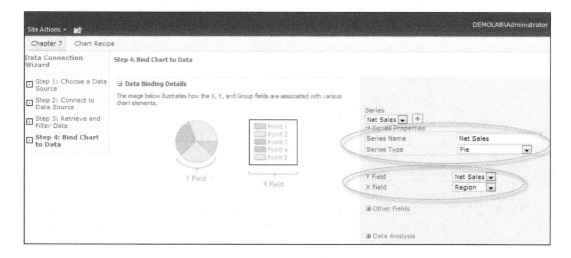

11. The chart will now be displayed in your SharePoint page. We will customize the appearance of the chart to make it 3D and display a title. Click on the **Data & Appearance** link above the chart.

12. Select the **Customize Your Chart** option.

13. The **Chart Customization Wizard** is displayed. In **Step 1: Select Chart Type,** select the **Standard Chart Types** tab.

   ❏ From the **Chart Type Categories**, select **Pie**

   ❏ Select the **3D Chart Types** tab and select **Pie**

14. Click on the **Next** button to continue.

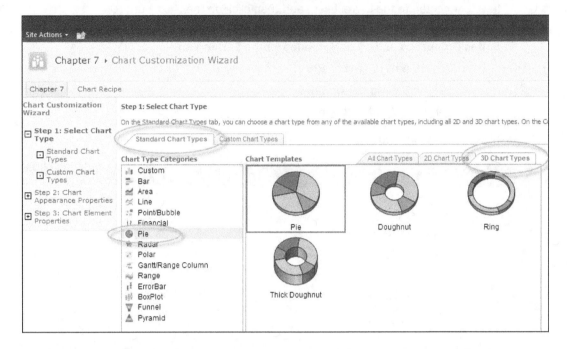

15. **Step 2: Chart Appearance Properties** is displayed. You can use this page to change the appearance and rendering of your chart if you wish. Click on the **Next** button to continue.

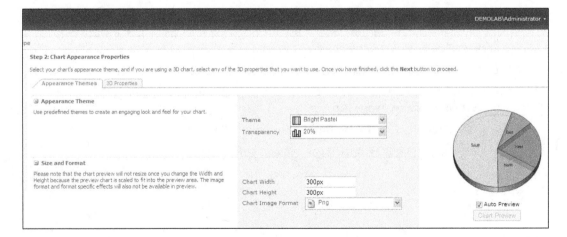

16. **Step 3: Chart element properties** is displayed. Tick the **Show Chart Title** checkbox and enter **Net Sales by Region**.

17. Click on the **Finish** button. The completed chart is now displayed in our SharePoint page.

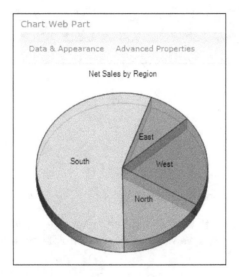

How it works...

The **Chart Web Part** provides a simple, wizard-driven interface that allows you to display data form a range of different data sources. It has an extensive array of charts to choose from including line graphs, bar charts, pie charts, and so on. The chart wizard presents many options that provide fine-grained control over how your chart is formatted and how it displays the data. The chart redraws each time you load the page, providing a simple but effective way to provide a real-time visualization of your data.

There's more...

In our recipe we have only plotted a single series of data (Net Sales). We could also hook our chart up to additional series, such as Budget, and plot both on the same chart for comparison.

The **Chart Web Part** is designed to chart data that has already been organized for charting. It is ideal for charting summary data held within a SharePoint list. Unfortunately, it will not roll up data to provide counts or totals. If you need roll ups or have large volumes of data, Excel Services or PerformancePoint Services (both described later in this chapter) provide better options.

See also

- ▶ *Creating an Excel spreadsheet to run on the server*
- ▶ *Creating a chart using the PerformancePoint Dashboard Designer*

Creating a Key Performance Indicator (KPI)

This recipe shows you how to create a Key Performance Indicator based on data held in SharePoint list.

Getting ready

This recipe works for:

- ▶ SharePoint 2010 Enterprise Edition
- ▶ SharePoint 2010 Online (Office 365 Edition)

You will require a SharePoint site where you intend to create the KPI and a SharePoint list containing the data to report on. We will use the SharePoint site and **Sales** data list from the previous recipe for illustration.

You will need the **Design** or **Full Control** permission level to run this recipe.

How to do it...

1. Navigate to your SharePoint site. Open the **Site Actions** menu and then click on **More Options**. Filter the list of available content by the **List** type and then choose **Status List**.
2. Name the list **Sales Status** and click on the **Create** button.

3. Once the **Status List** has been created click on the **New** link and select **SharePoint List based Status Indicator**.

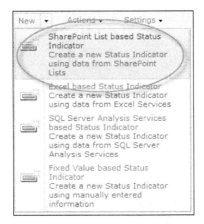

4. Enter the **Name** for your indicator as **Sales Targets**.

5. You need to provide a link to the SharePoint list containing the sales data for your indicator. Click on the **Browse** icon next to the **List URL** text box.

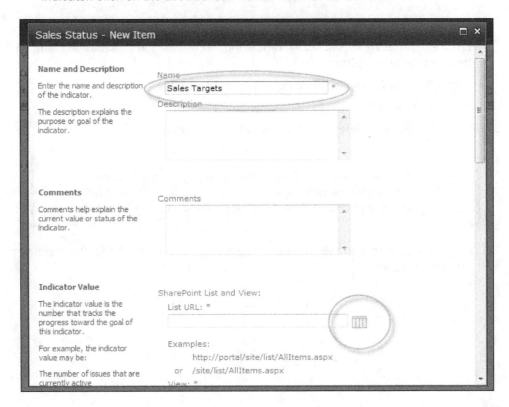

6. The **Select an Asset – Webpage Dialog** is displayed. Select the **Sales** list and click on the **OK** button.

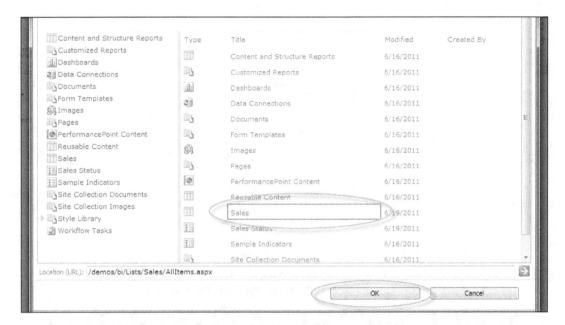

7. Ensure that the **View:** is set to **All Items** and then select the **Calculation using all list items in the view option**.

8. Select **Sum** from the drop-down list of calculation types.

9. Select **Net Sales** from the list of SharePoint columns.

10. Under **Status Icon Rules** select **Better Values are higher**.

> For this recipe, the higher the Net Sales figures are the better!
> You might choose **lower** in other scenarios, for example if KPI was
> displaying data on the number of accidents in your workplace.

11. Finally we need to manually enter our target values. Enter **20000** for the **warning** and **40000** for the **goal**.

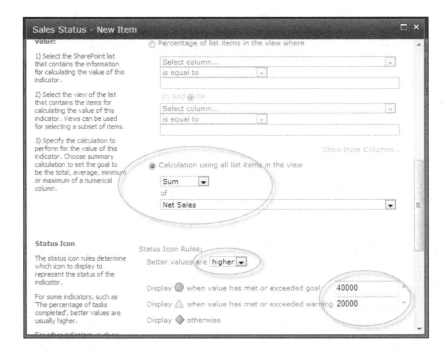

12. Click on the **OK** button.

13. The **Sales Targets** KPI is displayed as a green dot because the current **Value** of **Net Sales** is **61,000**, which exceeds the **Goal** of **40,000**.

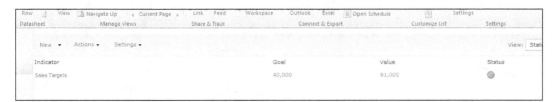

How it works...

Key Performance Indicators provide valuable summary information in a single row of a SharePoint list. In our example, the Sales Director can see instantly if the Net Sales target is being met or not. KPIs are ideal for use in management dashboards to present high-level summary information which can then be used make key business decisions. You can add as many different indicators to the list as you need.

You may see KPIs referred to as Status Indicators in SharePoint 2010.

There's more...

We can use the Status List Web Part to show the Status Indicator alongside the chart we created in the previous recipe. Edit the page containing the Chart Web Part from the previous recipe, select the **Insert** tab from the ribbon, and click on **Web Part**. Filter the list of available **Web Parts** by the **Business Data** category, select the **Status List** Web Part, and click on **Add**.

Once the **Web Part** has been inserted into the page, open the **Web Part Tools Pane** and enter the link to the **Status List** you created earlier. Once you've finished configuring the available options, click on **OK** at the bottom of the pane.

Your Sales Indicator is now displayed alongside the pie chart we created in the previous recipe. You have now created a dashboard showing Net Sales targets alongside a chart of the raw data!

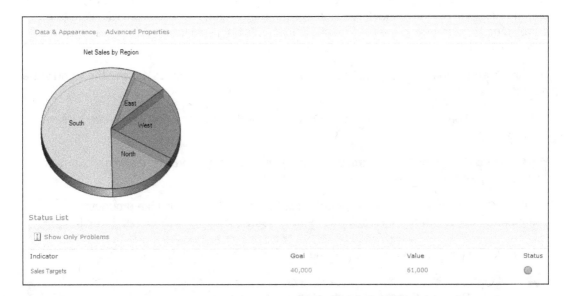

 The KPI is hooked up to the data in your Sales list in real time. Try changing the value of Net Sales for the South region to 11,000 and see what happens to the Indicator.

See also

▸ _Creating a chart using the Chart Web Part_

Creating an Excel spreadsheet to run on the server

In this recipe you will see how to upload your spreadsheet to the server and use the Excel Web Part to expose its information within your SharePoint pages.

Getting ready

This recipe works for:

- SharePoint 2010 Enterprise Edition
- SharePoint 2010 Online (Office 365 Edition)

You will need an Excel spreadsheet (containing your data) and a SharePoint site with a document library where you wish to upload your spreadsheet. Excel services will need to be enabled on the server and the document library set as a trusted location (check with your SharePoint administrator if you are unsure about this).

To publish and upload the spreadsheet you will need Microsoft Excel 2010 and the **Contribute** permissions level.

For the second part of this recipe you will need a SharePoint page where you wish to insert the Excel Web Part.

You will need **Design** or **Full Control** permission level to insert the Excel Web Part onto the SharePoint page.

For illustration, I have populated a spreadsheet with sales for various bike products using the data from an Adventure Works sample database freely available at Codeplex (http://msftdbprodsamples.codeplex.com/). The spreadsheet is shown in the following screenshot and is available in the download file available for this chapter.

Downloading the example code

You can download the example code files for all Packt books you have purchased from your account at http://www.PacktPub.com. If you purchased this book elsewhere, you can visit http://www.PacktPub.com/support and register to have the files e-mailed directly to you.

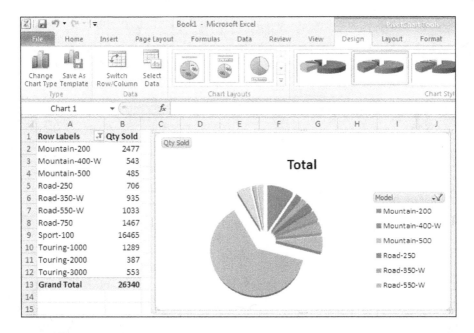

How to do it...

1. Upload the spreadsheet to your SharePoint document library (Refer to *Chapter 4, Uploading an existing document to a document library,* if you need instructions on how to do this).

2. Navigate to the page where you wish to display the spreadsheet information.

3. Click on the **Edit** button on the **Page** ribbon.

4. Locate the cursor where you want to display the spreadsheet.

5. Select the **Insert** tab of the **Editing Tools** ribbon and click on the **Web Part** button.

6. Click on the **Business Data** category. Choose the **Excel Web Access** Web Part and click on the **Add** button.

7. The Excel Web Part is inserted in the page. Click on the **Click here to open the tool pane** hyperlink.

8. The tool pane opens. Click on the browse icon to the right of the **Workbook** field.

9. The **Select an Asset – Webpage Dialog** is displayed. Navigate through the site hierarchy (in the left pane) to locate the document library which contains your spreadsheet.
10. Select the spreadsheet from the list of contents (in the right pane).
11. Click on the **OK** button in the **Select an Asset – Webpage Dialog.**
12. Click on the **OK** button in the **Web Part Tools** pane.
13. The spreadsheet is now displayed on the page.

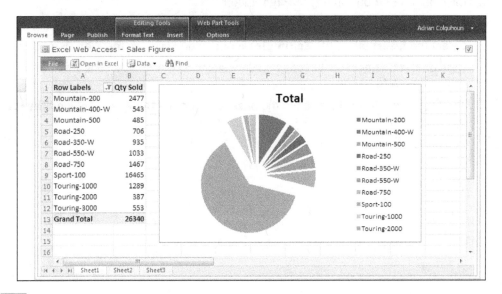

How it works...

Excel is the Power User's data analysis tool of choice. That's why Microsoft created Excel Services to provide special support for Excel in SharePoint. Excel Services allows you combine the power of Excel with all the benefits of SharePoint by creating spreadsheets that run on the SharePoint server. Excel Services allows Excel spreadsheets to be rendered in the web browser.

In this recipe, we first upload a spreadsheet in to a document library. By adding the spreadsheet to SharePoint we can take advantage of all the normal SharePoint document management features such as check in/out, versioning, content approval, security permissions, and so on that we have covered earlier in the book. If you click on the spreadsheet in SharePoint 2010, it will open and display in the web browser by default.

SharePoint 2010 includes the Excel web application that allows you to open spreadsheets directly in the browser. If this is configured and enabled on your document library, clicking on the spreadsheet that you uploaded will open it in the web browser. The Excel web application is turned on in Office 365 by default. If you want to check this setting on your document library, look at the **Opening Documents in the Browser** property on the **Advanced Settings** page for the list.

We then use the Excel Web Part to insert and display the spreadsheet data directly into a SharePoint page. This allows site visitors to easily view and interpret its information. Under the covers, SharePoint uses Excel Services to display the spreadsheet. The Excel Web Part is a great alternative to e-mailing spreadsheet reports around the organization and always wondering if you have the latest version.

To display a spreadsheet in the browser it must be added to a trusted location. All SharePoint 2010 document libraries are trusted locations by default. However, your SharePoint administrator may have changed this setting, so check with them if you encounter problems.

There's more...

Excel includes some great data visualization and charting features. Wouldn't it be great if you could include those charts in your SharePoint pages? Of course you can do this too. Add another Excel Web Part your page and select the **Sales Data** spreadsheet as before. Then enter **Chart 1** in the **Named Item** textbox and click on the **OK** button. This second Web Part only shows the chart from your spreadsheet, not the complete workbook as we had before. You can use this technique to display charts, pivot tables, named ranges of cells, and so on throughout many SharePoint pages, all powered from the data in a single spreadsheet that you upload to a document library.

If you don't like the name **Chart 1**, open your spreadsheet in Excel 2010, select the chart and then select the **Layout** tab in the ribbon. At the right-hand end of the ribbon controls you will see a **Chart Name** textbox. Type the new name of your chart here and then save your spreadsheet back to SharePoint.

Controlling what gets published to SharePoint

You may not want everything in your spreadsheet to be available in SharePoint. The trick is to specify which items that you want available to Excel Services (charts, named ranges, and so on) when you save the spreadsheet back to the SharePoint server.

First click on the **Sales Data** spreadsheet in its document library. The spreadsheet will open in the browser. Now select the **Open in Excel** button (top left of the spreadsheet) and select edit mode if prompted. The spreadsheet will open in Excel 2010.

Navigate to the backstage view (**File** tab) and select the **Save & Send** and then **Save to SharePoint** option. Select the **Publish Options** button on the right-hand side of the backstage view.

The **Publish Options** dialog box will be displayed. You can use this dialog to select which bits of your spreadsheet will be available in SharePoint. Change the drop-down list to **Items in the Workbook** and ensure that **Chart 1** is selected. Click on **OK** to close the dialog and then click on the **Save** button to save the spreadsheet back to SharePoint. Now only **Chart 1** is available for viewing in SharePoint, not all the workbook items that were previously available by default.

Unsupported features

Excel Services support most, but not all the features that you find in Excel 2010. Where unsupported features are detected, Excel Services will add a yellow warning bar at the top of the spreadsheet, but will still attempt to display the spreadsheet's information. Depending on how your connections are configured, functions such as the external data ranges (query tables) are not supported, so the spreadsheet will only show a snapshot of data based on the last time the connection within the spreadsheet was refreshed. In this case, the external data can be refreshed by opening the spreadsheet in the Excel 2010 client, refreshing the connections, and then saving it back to SharePoint.

See also

▶ *Uploading an existing document to a document library, Chapter 4*

Creating a report using Report Builder

If you need a traditional tabular report in SharePoint, then build it using Reporting Services. This recipe demonstrates how to create a simple report using the Report Builder 3.0 application.

Getting ready

This recipe works for:

▶ SharePoint 2010 Foundation

▶ SharePoint 2010 Standard Edition

▶ SharePoint 2010 Enterprise Edition

You will need an instance of SQL Reporting Services that has been configured and integrated with your SharePoint environment.

This recipe uses a SharePoint site created from the **Business Intelligence Centre** template (only available with SharePoint 2010 Enterprise) for illustration as all the required business intelligence features are automatically enabled on this site. However, any type of SharePoint site can be used, but the required features will need to be enabled manually.

You will need a document library with the **Report Builder Report** and Report Builder **Data Source** Reporting Services content types enabled on it.

Report Builder allows you to use a variety of data sources including SharePoint lists and SQL Server databases. In this recipe we connect to the **Sales** SharePoint list we created in the first recipe of this chapter. Modify the list to add an extra number column (**Sales Target**) and add a value of **10000** to each of the four rows in the list.

How to do it...

1. Navigate to your document library (**Customized Reports** if you are using the business intelligence site). Select the **Documents** tab of the **Library Tools** ribbon.

2. Open the **New Document** menu and select the **Report Builder Report** option. The Report Builder 3.0 application will now load on your computer. If you receive a security prompt click on the **Run** button.

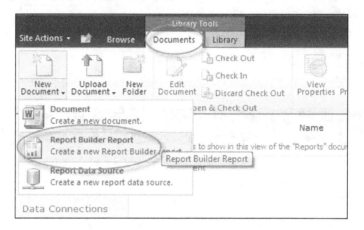

3. From the **Getting Started screen** (this screen can be turned off once you get more familiar with Report Builder) select **New Report** and click on the **Table or Matrix Wizard** option.

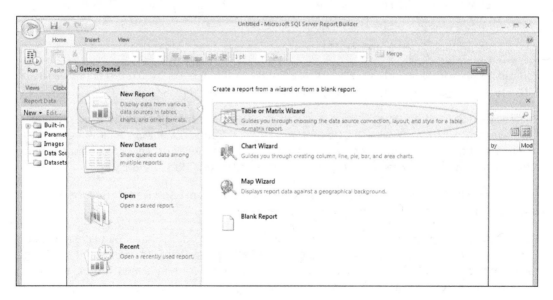

4. The **New Table or Matrix, Choose a dataset dialog** is displayed. A dataset is required to provide data for the report. As we don't have one yet, Select **Create a dataset** and click on the **Next** button.

5. The **Choose a connection to a data source** dialog is displayed. A dataset is created from a data source, but as we do not have a data source either, so let's create one now. Click on the **New** button.

6. First enter **Sales** as name for your data source (this name can be anything you like), select **SharePoint List** as the connection type.

7. Type the URL to the SharePoint site that contains your **Sales** list (for example, `http://portal.demolab.local/demos/bi`) in the **Connection string** textbox.

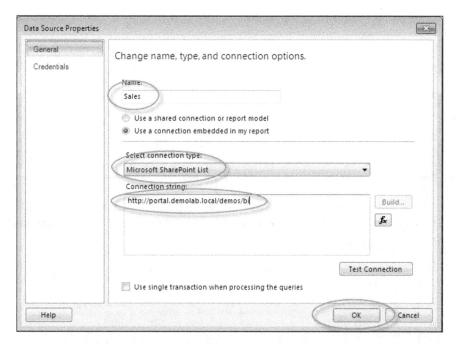

8. Select the **Credentials** tab and select a value suitable for your environment. This recipe uses the **Use current windows user** option. Another setting may be more appropriate in your environment, see the *How it works* section later in this recipe for more details.

9. Click on the **OK** button.

10. Your new **Sales** data source will now appear in the **Choose a connection to a data source screen**. Ensure the **Sales** data source is selected and then click on the **Next** button.

11. Now we select our dataset (the SharePoint list which contains our data). Select the appropriate SharePoint list (**Sales** in our example) and click on the **Next** button.

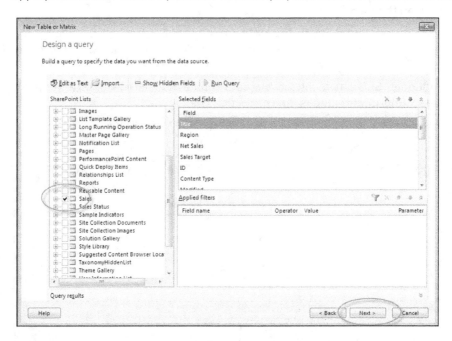

12. Now we choose fields and the layout for our tabular report. Drag the **Net Sales** and **Sales Target** fields into the **Values** box and drag **Region** into the **Row Groups** box.

13. Click on the **Next** button.

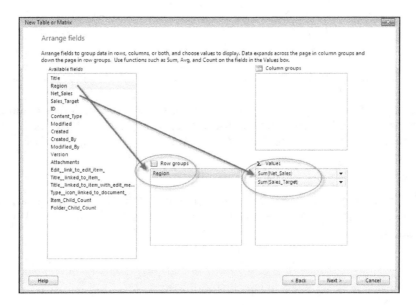

14. Now you can choose how you wish totals and subtotals to appear on the report. A preview of what the report will look like is shown in the **Preview** box. As we're using a list with limited data we have no further options for customization so just click on the **Next** button.

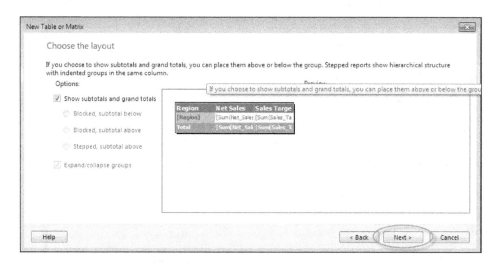

15. Finally, you can choose a color scheme for your report. Select **Slate** and click on the **Finish** button.

16. The basic report is now displayed in Report Builder. We can now use the Report Builder tools to make further enhancements to it.

17. Resize (drag) report detail table out to meet the right-hand edge of the page.

18. Change the text **Click to add title** to **Sales Targets by Region**.

19. Click on the **Run** button.

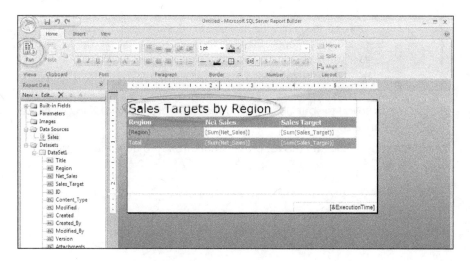

20. The reports will display the list data as it will be presented to our users.

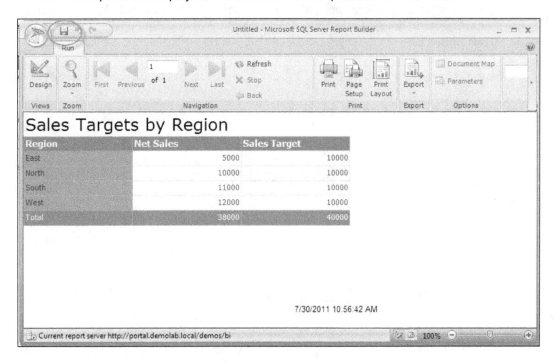

21. Click the **Save** icon at the top of the screen to save the report back to SharePoint. Select the document library (**AnalyticsReports**) where you want to save the report. If the library you need isn't displayed click on the **Recent Sites and Servers** option.

22. Provide a suitable filename for the report (for example, **cookbookSSRS.rdl**), and click on the **Save** button.

We need to specify the location to save the report, because we are using Report Builder for the first time. When you work with subsequent reports, Report Builder will have your location listed for you.

23. Your report is saved to your SharePoint reports library. Click on **X** (top right-hand side) to close Report Builder.

24. To run the report, click on the report hyperlink from the document library.

How it works...

Another great business intelligence tool at the disposal of the SharePoint user is **SQL Server Reporting Services** (**SSRS**). SSRS is part of MS SQL Server, but it is integrated with SharePoint to provide Power Users the ability to create a variety of reports and charts and display them on a SharePoint page. SQL Reporting Services is a professional reporting tool, which has been available for many years. Historically a developer was required to create reports. Now the combination of SharePoint integration and the Report Builder tool makes it easy for Power Users to author and deploy them. Reports can be created across a range of data sources (lists, databases analysis services cubes, and so on) and then published out for authorized end-users to consume.

Regardless of the data source used, conceptually the reporting process is the same. First select a report type, then select a data connection, create a dataset, design the report, and then save it to SharePoint.

One area that may trip you up is if you forget to set the credentials for your data connection. In a production environment you may simply be reusing data connections that an administrator has created for you, in which case everything will work fine. However, if you create a new connection you will need to specify one of the credential options. Depending on how your environment has been configured you may pass the identity of the current user through to the report, prompt the person using the report to enter credentials, always run the report as a particular user, and so on. Selecting the correct option is important to ensure that you don't make data visible in a report that users would not normally have permission to see. Get your SharePoint administrator to help you on this and always test your reports thoroughly.

There's more...

Report Builder is a great tool for building professional, print quality style reports, which can be made available through SharePoint on demand. Reports can also be scheduled to run at specific times and users can be alerted when their report is ready. Reports on large data sources can also be processed out-of-hours and made available as a snapshot so users do not need to wait for the report to be processed when they need it. Report Builder reports also have a wealth of export options to formats such as PDF and HTML. Report Builder also has a wide range of great-looking charts, gauges, and maps.

A map report can use geographical data to perhaps show the locations of your best sales overlaying a Bing Maps background.

See also

▸ *Creating a chart using the PerformancePoint Dashboard Designer*

Creating a chart using the PerformancePoint Dashboard Designer

PerformancePoint Services provides the ability to create a wide range of charts, KPIs, scorecards, and filters, and integrate them all together in a dashboard. In this recipe we learn how to use the Dashboard Designer tool to create and deploy an Analytic Chart to a SharePoint page.

Getting ready

This recipe works for:

▸ SharePoint 2010 Enterprise Edition

You will need SharePoint 2010 Enterprise with PerformancePoint Services configured. You will require a SharePoint site created from the **Business Intelligence Centre** template.

You need a compatible data source such as a Microsoft Analysis Services OLAP cube. In this example, we use the AdventureWorks Analysis Services database for illustration from (http://msftdbprodsamples.codeplex.com/).

You will need a SharePoint page that you want to insert your chart into.

How to do it...

1. Navigate to the **Data Connections** library in your SharePoint site. Select the **Documents** tab of the **Library Tools** ribbon.
2. Select **PerformancePoint Data Source** from the **New Document** menu.
3. Dashboard Designer will open on your machine. If you receive a security prompt click on the **Run** button.

4. The **Select a Data Source Template** is displayed. Select **Analysis Services** and click on the **OK** button.

5. You will now need to provide the details of your data source. This recipe demonstrates connecting to the AdventureWorks Cube. Provide the **Server**, **Database**, and **Cube** details that match your Analysis Services database settings. We set the authentication to be **Unattended Service Account,** which means SharePoint will always connect to the cube using a dedicated account as opposed to the user who is logged in.

6. You may also change the name of the data source from **New Data Source** (left pane) and then click on **Save** (top of the screen).

 Use the Test Data Source button to check you have entered the correct details.

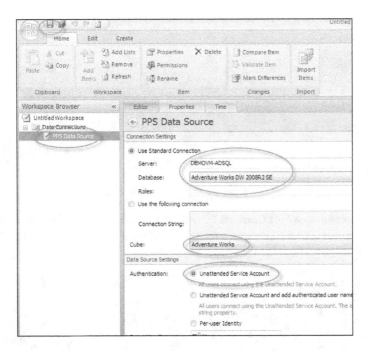

7. Now that we have a data source, we can create our chart. Charts are stored in a **PerformancePoint Content** list, which you will have in your Business Intelligence Centre SharePoint site. We need to add this to **Dashboard Designer**. Click on the **Add Lists** button from the **Dashboard Designer** ribbon, select your **PerformancePoint Content**, and click on the **OK** button.

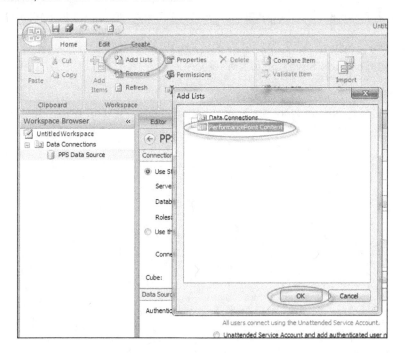

8. The **PerformancePoint Content** list will now appear in the **Workspace Browser** on the left panel within **Dashboard Designer**. Click the **Create** tab on the ribbon, and select **Analytic Chart**.

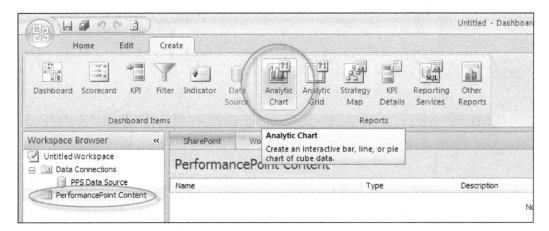

9. Next, select the data source we created previously and click on the **Finish** button.

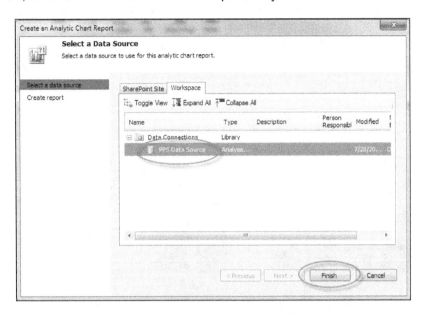

10. You are now presented with a design view for the chart. This will be blank until we drag on some measures and dimensions from our cube. From the **Details** pane on the right, expand the **Measures** group and drag **GrossProfit** onto the **Series** section of the report. The chart will update but there will be nothing visible just yet.

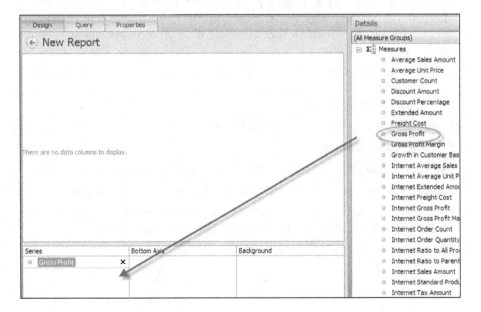

11. Expand **Dimensions** from the **Details** pane, and drag on a dimension (here we drag on Country from the Sales Territory dimension). Now we have at least one series and data for both axes, the chart will display. The initial look of the chart will depend on the way the cube is configured.

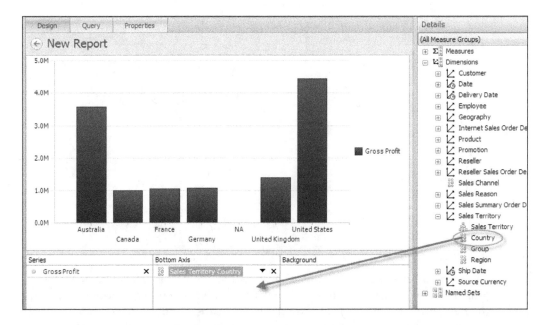

12. There are a number of options on the **Edit** tab of the ribbon to alter the look of your chart. You can also change the name of the chart through the **Properties** tab above the chart. When you're happy with the chart, click on the **Save** icon to save the chart back to SharePoint.

13. Optional: save the work we have done to a local workspace file (we will use this in the next recipe). Click on the **Office** button in the top left to reveal the file menu and select **Save Workspace As**.

14. Optional: Give your workspace a filename and save it to a location on your computer.

15. Exit **Dashboard Designer**.

16. Navigate to and edit the SharePoint page you wish to insert your chart into.

17. Select the **Insert** tab of the **Editing Tools** ribbon and click on the **Web Part** button.

18. Filter the list of Web Parts by the **PerformancePoint** category. Select the **PerformancePoint Report** Web Part and click on the **Add** button.

19. Click on the **Click here to open the tool** pane hyperlink.

20. Click on the orange browse button located to the right of the **Location** field at the top of the pane.

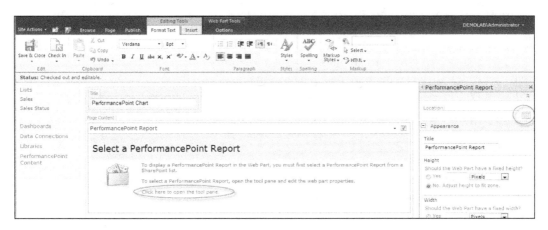

21. The **Select an Asset – Webpage Dialog** is displayed. Navigate to the list containing your chart item (**PerformancePoint Content**) and select the **PerfomancePoint Report**.
22. Click on the **OK** button to return to the tool pane.
23. Give you chart a suitable title in the **Title** textbox.
24. Click on the **OK** button to close the tool pane. The chart will be displayed on the page.
25. Save the SharePoint page.

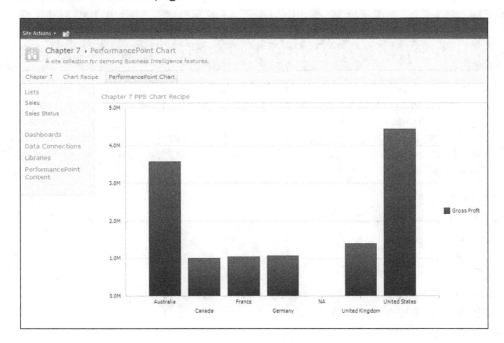

How it works...

A **PerformancePoint Analytic Chart** is a great way to visualize an Analysis Services **Online Analytical Processing** (OLAP) cube. Dashboard Designer provides a Power User with the ability to quickly build a chart from a cube without any knowledge of MDX (the OLAP query language). Any charts that are created are saved to SharePoint in a special PerformancePoint Items list where they can be managed like any other list item. PerformancePoint also provides a suite of Web Parts, one of which can be used to display the charts.

There's more...

In addition to bar charts, a chart can be displayed in a number of ways including stacked bar, line, pie, or tabular. There is also some control over the appearance such as font color and size, sorting/filtering, and legend position, however, the display options are not as extensive as Excel Services or even the Chart Web Part.

The chart does have an interactive menu system, where the user can perform a number of options such as drill-down, filtering, changing the chart type on the fly, and launching the Decomposition Tree, which provides another Silverlight-driven visualization for the user!

See also

 ▸ *Building a PerformancePoint business intelligence dashboard*

Building a PerformancePoint business intelligence dashboard

In the *Creating a chart using the PerformancePoint Dashboard Designer* recipe we demonstrated how to create an analytic chart using Dashboard Designer. However, this tool allows you to create many items (charts, KPIs, filters) and bring them all together in a dashboard. Your dashboard can be organized and deployed to SharePoint right from within Dashboard Designer, providing an alternative to manually configuring Web Parts as we did in the previous recipe.

Getting ready

This recipe works for:

 ▸ SharePoint 2010 Enterprise Edition

This recipe requires a SharePoint Enterprise environment with PerformancePoint Services configured.

You will require a SharePoint site created from the **Business Intelligence Centre** template as this contains all the lists and content types required for this recipe.

You will need access to the Sales SharePoint list and AdventureWorksOLAP cube data sources, which we have used in previous recipes.

You will need to know the URL of your Reporting Services Report Server (if you do not know this, your SharePoint Administrator should be able to help).

You will need the Dashboard Designer Workspace that was created and saved at the end of the previous recipe.

Finally, you will need the Microsoft Report Viewer 2008 installed on your computer (`http://www.microsoft.com/download/en/details.aspx?displaylang=en&id=3841`).

How to do it...

1. Locate the Dashboard Designer workspace file that was saved at the end of the previous recipe. Double-click the file to open it in **Dashboard Designer**.

 This is the quickest way to maintain your dashboards in SharePoint, as the workspace file understands all the PerformancePoint lists and libraries you are working with. Dashboard Designer should now open at the point we finished the previous recipe.

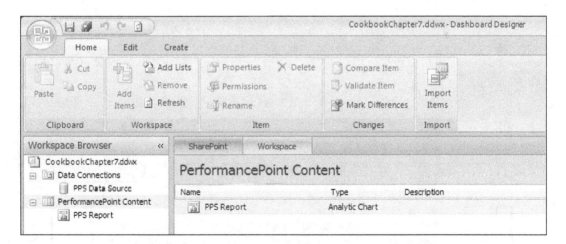

2. Now we will add the Report Builder report we created in a previous recipe. Click on the **Create** tab on the ribbon and select the **Reporting Services** button.

3. A form will appear requiring details of the location of your report. The keyboard cursor should be placed over the name of your report in the **Workspace Browser** pane on the left. Give your report a suitable name.

4. Set the **Server mode** to **SharePoint Integrated**.

5. Set the **Server Name** to the URL for your Report Server. Typically, this will be in the form `http://<servername>/reportserver`.

6. Type the full location of the report we created in a previous recipe. This will be in the form `http://<sharepointsite>/<reportslibrary>/<reportname>.rdl`

7. Click on the **Preview** button to show your report in the preview pane.

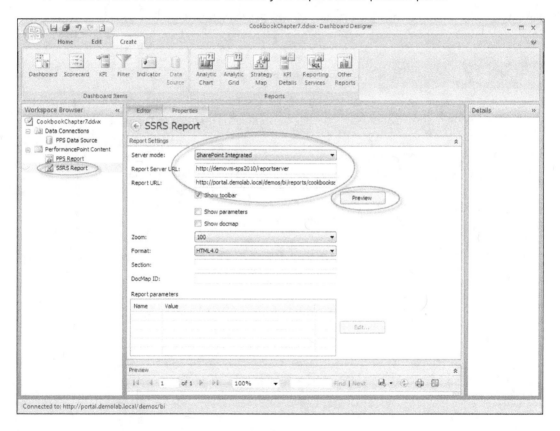

 If you can't see your report preview, try either double-clicking the chevrons in the top right-hand side of the **Report Settings** pane to move out of the way, or scrolling down the page.

8. We will now create the PerformancePoint dashboard. Select the **Create** tab of the ribbon and click on the **Dashboard** button.

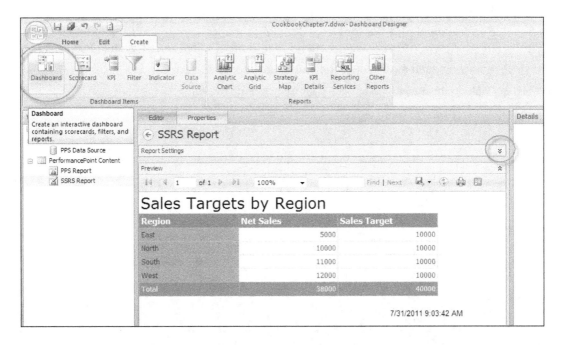

9. The **Select a Dashboard Page Template** dialog will be displayed. You will be prompted to select a Dashboard Template. Select the template for **2 Columns** and click on the **OK** button.

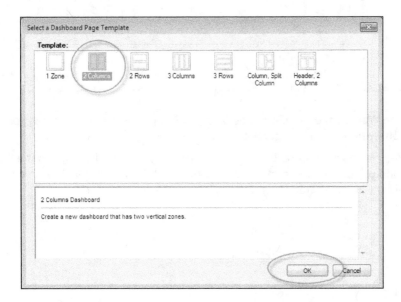

10. The dashboard editor screen will now be displayed. Change the name of your dashboard to something memorable.

11. Expand the **Reports** section on the right hand **Details** pane and then expand the **PerformancePoint Content** icon. Both PerformancePoint reports created during this chapter (the Analytic Report and your Report Builder report) should be visible.

12. Now drag each report to a zone on the dashboard screen.

13. Click on the **Save** icon to save your new dashboard item.

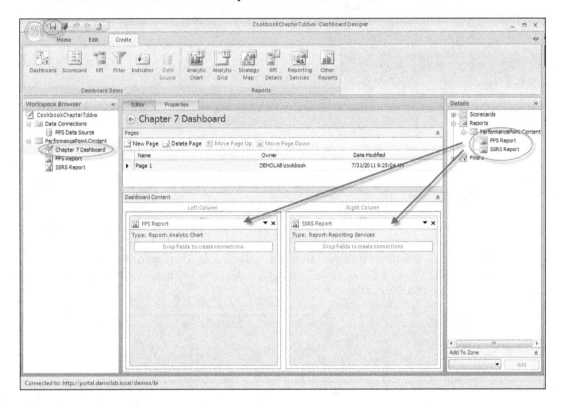

14. In the **Workspace Browser** pane, right-click your dashboard item and select **Deploy to SharePoint** from the pop-up menu.

15. Select your **Dashboards** Library from the list presented and click on the **OK** button. (When you create a SharePoint site from the BI Centre template, a Dashboards Library will be created for you.)

16. After a short while, your dashboard will be deployed to SharePoint and presented to you. You can Save your Dashboard Designer workspace file again, and come back to add more features at a later date.

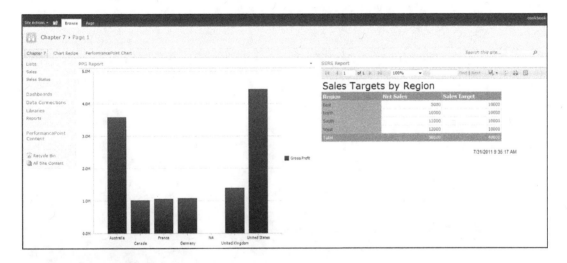

How it works...

PerformancePoint Dashboard Designer is used to create dashboards from a number of components. In this recipe we first pulled in the Report Builder report we created earlier and created a reference to it in Dashboard Designer. Dashboards can be created to position items on a page exactly how we want them to look on a SharePoint page. The deploy to SharePoint function creates a new SharePoint page, places PerformancePoint Web Parts on it, and links these Web Parts to our reports. This is a much quicker way of creating dashboards than manually positioning Web Parts in SharePoint.

There's more...

You could also use Dashboard Designer to pull in other report types such as our Excel Services report. There is also an option to create filters, which can be linked to reports, which allows users to change the appearance of a dashboard by selecting a new date, for example.

See also

- ▸ *Creating a Chart using the PerformancePoint Dashboard Designer*
- ▸ *Creating a report using Report Builder*

8

Automating Business Processes—Recipes for Electronic Forms and Workflows

In this chapter, we will cover:

- ▶ Creating an InfoPath form for a SharePoint list
- ▶ Creating a holiday request InfoPath form and publishing it to a Form Library
- ▶ Using the Collect Feedback workflow to receive feedback on a Microsoft Word 2010 document
- ▶ Creating a list workflow using SharePoint Designer 2010
- ▶ Using Microsoft Visio 2010 to model a SharePoint workflow

Introduction

The recipes in this chapter explore the technologies and options available for creating electronic forms and workflows in SharePoint 2010. Understanding the technologies explored in this chapter is key to building no-code composite applications, which automate the business process.

SharePoint 2010 uses InfoPath 2010 to create rich, powerful electronic forms. InfoPath forms can replace the default forms used for SharePoint lists or act as custom forms that provide the user interface and business rules required to run a custom business process. The first two recipes of the chapter show you how to create, publish, and consume InfoPath forms in SharePoint.

When automating business processes, we automatically think of workflow. SharePoint 2010 supports many different workflow and task-management scenarios. There are a number of out of the box workflows that can be used to perform tasks such as to requesting feedback or approval for a document. Where these workflows don't suffice, they can be copied, modified, and extended, or completely new custom workflows can be constructed. These custom workflows can perform a range of custom actions, allocate tasks to users, or automate an end-to-end business process as required.

SharePoint 2010 provides a number of different tools to build workflows, including SharePoint Designer 2010 and Visio Premium 2010. Workflows can be started from SharePoint 2010 or directly from client applications such as Microsoft Word 2010. The remaining recipes of this chapter provide a deep dive into some of the most important SharePoint 2010 workflow features, demonstrating the approach required and the toolsets used to create, publish, monitor, and run SharePoint 2010 workflows. By the end of this chapter you will have a good understanding of what you need to do to start adding electronic forms and workflows to your own composite applications. We revisit the forms and workflows developed here when we explore building composite applications in the *Appendix*.

InfoPath forms and SharePoint workflows are very big subjects. Both could command books in their own right. The recipes presented in this chapter are not comprehensive treatments. Instead, what you will find is coverage of the most useful features and concepts, intended to allow you to quickly become productive. However, to become an effective Power User I strongly recommend more study and practice in these areas. You will find more information and resources to help you do this on my blog at `http://www.sharepoint-mentor.com`.

Creating an InfoPath Form for a SharePoint List

You can replace the default SharePoint list forms with an InfoPath form on any SharePoint list. This gives you much more flexibility and control over how you edit and display the data.

Getting ready

This recipe works for:

- SharePoint 2010 Enterprise Edition
- Office 365 (SharePoint Online)

You will need a SharePoint List where you want to create an InfoPath form.

You will need the **Design** or **Full Control** permission level to run this recipe.

You will need InfoPath Designer 2010 installed on your client machine.

This recipe uses a SharePoint 2010 Team Site with a contacts list added for illustration. You can add a Contact lists to any site using the recipe *Creating a SharePoint contact list and connecting it to Outlook 2010* in *Chapter 2* of this book.

How to do it...

1. Open Internet Explorer and navigate to your SharePoint 2010 Team Site.
2. Select the **Contacts** list from the **Quick Launch** menu.
3. Select the **List** tab of the **List Tools** ribbon.
4. Select the **Customize Form** icon.
5. InfoPath Form Designer 2010 will open displaying an auto-generated InfoPath form for the contacts list.

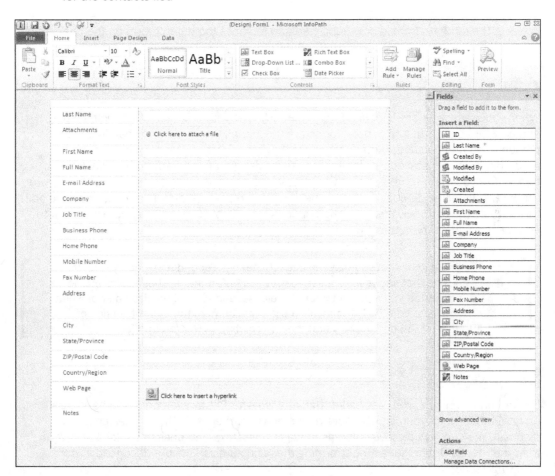

6. Select the **File** tab in the ribbon to access the backstage view.

7. Select the **Quick Publish** button.

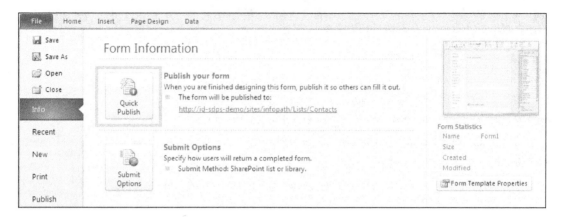

8. The InfoPath form is now published and replaces the default form on the SharePoint list. Click on the **OK** button in the **Publish** dialog displayed.

How it works...

When you create a SharePoint list, SharePoint automatically creates default edit, display, and new forms for you. While these forms are functional, they are somewhat limited in the presentation and customization options that they provide. If you have SharePoint Server Enterprise Edition installed, you replace these forms with an InfoPath 2010 form. InfoPath forms offer you many more options for creating and controlling how you edit and display your list data. This recipe demonstrates the mechanics of replacing the forms; once you have done this a whole range of new customization options is available to you. Every time you want to edit the form, just repeat this procedure.

One gotcha that you may run into is if you have added a taxonomy field (that is, one that shows a term set) to your list. Unfortunately these fields are not supported in the current InfoPath release, and you will receive an error when you try to edit the list form. It's a big omission from the current version of SharePoint, and not one that there is an obvious workaround for.

There's more...

Having run this recipe, you may be left thinking "*so what?*" However, once you have created an InfoPath form for your list, you have all the power of the InfoPath form designer at your disposal. You can now remove columns, add graphics, text, and business rules to the form to fit your needs. Techniques for performing these customizations are described in the following sections.

Removing columns

It's quite common to have columns in a list that you don't want the user to fill in. When you have an InfoPath attached to the list, simply open the form, delete the field that you don't want the users to edit, and republish.

If you have used the table-editing tools in Microsoft Word, you will find the InfoPath experience very familiar. The following screenshot shows the **Attachments** row being deleted from the form:

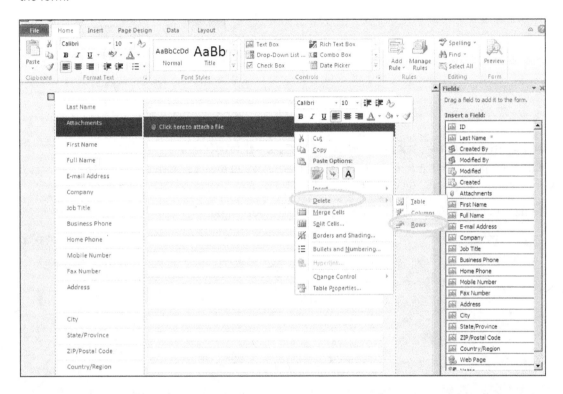

It's important to realize that you are only removing columns from the form, not from the underlying list itself. Also, if you add a new column to your list after you have customized the form, SharePoint won't automatically add the new column to your form for you. It will prompt you that there are new columns available the next time you open the InfoPath form designer. Click on **Yes** to update the fields list.

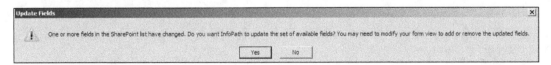

You can then select the new fields that you require and drag-and-drop them into the form.

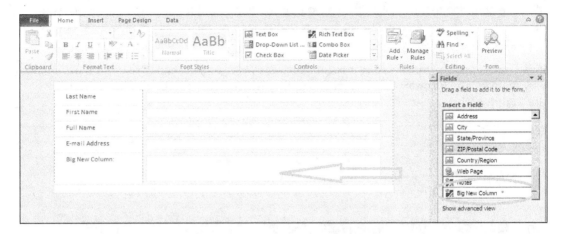

Adding images, explanatory text, and tooltips

Normal SharePoint list forms are a bit dull. Now that you have an InfoPath form, you can start to brighten things up. You can change colors, fonts, add images, text, and tooltips.

To add an image, use the **Picture** button on the **Insert** ribbon.

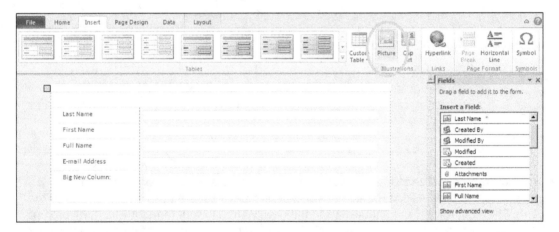

Then simply browse to the picture that you want to add and republish the form.

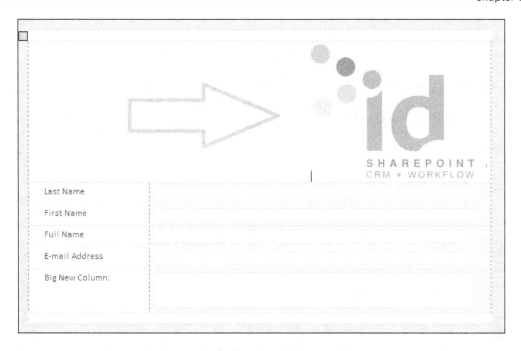

Adding text to your form can help guide your users when they are filling it in. You can add the text directly to the form or you can add it to the controls **ScreenTip.**

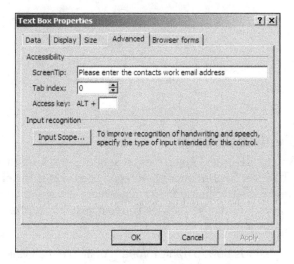

The **ScreenTip** text will only be shown when the user's mouse hovers over the control in the browser. This helps your users without cluttering up your form.

Adding rules to validate data

InfoPath forms allow you to add rules. Rules can be added to the form to validate data, apply custom formatting, or perform custom actions. You can use actions to set field values, switch views, submit form data, and so on. InfoPath form rules are the way to implement and enforce custom business logic in your forms, so I advise you to invest some time learning how to build them up and exploring what they can do.

The following screenshot shows how to apply InfoPath built in e-mail validation rule to the e-mail textbox field. This rule uses a regular expression to ensure that the value entered is in a valid e-mail format, and shows a validation error if it is not.

InfoPath Designer versus InfoPath Filler

You may notice two Microsoft Office InfoPath programs on your computer, **Microsoft InfoPath Designer 2010** and **Microsoft InfoPath Filler 2010**. When creating forms for use in SharePoint, InfoPath Designer 2010 is the application you need to use. InfoPath is a standalone forms technology, while InfoPath Filler 2010 exists to allow users to fill in InfoPath forms without the use of SharePoint. That isn't something we cover in this book, though it's useful to know that you can use this if you need to.

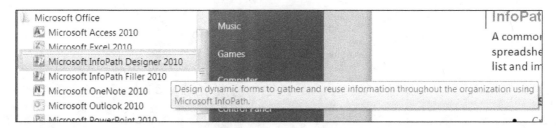

See also

▶ Creating a Team Site, Chapter 2

▶ Creating a SharePoint contact list and connecting it to Outlook 2010, Chapter 2

▶ Creating a holiday request InfoPath form and publishing it to a form library

Creating a holiday request InfoPath form and publishing it to a form library

InfoPath forms are capable of containing repeating data, optional fields, and presenting different views to different users. To access the full power of InfoPath, you will want to create a custom form and publish it to a SharePoint form library. In this recipe we learn how to create a holiday request form and publish it to SharePoint.

Getting ready

This recipe works for:

- ▸ SharePoint 2010 Enterprise Edition
- ▸ Office 365 (SharePoint Online)

You will need a SharePoint site where you want to create an InfoPath form. This recipe creates a holiday request form for illustration.

You will need the **Design** or **Full Control** permission level to run this recipe.

You will need InfoPath Designer 2010 installed on your client machine.

How to do it...

1. Open the **Microsoft InfoPath Designer 2010** on your computer.

2. The backstage view is displayed. Double click the on **SharePoint Form Library** button.

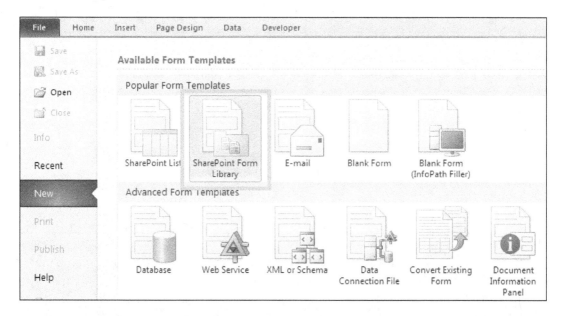

3. A new blank form opens. Change the form title to **Holiday Request**. Change the first subheading to **Employee Details**.

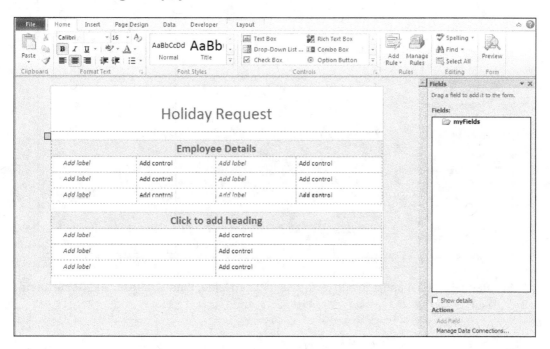

4. Place the cursor on the first **Add control** cell in the **Employee Details** table. Click on **Text Box** in the **Controls** section of the **Home** ribbon. A new textbox will be inserted into the form (**field1**) and a new field is added to the forms data source (**Fields** view).

5. Double on click **field1** in the **Fields** view to open the properties dialog. Rename the field to **FirstName** and click on the **OK** button.

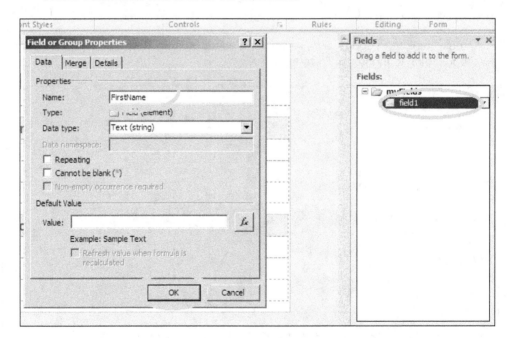

6. Repeat steps 4 and 5 to add textboxes for **LastName, EmailAddress,** and **Department**.

7. Add labels to the form for each of the textboxes that you have added.

8. Highlight the last row in the **Employee Details** table and delete it.

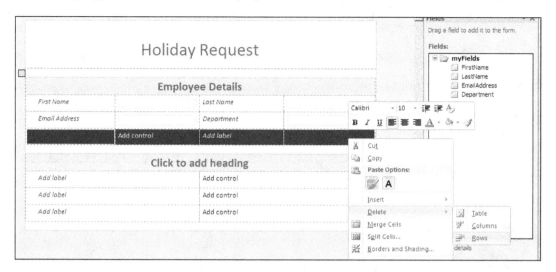

9. Rename the next section in the form **Holiday Details**. Add labels for **Start Date** and **End Date**.

10. Expand the Controls section in the ribbon. Select the **Date Picker** control. Add date controls for **StartDate** and **EndDate** to the form.

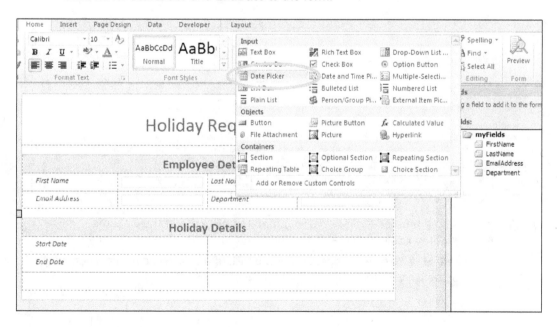

11. Click on the **File** tab to access the backstage view. Click on the **Publish** button.

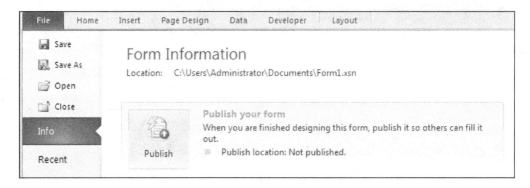

12. The **Publish** options are displayed. Click on the **SharePoint Server** button.

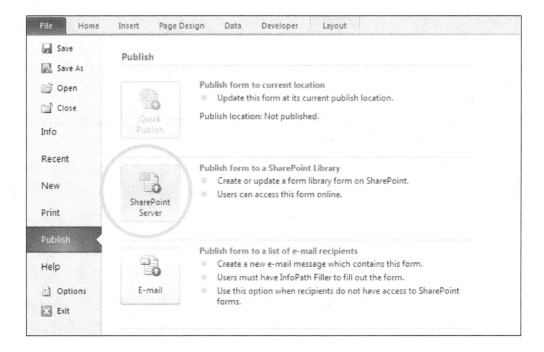

13. You will be prompted to first save your form template. Enter the filename **holidayrequest.xsn** and click on the **Save** button.

14. The **Publishing Wizard** will open. Enter the URL of the SharePoint site where you want to publish your form and click on the **Next** button.

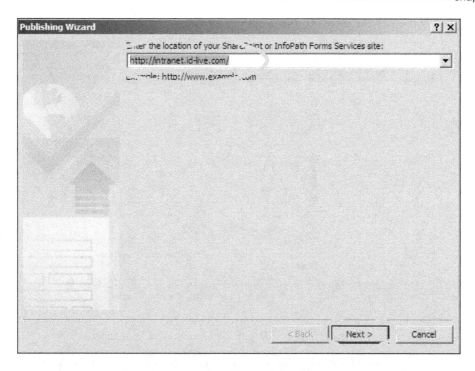

15. Tick the **Enable this form to be filled out using a browser**.

16. Select the **Form Library** option.

17. Click on the **Next** button.

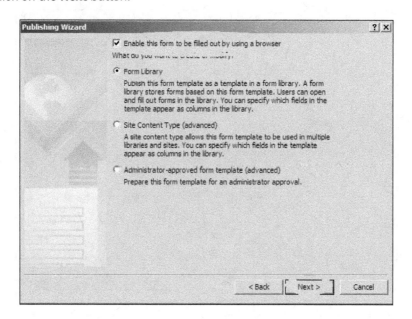

18. Select the **Create a new form library** option.

19. Click on the **Next** button.

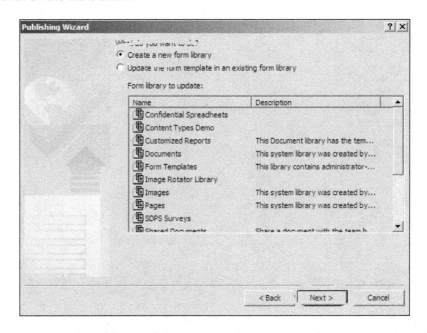

20. Name the new library **Holiday Requests**.

21. Click on the **Next** button.

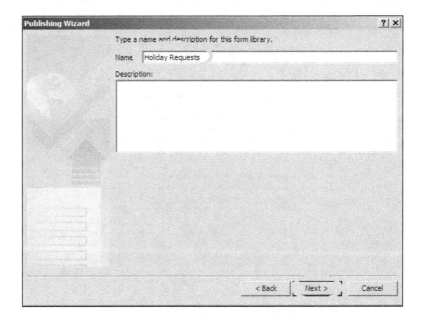

22. To promote data items in the form to SharePoint list columns, click on the **Add** button.

23. Select the **FirstName** column and click on the **OK** button. Repeat for the **LastName**, **EmailAddress**, **Department**, **StartDate**, and **EndDate** fields.

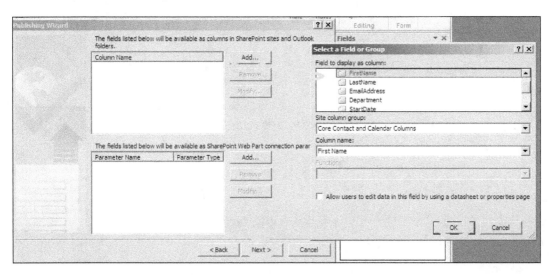

24. Click on the **Publish** button.

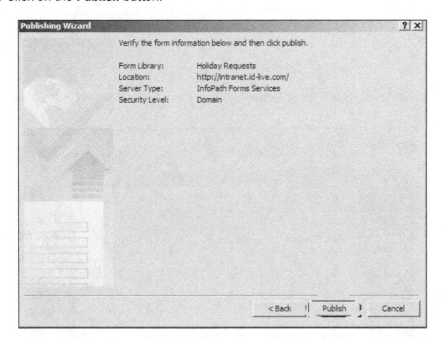

25. The form is published to SharePoint. Click on the **Open this form in a browser link**. The InfoPath form opens in the web browser.

26. Enter some data to test the form and click on the **Save** button.

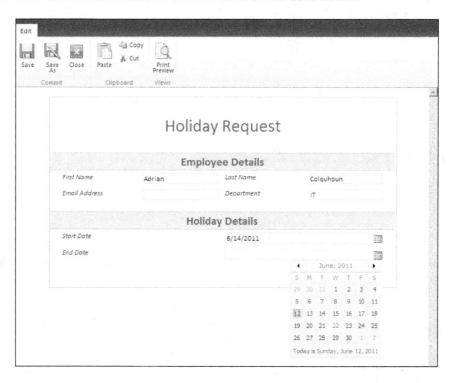

27. You will be prompted for a filename for your form. Enter **request1** and click on **Save**.

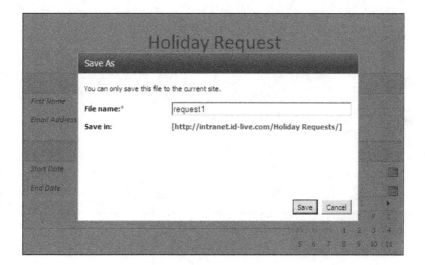

28. Your holiday request is saved to the form library. Click on the **Close** button.

How it works...

When we design our InfoPath forms directly, we have far more options and possibilities than if we just promote the form for a SharePoint list (as we did in the previous recipe). This recipe illustrates the key steps involved, such as adding controls to the form, building up the data structure that underlies the form, and so on. Once you get proficient with these, there are even more goodies to explore, such as repeating sections, optional sections, themes, and views.

The recipe then shows you how to publish the form to a SharePoint 2010 form library. By doing so, we take advantage of the tight integration between SharePoint 2010 and InfoPath 2010. Data can be collected from your users in InfoPath, and that same information appears in the columns of the SharePoint form library. All this magic happens because we promoted those fields out of our InfoPath form during the publishing process. We can even change the data in SharePoint and have it automatically synchronized back to our form if we want to. This is an important approach, as it allows us to run workflows against our form data. You will see this demonstrated in the *Creating a list workflow using SharePoint Designer 2010* recipe later in this chapter.

There's more...

One of the key concepts to grasp in InfoPath is the difference between the form itself (that is, the bit you can see) and the form data shown in the Fields view. This can include data that the users don't enter and data that we don't even show in the form. The data could come from a secondary data source (such as a database or SharePoint lookup) or be updated by a workflow that runs on the form after we submit it to SharePoint. One common example is to include a workflow status field that we update using a SharePoint 2010 workflow. I will illustrate that later in this chapter.

Tip: Build the form data structure first

When you become more practiced at building InfoPath forms, you may find it easier to design and build the form's data structure first. For complex forms, you will find it much easier to group together related fields. Add the fields that you require, then drag-and-drop those fields directly into your form. InfoPath will automatically generate the most appropriate controls and labels for you. It is a great timesaver. For an example of how a remodeled holiday form data structure might look, see the next screenshot. If you want to go one step further, investigate InfoPath form **Template Parts** too—they allow you to pre-create data field and form control snippets that you can use as building blocks over and over again.

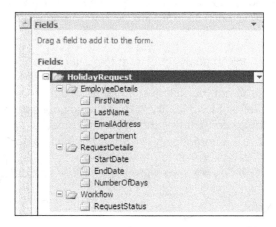

Within our InfoPath form itself, we can create many different views. Those views can be used to present different subsets of the form data. For example, we often create summary views, or create a read-only view of the form once it has been submitted. We can use rules when the form is opened to switch to the correct view according to the logic in our business process.

List Forms versus Form Library forms

You may be wondering when you should customize the form on a list (as explained in the previous recipe) or when you should use a form library (as described here). The answer (like so many things in SharePoint) is it depends. List forms are simpler and quicker to create, but will only support data structures that you can easily represent in a list. What's more, every piece of data you capture must go in the list. By contrast, a form library form may capture information that remains hidden in the form and isn't exposed to SharePoint at all. You can use complex logic, repeating sections, optional sections, views, and so on. My advice is if in doubt—try it out! It's very easy and quick to prototype your form using both approaches to find which one works best for your particular scenario.

Configuring submit options for the holiday request form

The form presented in this recipe is overly simple, designed only to illustrate key InfoPath concepts. Although the form created in this recipe can be saved to the **Holiday Requests** form library, typically what we require is that the form be submitted by the user through the use of a **Submit** button. At the same time, we don't want the users to type in an arbitrary filename for their request, and we will also want to remove the save buttons that InfoPath shows by default. There are number of steps required to achieve this outcome.

1. Configure a submit connection to our holiday request library.
2. Add a formula that generates unique filenames for the submitted forms.
3. Add a **Submit** button to our form and connect it to the submit connection.
4. Remove the default InfoPath buttons.

To configure the submit connection; first select the **File** tab in InfoPath Designer. Click on the **Submit Form** button and select the **To SharePoint Server** option. A dialog opens similar to the publishing dialog that we encountered earlier. You will need to enter the URL of the holiday request library where you want to submit the forms.

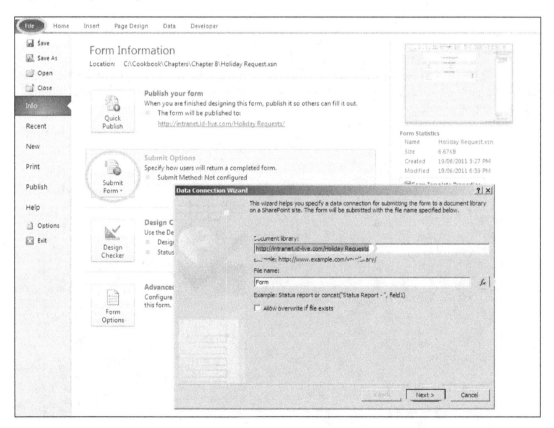

With the dialog open, you can create a formula that assigns each submitted request a unique value. Click on the **fx** button to open the formula editor. The easiest way to do this is to enter a formula that combines some of the fields entered onto the form with a timestamp, as shown in the next screenshot. Once the formula is added you can complete the submit connection wizard. Name the submit connection **HolidayRequestSubmit**.

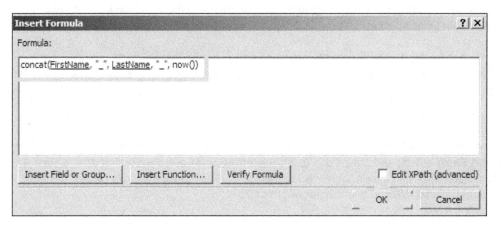

To add a **Submit** button, add a button control to the bottom of the form in the same way as you added the textbox and the date picker controls earlier in the recipe (you may have to expand the controls ribbon to see all the available controls). Access the button's properties using its context menu. Name the button **Submit** and ensure that its **Action** is set to **Submit**. Open the **Submit Options** dialog and ensure that it is configured as shown in the following screenshot:

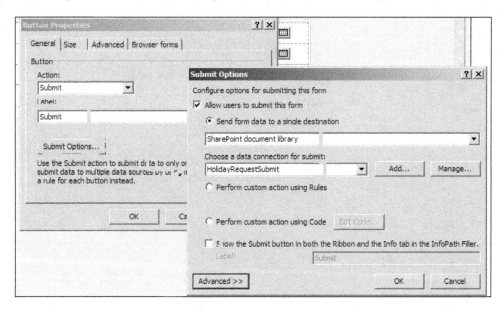

To remove the default InfoPath form buttons, click on the **Form Options** button on the **File** tab to open the **Form Options** dialog. You will need to uncheck the **Show InfoPath commands in ribbon or toolbar** option and click on the **OK** button. **Quick Publish** the form. Now when the users add new holiday requests they will be able to submit the requests using the **Submit** button.

See also

- ▸ *Creating an InfoPath form for a SharePoint list*
- ▸ *Creating a Team Site, Chapter 2*

Using the Collect Feedback workflow to receive feedback on a Microsoft Word 2010 document

SharePoint 2010 provides a number of workflows ready to use out of the box. In this recipe, we learn how to use the collect feedback workflow to get feedback on a Microsoft Word 2010 document.

Getting ready

This recipe works for:

- ▸ SharePoint 2010 Standard Edition
- ▸ SharePoint 2010 Enterprise Edition
- ▸ Office 365 (SharePoint Online)

You will need a document library to attach the collect feedback workflow to. You will need a document in that document library to run the collect feedback workflow against. This recipe uses a SharePoint 2010 Team Site with a Sales Proposals document library added for illustration.

How to do it...

1. Open Internet Explorer and navigate to your SharePoint 2010 Team Site.
2. Select the **Sales Proposals** list from the **Quick Launch** menu.
3. Select the **Library** tab of the **Library Tools** ribbon.

4. From the **Workflow Settings** button, activate the **Add a Workflow** option.

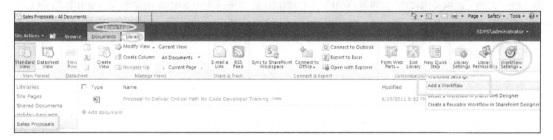

5. Select the **Collect Feedback – SharePoint 2010** template from the **Select a workflow template:** list.

6. Name the workflow **Sales Proposal Feedback Workflow**.

7. Set the **Select a task list:** drop-down to **Tasks**.

8. Set the **Select a history list:** drop-down to **Workflow History (new)**.

9. Ensure that the **Allow this workflow to be manually started by an authenticated user with Edit Item permissions** checkbox is ticked.

10. Click on the **Next** button.

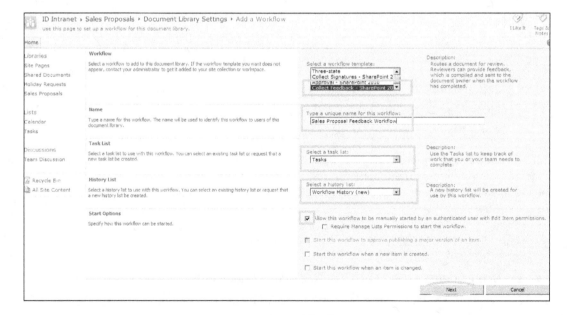

11. The workflow association form is displayed. Enter the text **Please provide feedback on this sales proposal** in the **Request** textbox.

12. Set the **Duration Per Task** to **5**.

13. In the **End on Document Change** row of the form, ensure that the **Automatically cancel the workflow if the document is changed before the workflow is completed** checkbox is ticked.

14. Click on the **Save** button.

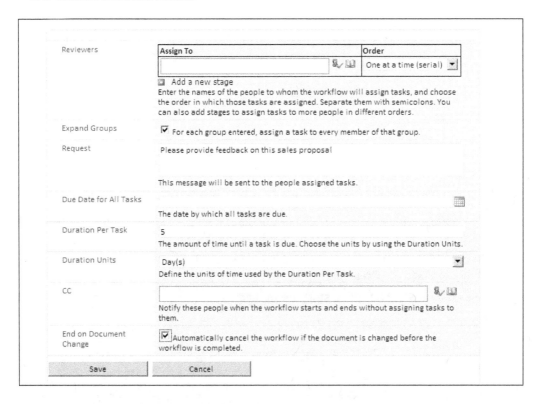

15. Open the **Sales Proposals** Library and select the document that you wish to run the Collect Feedback workflow on.

16. Select the **Workflows** button from the **Library** tab of the **Library Tools** ribbon.

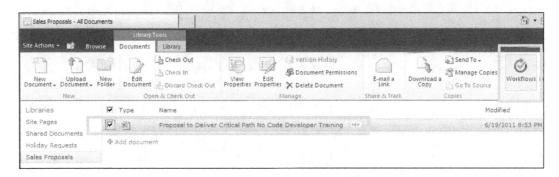

17. Click on the **Sales Proposal Feedback Workflow** hyperlink in the **Start a New Workflow** section.

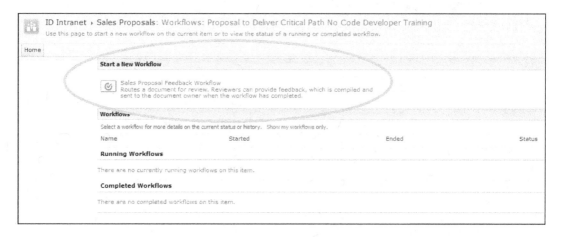

18. The workflow initiation form is displayed. Enter the users who you want to collect feedback from. Set the **Order** drop-down list to **All at once (parallel)**.

19. If you require any users to be copied in on the progress of this workflow, then add their details to the **CC** box.

20. Click on the **Start** button to start the workflow.

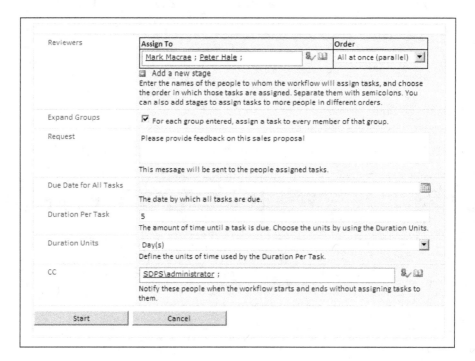

How it works...

SharePoint 2010 provides a number of workflow templates out of the box. The three features that you will use most commonly are:

- ▸ Approval – SharePoint 2010
- ▸ Collect Feedback – SharePoint 2010
- ▸ Collect Signatures – SharePoint 2010

To use a SharePoint workflow, you first need to create an **association** between the workflow template and the document library (site or content type) that you want it to act upon. The first steps in this recipe show you how to create the association between the **Collect Feedback Workflow – SharePoint 2010** and the **Sales Proposals** document library in our Team Site. As we create the association, SharePoint displays the workflow association form, which in turn prompts us for various pieces of information about how we want our workflows to run. We can set the task list where we want any tasks generated by the workflow to be placed, the history list where we want it to log out messages that track its execution history, decide if we want the workflow to be started automatically, and so on. If our workflow has an initiation form (that is, a form that will be displayed to our users each time they start it), we can set default values and options for the form as we create this association. The association between the document library and the workflow only needs to be created once. As soon as the association has been created, the Collect Feedback workflow is read to be run against any of the documents that exist in the Sales Proposals Document library.

[

Workflow associations allow the same workflow template to be reused multiple times in the same document library. Each different association has a different name and allows different configurations and default values to be set.
]

The second part of this recipe shows you how to run the collect feedback workflow against an individual document in the document library. In this case the workflow is started manually, but depending on how you create the association above, you could choose to have the workflow start automatically when a new document has been created, is updated, or published.

When you start the workflow, SharePoint 2010 displays its (InfoPath) initiation form. In this workflow, the initiation form is the same form as we saw earlier for association, except this time the values we set previously are already filled in. Each of the reviewers that you enter will be allocated a task to provide feedback on your document. Assuming outgoing e-mail is configured for your SharePoint farm, they will also receive an e-mail notifying them of the task as well. Once all the tasks are complete, the feedback provided is returned to you.

If you assign your task to a SharePoint group, the workflow is smart enough to go through the group's membership and assign a feedback task to each of the group members. However, it won't expand **Active Directory** (AD) groups, so if you have any AD groups within your SharePoint groups, users in the AD groups don't get allocated the tasks.

There's more...

It's all very well starting the Collect Feedback workflow, but how do you know what it has done and what its current status is? If you have a look at the Shared Documents library after you have created the workflow association, you will notice a new column **Sales Proposal Feedback Workflow** has been added. SharePoint creates this association column automatically and uses it to keep track of the execution history of the workflows that you start.

Click through the **In Progress** link in the association column and you will be taken to the page. Here you can see the history of the workflow's execution, including the messages that it has logged out and the Feedback tasks that it has allocated.

The **Workflow Information** section in this page displays basic information about the workflow (such as its current **Status**, the **Document** that it is acting upon, and so on).

The **Workflow Visualization** section displays a graphical representation of the workflow's progress, rendered through SharePoint's Visio Services (you will see an error if this isn't configured correctly). These graphics are a great way to show a workflow's progress. You'll learn how easy it is to create them for your own workflows in the next recipe.

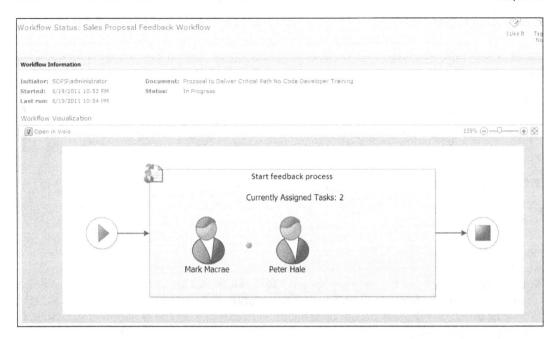

Scrolling further down the page, you will find details of the **Tasks** that the workflow has created, as well as any messages that have been logged out to the **Workflow History** list.

When allocating workflow tasks, you may prefer to have all your workflows write their tasks to the same place, so that users only have to refer to one task list to see what they have to do. However, with the history list, the reverse is usually true. Use a new history list for each workflow association that you create—you will find it easier to see the messages that way.

 Do not rely on the **Workflow History** list as an audit record of your workflow's execution history. By default, its contents get deleted 60 days after the workflow completes.

Starting workflows from Microsoft Word 2010

One of the great features of the Microsoft Office 2010 product suite is the way that it integrates with SharePoint 2010 without you necessarily having to actually visit the SharePoint site. This is definitely true for workflows. If you edit a document from your Sales Proposals document library after running this recipe, you will be able to start the collect feedback workflow directly from Microsoft Word 2010. To do this, click on the **File** tab. In the **Save & Send** section you will see the **Sales Proposal Feedback Workflow** listed under the **Workflows** heading. Click on the workflow to make the **Start Workflow** button visible. Click on the **Start Workflow** button to bring up the workflow initiation form and start the workflow in the same way as you did above.

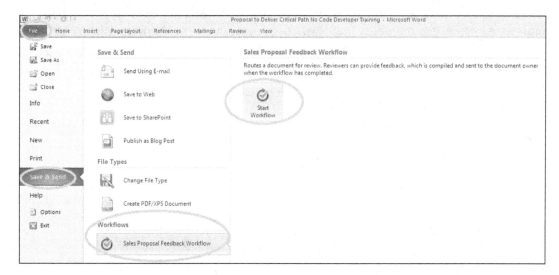

 The Collect Signatures workflow can only be started from within Microsoft Word 2010.

Customizing the out of the box workflows

SharePoint 2010 allows any of the out-of-the-box workflows to be customized. You can add extra steps or tweak the current processing to better suit your needs. SharePoint Designer 2010 contains a menu option that allows you to **Copy and Modify** the workflow, and then you can make whatever changes you require (there are more details on the available changes later in this chapter). The golden rule here (as with most things in SharePoint)—never try to modify the built-in workflows directly!

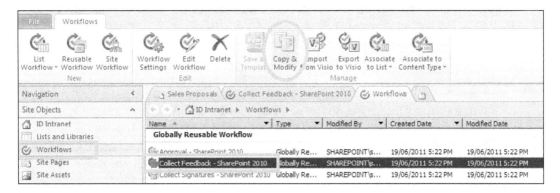

See also

▸ *Creating a list workflow using SharePoint Designer 2010*

▸ *Using Microsoft Visio 2010 to model a SharePoint workflow*

Creating a list workflow using SharePoint Designer 2010

Earlier in this chapter we created a holiday request InfoPath form and configured it to post into an InfoPath from library. In this recipe, we will learn how to attach a custom workflow to that library to custom approval on each holiday request when it is received.

Getting ready

This recipe works for:

▸ SharePoint 2010 Standard Edition (standard lists and libraries only)

▸ SharePoint 2010 Enterprise Edition

▸ Office 365 (SharePoint Online)

You will need the **Design** or **Full Control** permission level to run this recipe.

You will need SharePoint Designer 2010 installed on your client machine.

This recipe uses the holiday request InfoPath form library created earlier in this chapter for illustration. However, the same approach can be used to add a custom workflow to any SharePoint list or library. The earlier form has been slightly modified to include a **Number Of Days** field in the form itself and a **Request Status** field in the form's data structure. When republishing the form, both fields have been promoted to the **Holiday Requests** InfoPath form library. Additionally, when promoting the **Request Status** field, the Option **Allow users to edit data in this field by using a datasheet or properties page** was checked, allowing us to update that field using the workflow that we will create in this recipe. Please refer to the earlier recipe for more details on how to make these customizations.

How to do it...

1. Open your Team Site using SharePoint Designer 2010. Navigate to the **Holiday Requests** form library and click on the **List Workflow** button from the **List Settings** ribbon.

2. **Name** the workflow **Holiday Requests Approval Workflow**. Optionally enter a **Description**.

3. Click on the **OK** button to continue.

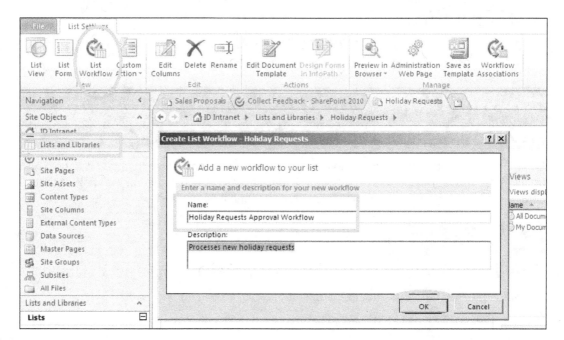

4. The workflow designer will be displayed.

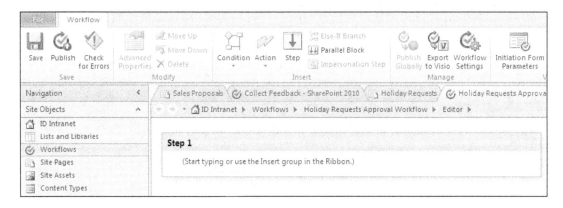

5. Click inside **Step 1** and rename this step **Acknowledge Holiday Request**.

6. Click on the **Step** button on the **Workflow** ribbon to add a second step into the workflow.

7. Rename the second step **Apply Approval Logic**.

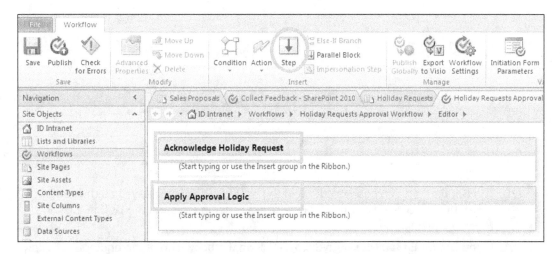

8. Place your cursor inside the **Acknowledge Holiday Request** step (use the flashing orange bar to locate the correct insertion point in the workflow designer).

9. Expand the **Action** button on the **Workflow** ribbon. Select the **Send an Email** action form the **Core Actions** section.

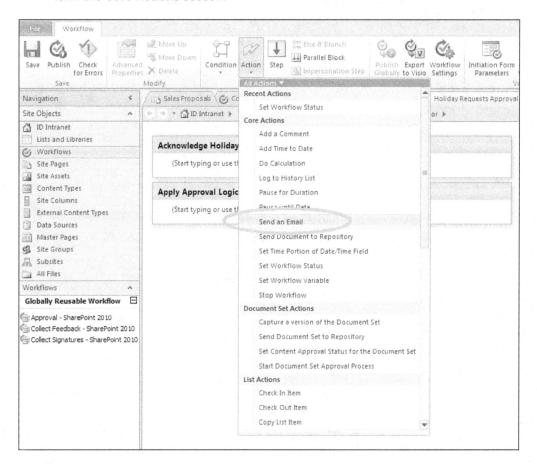

10. The **Send an Email** action is added to the workflow and is displayed as the sentence **Email these users**. Click on the **these users** hyperlink to open the **Define E-mail Message** dialog.

11. In the **Define E-Mail Message** dialog, click on the book icon at the end of the **To** line.

12. In the **Select Users dialog**, select the **Workflow Lookup for a User** option.

13. In the **Lookup for Person or Group** dialog, set the **Date source** to **Current Item**. Set the **Field from source** to **Email Address**.

14. Click on the **OK** button to close the **Lookup for Person or Group** and the **Select Users** dialog.

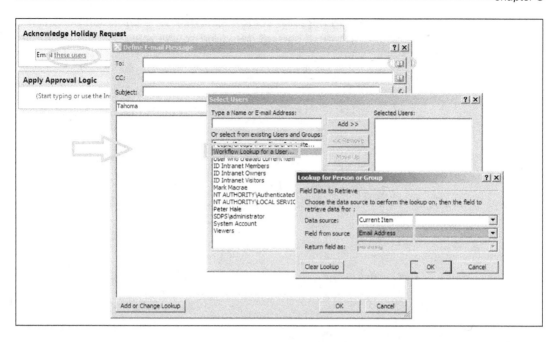

15. Continue to define the e-mail address as shown in the following screenshot. Use the **Add or Change Lookup** button to add lookups for **First Name**, **Number of Days**, and **Start Date** from the current item.

16. Click on the **OK** button.

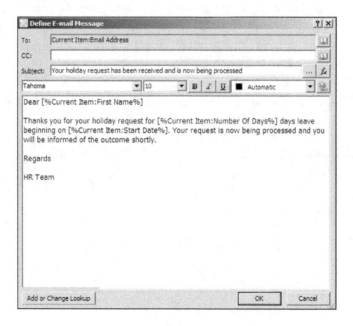

17. Inset your cursor in the **Apply Approval Logic** step. Expand the **Condition** button on the **Workflow** ribbon. Select the **If current item field equals value** condition from the **Common Conditions** section.

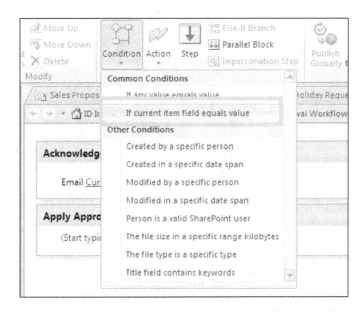

18. A new condition is placed in the workflow. Use the hyperlinks in the conditions text to set the condition logic as shown in the following screen shot.

19. Add a **Send an Email** action to the **If** branch. Configure it as described previously above, but set the subject and body to **your request has been rejected**.

20. Place the insertion point outside the **If** condition. Right-click to bring up the context menu. Select the **Else-If Branch** option.

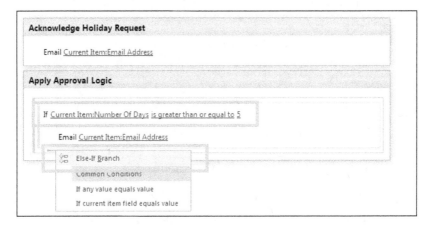

21. Add a **Send an Email** action to the else branch. Configure it as described previously above, but set the subject and body to **your request has been approved**.

22. Place the cursor immediately beneath the **Send an Email** activity in the **Acknowledge Holiday Request.** Expand the **Action** button on the **Workflow** ribbon. Scroll down and select the **Update List Item** action form the **List Actions** section.

23. The **Update List Item** action is added to the workflow and is displayed as the sentence **then Update item in this list**. Click on the **this list** hyperlink to open the **Update List Item** dialog.

24. Set the **List** to **Current Item** and click on the **Add** button.

25. The **Value Assignment** dialog is displayed. Set the **Set this field** drop-down to **Request Status** and set the **To this value** drop-down to **In Progress**.

26. Click on the **OK** buttons to close the dialogs.

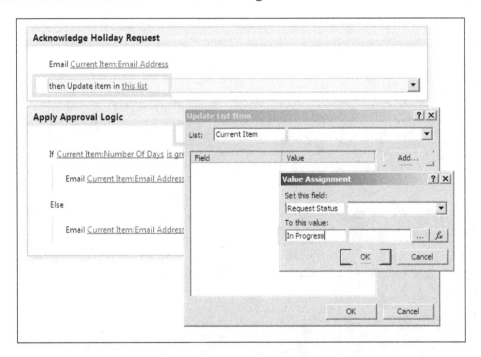

27. Repeat steps 22–26 above to add **Update List Item** actions beneath the **Send Email** actions in the **If** and **Else** branches of the **Apply Approval Logic** step. Set the **Request Status** value to **Rejected** and **Approved** respectively.

28. Click on the **Check for Errors** button in the **Workflow** ribbon. Ensure that there are no errors present.

29. Click on the **Publish** button. The workflow is published to the **Holiday Requests** library and is ready to use.

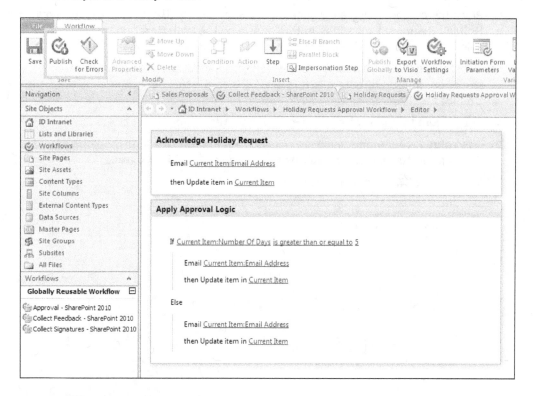

How it works...

SharePoint Designer 2010 allows us to quickly assemble SharePoint 2010 workflows without writing any code. In this recipe, you are introduced to the key building blocks of those workflows:

- ▶ **Steps**
- ▶ **Actions**
- ▶ **Conditions**

Steps are used to divide workflows up into logical units, making them easier to create, maintain, and understand. This workflow is a custom approval workflow designed to process new holiday requests. It is divided into two steps:

- ▶ Acknowledge Holiday Request
- ▶ Apply Approval Logic

In the first step, the request is acknowledged by an e-mail and the **Request Status** field on the form library is updated to note that the request is in progress. Both these jobs are performed by adding pre-built actions to the workflow and then configuring the actions' properties. In each case the action adds a sentence to the workflow designer surface (such as **Update item in this list**). The actions' configuration dialogs are accessed by clicking on hyperlinks presented in this sentence. Once the configuration options are set, the sentence is updated accordingly. There are a large number of actions available in SharePoint Designer. The actions you can choose from will depend upon the current context that you are working in. If you can't find an action that does what you want, you will need to call upon the services of a SharePoint developer or install a third-party workflow power pack to give you the extra actions that you require.

The second step of the workflow implements the approval logic through the application of a simple condition. There are a number of different conditions to choose from in the designer. Thus we build up our workflow processes through the combination of steps, actions, and conditions that allows us to achieve the results we need.

 Simplify your business processes before trying to automate them in SharePoint. Keep your workflows simple and do not try to automate every possible nuance of your process. Going from no automation to some automation is a far better outcome than failing to deliver anything because your workflow is over-engineered and too complicated to be run.

This workflow makes use of the update list action to update the **Request Status** field in the form library. Though we do not make any further use of that field here, we will revisit this workflow again in the *Appendix*, where you will learn how this field is invaluable when developing our composite applications.

There's more...

Once you have completed your workflow and thoroughly tested it, you will want to configure it to start automatically when a new holiday request is received. To do this, adjust the workflow start options in SharePoint Designer and then republish it.

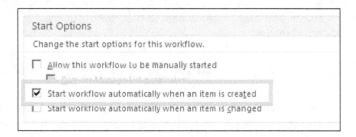

Many Power Users fail to appreciate the importance and complexity of the testing required for custom workflows. You should endeavor to test every possible execution path, not just the happy path that you expect your requests to take. Ensure that you include test cases which exercise all possible outcomes for each condition that you introduce. Make sure you have data that tests each condition's boundaries (for example, if a condition tests for a number smaller than 5, feed your workflow with test data that includes four and five to make sure you have entered the condition correctly). Start your workflows with rubbish or missing data and see how they respond. Make sure you use test e-mail addresses while you are developing and testing the workflow logic if you don't want your users being bombarded with meaningless messages. Don't forget to replace these with the real addresses before your workflow goes live (workflow variables can really help you with this). All software has bugs and your custom workflows will be no exception to this. Test, test, and test again, because an automated workflow process with a bug in it can make a very big mess in a very short period of time.

As this recipe is designed to illustrate the mechanics of workflows, the logic it contains is a bit contrived. It wouldn't make sense to automatically reject all leave requests over five days (although I did once work for a boss who would have loved to do this).

Also, the workflow designer, though functional, is a bit limited when it comes to visualizing what is actually going on in the workflow. In the next recipe we will learn how we can import this workflow into Visio Premium 2010. Once there we can create a much more visually appealing representation and improve the leave-approval logic along the way.

There are a few other SharePoint workflow areas that you will want to explore as your proficiency increases. I recommend that you investigate using workflow variables to pass data around and designing custom forms to interact with your users. You will definitely want to spend some time investigating the task process designer (that's just like the workflow designer we have seen here, but purely focused on the logic surrounding a task process). Unfortunately we don't have the space to explore it here. One of the best ways to start to understand how this works is to copy and modify the existing out-of-the-box approval workflow and explore how the SharePoint team have designed their task process. You'll also find some resources on my blog that will help.

Understanding different workflow types: reusable and site-level workflows

When you create a list workflow, it can only be used on the list where it was created. If that's all you need then great, but there will often be times where you want your workflow to be more widely applicable. To achieve this, you will need to create a reusable workflow. This type of workflow isn't bound directly to an individual list, but is instead created against a content type. Once created, the workflow can be used wherever that content type is applied in SharePoint.

Before SharePoint 2010, workflows could only be run against particular items in a list or library. However, we now we have another option, the site workflow. These workflows exist at the site level and must be manually started by a site administrator. Site-level workflows are useful for scenarios where you want to work across multiple lists or perform actions that are independent of any particular list item.

Getting Visual: tracking your workflow execution status with Visio

The Collect Feedback workflow presented in the previous recipe displays a Visio Services representation of progress as the workflow executes. You can achieve exactly the same effect with your custom workflows. The only caveat is that the person publishing the workflow must have Visio 2010 Premium Edition installed on their computer, otherwise it won't work.

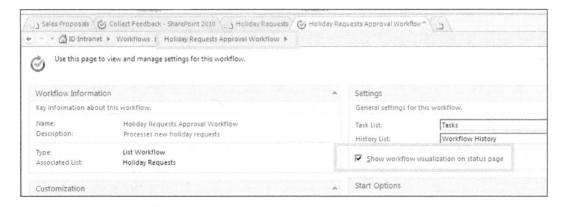

See also

▶ *Using the Collect Feedback workflow to receive feedback on a Microsoft Word 2010 document*

▶ *Using Microsoft Visio 2010 to model a SharePoint workflow*

Using Microsoft Visio 2010 to model a SharePoint workflow

SharePoint 2010 workflows can now be modeled in Microsoft Visio 2010. In this recipe we take the custom workflow created in the *Creating a list workflow using SharePoint Designer 2010* recipe, export it to Visio, and enhance it. We then send it back to SharePoint Designer where it can be further configured before being published back to SharePoint.

Getting ready

This recipe works for:

- SharePoint 2010 Standard Edition
- SharePoint 2010 Enterprise Edition
- Office 365 (SharePoint Online)

You will need the **Design** or **Full Control** permission level to run this recipe.

You will need SharePoint Designer 2010 installed on your client machine.

You will need Visio 2010 Premium Edition installed on your client machine.

This recipe makes use of the holiday requests workflow created in the previous recipe.

How to do it...

1. Open the holiday approval workflow created in the previous recipe in SharePoint Designer.

2. Click on the **Export to Visio** button in the **Workflow Settings** ribbon.

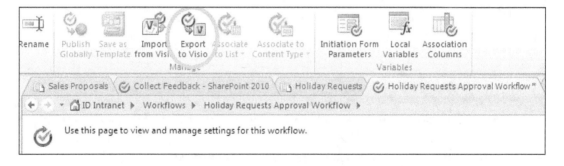

3. The workflow will be exported as a Visio Workflow Interchange file. Save the file as **Holiday Requests Approval Workflow** on your local computer. Close SharePoint Designer.

4. Open Visio 2010 Premium Edition and create a **new Microsoft SharePoint Workflow** (located in the **Process** templates).

5. Switch to the **Process** ribbon and click on the **Import** button. Browse to the location of the **Holiday Requests Approval Workflow.vwi** file created above and click on the **Open** button.

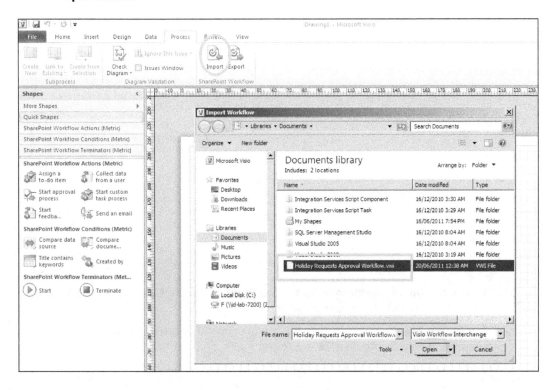

6. The workflow opens in Visio.

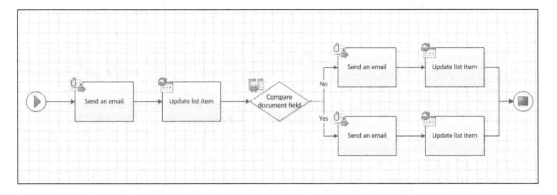

7. Edit the boxes in the workflow to display more meaningful descriptions of what is taken place in each step, as shown in the next screenshot.

8. Delete the **Send an Email** action on the **Yes** conditional branch.

9. Drag a new **Start Approval Process** shape from the Visio **SharePoint Workflow Actions** toolbox and add it to the workflow.

10. Modify the **Update List Item** shape to **Set Request Status = Manager Approval Required**.

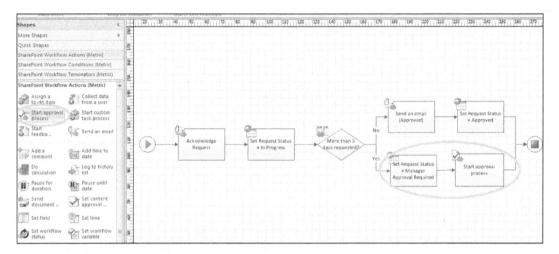

11. Click on the **Check Diagram** button in the **Process** ribbon. Ensure that there are no errors in the modified workflow diagram.

12. Click on the **Export** button to save the modified workflow as a VWI file (you can overwrite the file created earlier if you wish).

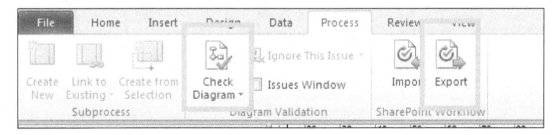

13. Open SharePoint Designer and navigate to your Team Site. Select **Workflows** in the **Site Objects** pane to activate the **Workflow** ribbon.

14. Click the **Import from Visio** button. The modified workflow is imported back into SharePoint Designer.

How it works...

Visio Premium 2010 includes the ability to design SharePoint 2010 workflows visually. It is intended to be a complimentary tool to SharePoint Designer 2010. In SharePoint Designer, we add the nuts and bolts of the workflow, set the configuration properties that we want, and publish the workflow to SharePoint so that it can be run. In Visio, we are more concerned with the big picture, modeling the workflow visually. Visio workflow diagrams are great for communicating to and designing workflows with other business stakeholders. The important thing to realize here is that Visio SharePoint workflow diagrams cannot be published to SharePoint directly; they must be exported to SharePoint Designer and further configured before they can be run. To facilitate this process, Microsoft has created the Visio Workflow Interchange File format that is understood by both applications.

This workflow demonstrates both the remodeling the logic of the holiday workflow in Visio as well as improving the annotation of the existing logic so that the workflow's intention and processing are easier to understand.

See also

- *Using the collect feedback workflow to receive feedback on a Microsoft Word 2010 document*
- *Creating a list workflow using SharePoint Designer 2010*

Joining the Dots— Creating Composite Applications

Taken individually, the recipes in this book can help you solve everyday SharePoint problems. However, by learning how to combine their tools and techniques you will be able to create powerful "no code" composite applications to automate and control business processes and functions. This chapter is designed to illustrate how to achieve this.

Introduction

Before we start, it is important to understand what is and isn't a composite application. The first few sections in this chapter introduce you to composite applications, explaining their background and the key underlying concepts. Studying these sections will allow you to determine if your particular problem should be solved by creating a composite application, or if another approach would be more appropriate.

Assuming that a composite application fits your needs, we then explore the approach you should apply to build one. There are some best practices that you should apply, and pitfalls that you will want to avoid. I have created a checklist of questions to ask to make this easier.

The second half of this chapter presents three simple composite applications covering:

- Project Management
- Customer Relationship Management (CRM)
- Human Resources (HR)

Each application is designed to illustrate a few key concepts that you should consider applying when building your own applications. For each application, I first outline the business problem to be solved, describe the composite application solution, provide some high-level instructions on how to build it, discuss how it works, and highlight the key learning points. These applications aren't intended to be comprehensive solutions. There isn't enough space to detail step-by-step how to build each application (that would require another book in itself). Think of each application as a starting point that you may extend to solve your own particular business problem. However, the information that you need has already been covered in the recipes previously presented in the book. Each composite application contains a list of the recipes that you should reference to help you.

At the end of the chapter you will find my closing thoughts, summarizing what we have learnt so far, along with some advice on how to continue your SharePoint Power User journey.

Understanding composite applications

A composite application is a quick, simple, "no code" SharePoint application intended to provide a solution to a particular business problem. It is constructed by a SharePoint Power User possessing an intimate knowledge of the problem to be solved. A composite application draws upon any or all of the SharePoint features explored in this book, melding them together until a satisfactory solution is produced. There is no right or wrong way to do this. Composite applications are normally developed through "trial and error"—prototyping and evaluating the application until something useful is produced.

The best types of composite applications to create on SharePoint are those which require collaboration, the sharing of documents, tasks, electronic forms, and simple workflows. SharePoint provides extensive out of the box tools and functionality to do this.

Powerful as composite applications are, it is also important to appreciate what they are not and to know where to draw the line between an informal Power User development and a formal software engineering project, with all the project management, governance, rigorous process, costs, and resource, which that entails.

Please don't read this chapter thinking that you can construct a new banking system, sophisticated payroll, or accounting solution as a composite application. You can't. You may be able to build solutions to those problems on SharePoint, but you will need a formal project, team-based development, designs, test plans, and lots of resources to be successful. You will definitely need to write code and will more than likely need to involve a whole range of other technologies as well. SharePoint may well make building those applications easier too, but that is not what this book is about.

How to design and build composite applications

There is no "right" or "wrong" way to build composite applications. SharePoint offers many different tools and techniques that may be used to achieve the same result. It is often difficult to know which technologies to choose, or where to start.

Regardless of the specific details of the particular composite application that you wish to build, you should seek to apply a consistent methodology and approach. This section describes my recommended approach to building composite applications. Before attempting to build a composite application, ask yourself the following questions:

- Is the problem simple and well defined?
- What are the risks if my application goes wrong?
- Who will use my solution and what roles will they play?
- Has somebody else already built a solution to my problem?
- Do I have the necessary time, skills, and resources required?
- Should this solution really be built without code?
- How can I test my application to be sure that it works?

The answers to these questions will help you decide if and how you should build your application. When building your application, don't expect (or even try) to get it right the first time. Create prototypes, test them, and get feedback until you have created a composite application that does just enough to solve the problem.

Is the problem simple and well defined?

No one has ever successfully built a composite application for a business problem that they didn't understand. If there are bits of business process, rules, and logic that are unclear, then try to resolve those questions before you proceed. If there are a number of suitable options, then build simple prototypes to refine your ideas as you proceed.

The most successful composite applications are the ones that really don't do very much. Simple, well-defined business problems lead to successful composite applications. Complicated business processes with many variants are impossible to build. Simplify processes before trying to automate them and don't try to cater for every possible scenario.

What are the risks if my application goes wrong?

Before embarking on any composite application development, consider the importance of the application to the business, particularly the risk and impact on the business should it all go wrong. Complex, high profile, high-risk projects are not suitable candidates for composite application development. Don't try to build them this way; you are just setting yourself and business up for failure.

Who will use my solution and what roles will they play?

Always think about who will use your solution and what roles they will play. For example, will everyone be allowed to see all the documents in a site? The answers to these questions will enable you to create the right functionality and inform the security model that you will need to apply to make sure people can do only what they are supposed to do in your application.

Has somebody else already built a solution to my problem?

The best composite applications are the ones that you never build. Why reinvent the wheel if someone else already has already created a solution to your problem? Start by opening your favorite search engine. Look for blogs, articles, and forum posts that might help. Check if someone has created a **Sandbox Solution** that you can download and install. Do some research to see how others have tackled your problem and consider purchasing third-party products or toolkits before trying to build your own.

 SharePoint 2010 allows Power Users to upload custom applications without having to ask permission from SharePoint administrator. These applications run in a sandbox that restricts what they can and can't to do on the server, making sure they can't do any damage, hence their name *Sandbox Solutions*.

Do I have the necessary time, skills, and resources required?

This book is all about giving you the skills to build composite applications, but do you have access to SharePoint and the power to make the changes you need? Are the right licenses in place to give you electronic forms and business intelligence capabilities? Do you have the necessary time to devote to creating the solution? If the answers to these questions are no, then you are probably on the road to failure.

Should this solution really be built without code?

No-code applications are an attractive proposition, but it is important not to make the mistake of rigidly applying a "one size fits all" approach. There are some applications that should not be built on SharePoint and others that should not be built without code. It is like cutting the grass with a pair of scissors; you can do it but you really shouldn't. Some problems that are very hard to achieve in the "no code" world are very simple to solve with the introduction of a little code. If you have SharePoint administrators, designers, and code developers at your disposal, then use them. You will invariably come out with a better solution.

How can I test my application to be sure that it works?

One of the biggest mistakes I see Power Users make is that they fail to test their applications adequately. When you build a composite application, you are still developing software (albeit without writing any code). You must plan to test your application thoroughly. Of course, you should test that your application does what you intend it to do. Ensure you test all the roles that you have identified and make sure you log in as different users to ensure that the security model you have implemented is working correctly.

Beyond this, you should expect that you will have made mistakes when building your application. Create different scenarios that test your logic thoroughly. Never underestimate the ability of your users to throw rubbish data into your application and to use it in ways that you don't expect. You need to repeat your testing each time you make major changes. Each time you add new functionality into your application; ask yourself "how will I test this?"

Composite applications are never "right first time" nor are they meant to be inflexible unchanging beasts. Composite applications can be expected to change over time, being constantly changed and tweaked as business rules change and processes evolve. The "no code" rapid development tools that SharePoint provides help us in changing our composite applications as we go, providing a level of flexibility that is impossible to achieve with traditional code-based applications.

 With great power comes great responsibility. The ability to change live business processes "on the fly" is fraught with danger. Make sure that you think through changes before you make them, test thoroughly, and have a back-out plan ready just in case things don't turn out quite as you expect.

Project Management composite application

Composite applications do not need to be complex. This example shows you how to combine existing SharePoint functionality in a SharePoint 2010 Team Site to create a simple but effective Project Management solution.

The problem

My company has decided to create a SharePoint Power User portal on the Internet to support this book. We have created the high-level concept ("SharePoint Mentor") but now need to set up and execute a project to turn our concept into reality. We need to be able to assemble our project team, create a simple project plan, allocate and track tasks, share documents and knowledge, capture and discuss ideas, and track our progress against the project goals and deadlines.

Our solution

Our solution is to create a SharePoint 2010 Team Site and then customize it to fit our needs. The Team Site template gives us a great starting point, providing most of the functionality required to solve our problem. We first remove the things that we don't want and then add new pages, lists, and libraries as required.

For our security model, everyone should be able to read the site, but we only want our project team to be able to upload and update its information. We want to keep our security model as simple as possible. We deploy our project site in our existing intranet site collection, but break the security inheritance at the site level. We add the project leader who will be the owner of the site. We will add all our project team members as contributors and the rest of the organization as readers.

To allow us to coordinate the work that needs to be done in our project, we will use the tasks list. We add the tasks that need to be done and assign them to members of the project team.

To capture and share knowledge of the project, we will use a number of complementary approaches:

- ▸ Wiki pages
- ▸ Documents library
- ▸ Discussion boards
- ▸ Project blog

The project home page is a wiki page. This is modified to replace the placeholder data that the Team Site template provides with information that shows the goals and status of, and important information for, the project. We add and link to other pages as we need them.

Project documentation is captured in the existing Shared Documents library. As we don't want to lose important information and change history as the project progresses, we configure this library to track versions, require checkout, and enable content approvals. We will also want to collect feedback on and seek approval for the various project documents as the project progresses. We use the out of the box Collect Feedback and Approval workflows for this.

There will be things that our project team needs to work out as they go along. A discussion board is an ideal medium for this. The Team Site template provisions the Team Discussion board ready for use. However, as our SharePoint mentor concept isn't thought out in any detail, we also want to capture the ideas from the rest of the company as well. We will add a second Ideas Discussion board for this and tweak the security permissions on this board to allow everyone in the company to contribute to it.

To complete our knowledge sharing, we add a project blog. The project leader will periodically post project updates to the blog, keeping the project team and the wider project stakeholders informed of the project's progress.

Getting ready

This recipe works for:

► SharePoint 2010 Foundation (not workflows)

► SharePoint 2010 Standard Edition

► SharePoint 2010 Enterprise Edition

How to do it...

 These instructions are intended to guide you through the key steps that you should perform to build this composite application. They are not a comprehensive guide like the recipes presented earlier. You will need to apply the knowledge you have learned and refer back to the recipes presented earlier to successfully build this application. Recipes that will be particularly useful to you are listed in the *Recipes that will help you build this application* section later in this chapter. I recommend that you also read the *How it works* section of this recipe first to gain further insight before trying to recreate this application.

1. Create a new SharePoint 2010 Team Site for the SharePoint Mentor project. Set the site to **Use unique permissions** when you create it (using the **More Options** dialog).

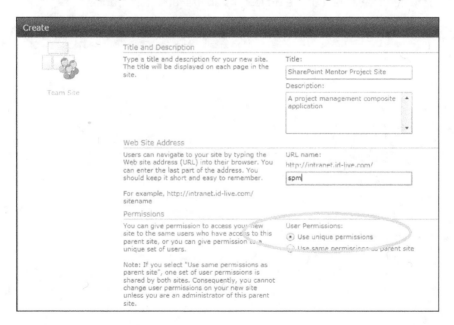

2. Create new groups for the **Owners** and **Members**; inherit the **Visitors** group form the parent site.

3. Add the project manager to the site owner's group. Add each member of the project team to the site member's group.

4. Edit the site home page to remove the placeholder information and pictures. Add some information about the project, its goal/s, and deliverables.

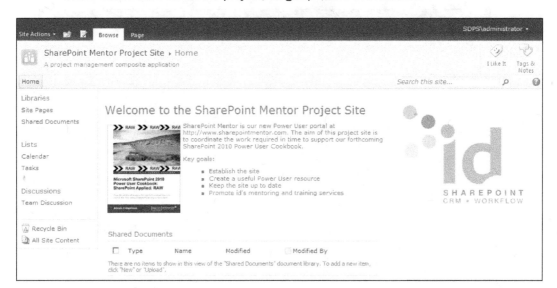

5. Adjust the settings on the **Tasks** list to send an e-mail when ownership of a task is assigned. Add any existing tasks to the list.

6. Add a view of the task list to the home page.

7. Edit the **Shared Documents** library settings to require checkout, enable versioning, and content approval.

8. Adjust the **Shared Documents** and **Tasks All Items** view to only show relevant columns.

9. Create workflow associations for the **Collect Feedback** and **Approval** out of the box workflows on the **Shared Documents** library.

10. Upload any existing project documents to the library.

11. Add a **Discussion Board** named **Ideas**.

12. Break inheritance on the **Ideas Discussions Board**. Edit the **Visitors** group permissions to give them access to this list.

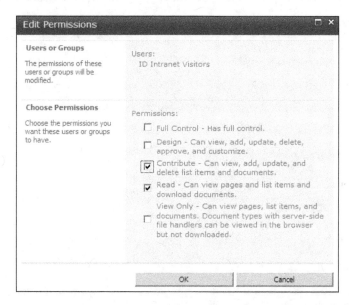

13. Add a new blog site under the Team Site named **Projcot Updates**. Use unique permissions for the site. Use an existing group for both the members and owners of the blog. Set this group to the **SharePoint Mentor Project Site Owners**. Use an existing group for the visitors to the site; use the same **intranet visitors group** as is used for the parent site.

14. Configure the blog, remove the placeholder post, and set up its categories.

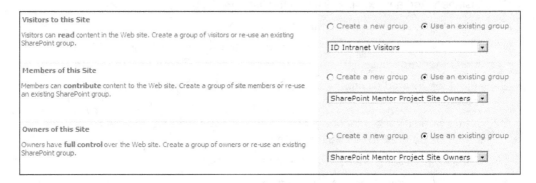

15. Add any project-related meetings and events to the **Calendar**.

16. The final application should look something like the following screenshot:

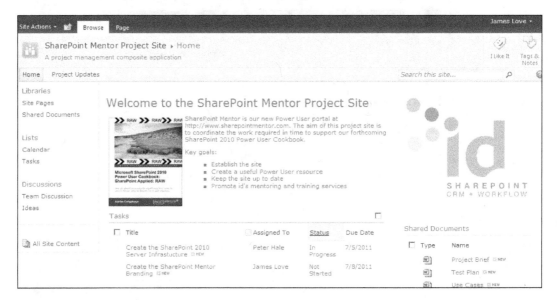

How it works...

The SharePoint 2010 Team Site template gives us a great starting point for creating collaborative applications. Many business problems can be solved by customizing this site. SharePoint makes these customizations very easy to perform. In this example, everything we need to manage our project can be obtained by creating and lightly customizing a Team Site.

The customization process starts when we create the Team Site. We know that our scenario demands a custom security model and that we will not inherit the security permission for our parent site. The **More Options** dialog makes it easy to apply unique permissions as we create the site. It also means that no-one else can see our site and accidentally start using it before we have finished configuring and testing it. Further security tweaks are made to the **Ideas Discussion Board** (so that all intranet visitors can post ideas) and to the **Project Updates Blog** (so that only the project manager can post updates about the project).

Collaboration and coordination of the project is achieved by sharing tasks through the **Tasks** list, documents through the **Shared Documents** library, and events though the **Calendar**. Team members automatically receive an e-mail whenever a task is assigned to them. For convenience, all team members can connect to the tasks list, shared documents library, and calendar. Project documents are versioned, require content approval, and must be checked out before they can be edited. The out of the box workflows are used to seek feedback and approval for project documentation changes.

The team shares ideas and resolves problems through posts in its **Team Discussion** board. Again, this list is synchronized to Outlook 2010, allowing team members to be informed of and reply to new posts as soon as they occur without having to visit the site.

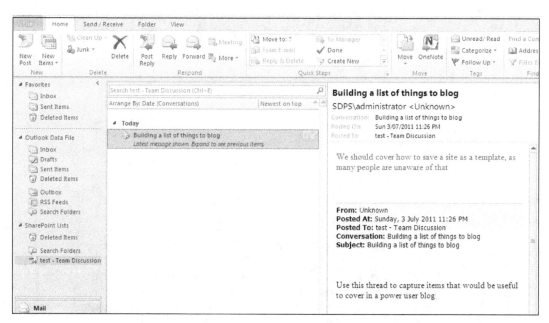

 You can use Outlook 2010's folder function to move e-mail messages to discussion boards that you are connected to. The e-mail message will then appear as a new post in the board.

Weekly project updates are posted by the project manager on the **Project Updates** blog using Microsoft Word 2010. Stakeholders who wish to be informed of a project's progress register for an alert on this blog.

Reusing the site as a template

Creating a custom project site is all very well, but you really don't want to go through this process every time a new project comes along. Wouldn't it be great if you could just save the new, preconfigured project site as a template? You will be happy to know that SharePoint provides exactly that functionality. You will find the option under the **Site Actions** group on the **Site Settings** page. You can save your project site as a template and then create as many new project sites from that template as you wish. You can even choose to include your existing data in the template, so if there are tasks that you always perform on every project, add those to your site before you save the template and then include them in it. Each project site you create from then on will include those tasks already created. It is all designed to save your work and get your projects off to a flying start.

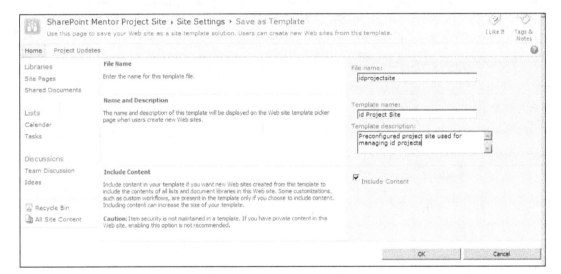

 Not everything saves across to your site template, for example the blog sub site is lost through this process. Spend some time testing any site templates that you create as SharePoint doesn't always create them quite how you might expect.

What we have learnt

Composite applications do not have to be complex. Always start with the out of the box site template that best fits your needs and then work from there. We could have over-engineered (or paid for) an elaborate project management solution, but there really is no need. This project management site is quick to create, functional, and helps us get the job done. A Team Site with some minor changes and a tweaked security model is all that we need.

We typically require some custom security permissions in our composite applications. These are easy to create, but best practice is to keep these changes as simple as possible.

When we have created a custom project site that we are happy with, we can save it as a template so that we don't have to reinvent the wheel each time we need a new project site.

Recipes that will help you build this application

- ▶ *Create a SharePoint list, Chapter 1*
- ▶ *Creating a Team Site, Chapter 2*
- ▶ *Adding users to a Team Site, Chapter 2*
- ▶ *Adding a new page to a Team Site, Chapter 2*
- ▶ *Creating a new task and assigning it to another user, Chapter 2*
- ▶ *Using the datasheet to bulk edit tasks in a task list, Chapter 2*
- ▶ *Uploading an existing document to a document library, Chapter 4*
- ▶ *Uploading multiple documents to a document library, Chapter 4*
- ▶ *Requiring users to check out a document before they can edit it, Chapter 4*
- ▶ *Enabling versioning on a document library, Chapter 4*
- ▶ *Publishing a major version of a document, Chapter 4*
- ▶ *Enabling content approval on a document library, Chapter 4*
- ▶ *Creating a blog in my My Site, Chapter 5*
- ▶ *Posting to my blog from* Microsoft *Word 2010, Chapter 5*
- ▶ *Using the Collect Feedback workflow to receive feedback on a Microsoft Word 2010 document, Chapter 8*

CRM composite application

If you need a simple application to keep track of customers, then deal with their enquiries, keep track of their orders, and quickly generate Sales Pipeline reports, this recipe will show you how it can be done.

The problem

Based on the success of our Power User cookbook, my company is launching a new SharePoint 2010 training business. We need a simple CRM application to help us keep track of it. We want to maintain a list of customers, a calendar of our public training courses, be able to quickly respond to course enquiries, track our customers' orders, and invoices for training places. We need some simple reports and charts that quickly give us an overall picture of how the training business is performing.

Our solution

Building on the previous recipe, we again create a custom SharePoint 2010 Team Site as the starting point of our solution. In this case, we add and customize a contacts list to track the details of our training course customers. We use the calendar list to record the public schedules of the courses we intend to present. We remove the Shared Documents library that was created automatically and replace it with two new document libraries designed to store sales resources and customer documents respectively.

The Sales resources library is used to store course information, company fliers, and other sales documents that we want to be able to quickly send out to customers in response to course enquiries.

The customer documents library is used to store the documentation related to existing customers. We create add content types for customer documents such as quotations, orders, and invoices, allowing us to capture different metadata for each document type. Our documents are generated in Word and uploaded to the library. We create a lookup field in each content type that links the documents to our customer list. We add a new web part page to the site and use connected web parts to give us a filtered view showing each customer's documents.

Getting ready

This recipe works for:

- SharePoint 2010 Foundation
- SharePoint 2010 Standard Edition
- SharePoint 2010 Enterprise Edition

How to do it...

These instructions are intended to guide you through the key steps that you should perform to build this composite application. They are not a comprehensive guide like the recipes presented earlier. You will need to apply the knowledge you have learned and refer back to the recipes presented previously to successfully build this application. Recipes that will be particularly useful to you are listed in the *Recipes that will help you build this application* section at the end of this recipe. This recipe assumes the knowledge presented in the earlier *Project Management composite application* section. I recommend that you also read the *How it works* section of this recipe first to gain further insight before trying to recreate this application.

1. Create a new SharePoint 2010 Team Site for the SharePoint 2010 training site. Customize the site's home page to remove the out of the box placeholders and add relevant information. Apply an appropriate security model.

2. Add details of the public training schedule to the **Calendar**. Add a view of the **Calendar** to the home page of the site. Change the title of the **Calendar** to **Course Schedule**.

3. Create a new **Contacts** list named **Customers** to store customer details. Remove any columns from the list that are not required.

4. Delete the **Shared Documents** library and add two new document libraries named **Sales Resources** and **Customer Documents** respectively.

5. Upload any sales resources, such as course outlines, to the **Sales Resources** library.

6. The home page of the site should look like the following screenshot:

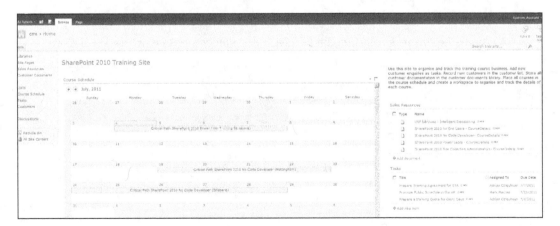

7. Create document content types for **Quote**, **Order**, and **Invoice**. Add appropriate metadata columns and document templates. Ensure that each content type contains a **Total** column (currency).

8. Enable content types for the **Customer Documents** list. Add the **Quote**, **Order**, and **Invoice** content types. Make **Quote** the default content type and then delete the **Document** content type from the list. When you have finished the **New Document** menu for the list, it should look like the following screenshot:

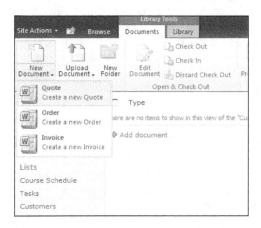

9. Create a new lookup column named **Customer** in the **Customer Documents** list and connect it to the **Company** field in the **Customers** list.

10. Set **Require that this column contains information** to **Yes** and **Enforce unique values** to **No**.

11. In the **Add a column to show each of these additional fields**, check the **Last Name** and **First Name** options.

12. Check the **Add to all content types** and **Add to default view** options.

13. Check the **Enforce relationship behavior** and select the **Restrict delete** option.

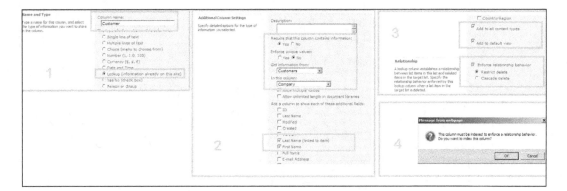

14. Add details of existing customers to the **Customers** list.

15. Upload any existing customer documentation to the **Customer Documents** library. Set the **Content Type** and metadata for each document uploaded.

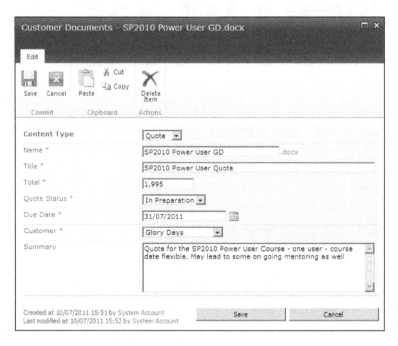

16. Create new **Standard Views** on the **Customer Documents** library to show **Quotes**, **Orders**, and **Invoices** respectively. For each view, set the **Filter** value to select the correct content type (you will have to type in the content type's name as text), and add the content type specific columns to the views (for example, **Quote Status** to the **Quotes** view). In the **Inline Editing** section, check the **Allow inline editing** checkbox. In the **Totals** section, add a **Sum** to the **Total** column. The quotes view is shown in the following screenshot:

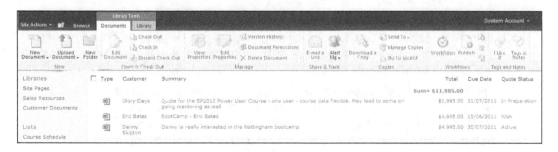

17. Using your web browser, add a new **Web Part Page** to the site and call it `CustomerView.aspx`. Select the **Header**, **Left Column**, and **Body** layout. Save the page in the **Site Pages** library.

18. Add list view web parts (**Lists** and **Libraries**) to the page for the **Customers** list (left column) and three separate views of the **Customer Documents** library (that is, add the same library web part three times) to the body.

19. Edit the **Customers** web part. Set the **Title** to **Select Customer** and set the **Chrome Type** to **Title and Border**.

20. Edit each of the **Customer Documents** web part properties in turn. Set the **Title** of the first web part to **Quotes** and the **Selected View** to **Quotes**. Repeat for the second and third web parts, setting the corresponding properties to **Orders** and **Invoices** views respectively. Set the **Chrome Type** on each web part to **Title plus Border**.

21. Your web part page should look somewhat similar to the following screenshot, displaying the list of customers together with different views showing all the quotes, orders, and invoices stored on the site.

22. Edit the `CustomerView.aspx` page using SharePoint Designer 2010. Highlight the **Select Customer** web part and click on the **Add Connection** button from the **Options** tab of the **List View Tools** ribbon.

23. The **Web Part Connections Wizard** is displayed. Connect the **Select Customers** web part to the **Quotes** web part by joining the **Company** and **Customer** columns as shown in the following series of screenshots. Repeat this process to connect the **Select Customer** web part in turn to the **Orders** and **Invoices** web part.

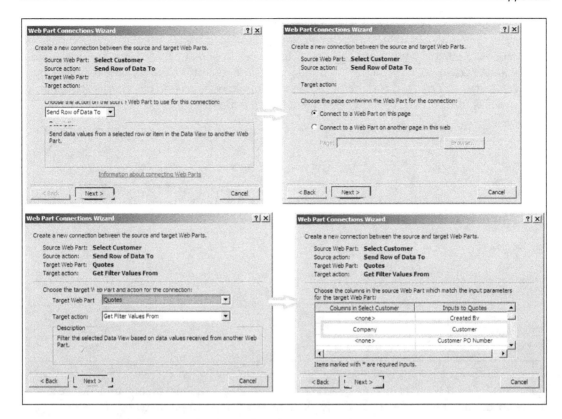

24. Save the page. It now displays a filtered view of customer documents, according to the customer that you select, as illustrated in the following screenshot:

How it works...

This composite application combines a custom Team Site, content types, and connected web parts to create a powerful yet simple CRM application.

The sales process starts when an enquiry is received from a potential training course customer. An initial e-mail response can quickly be produced using Outlook 2010. Because the course schedule calendar and the Sales Resources document library from the site can be connected to Outlook 2010, all the information required to craft an appropriate response is automatically synchronized and readily available. Course outlines and company information can be easily dragged and dropped into the outgoing e-mails.

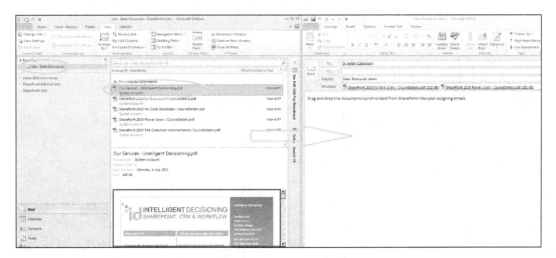

Positive enquiry responses can be converted into formal quotations, orders, and invoices. This application makes use of content types to allow all these different types of customer documents to be stored in the same document library, whilst at the same time employing different document templates, capturing different metadata, applying different workflows, and so on. Content types allow composite applications to successfully model and manage these real world entities. You should seek to employ them wherever possible.

> SharePoint 2010 allows a site collection to be designated as a **content type hub**. Content types defined in the hub can be published and shared across your SharePoint installation, providing consistency in metadata, document templates, information management policies, and associated workflows wherever that content type is consumed.

New invoices, orders, and quotations can be quickly generated in Microsoft Word 2010 by using the templates saved to their corresponding content type. The metadata required is prompted for and can be entered directly within the document information panel within Word documents themselves.

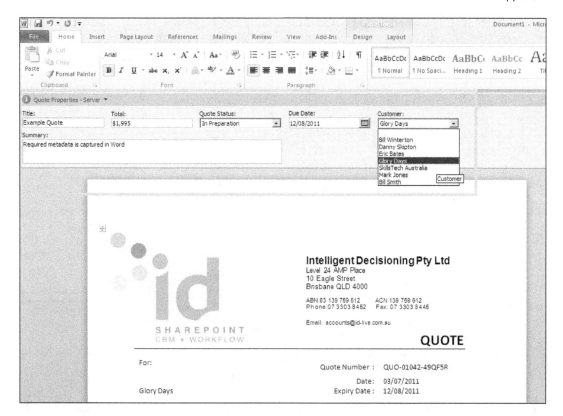

 You can use the **Quick Parts** within the **Insert** ribbon in Microsoft Word 2010 to embed the metadata from your content types directly into the body of your documents.

The content type in this application ensures that sales documents are captured in a structured way. Each content type has a lookup column on the customers' list, allowing all sales documents to be related back to their parent customer. This fact is exploited in the Customer View web part page to create a **customer dashboard** showing filtered views of selected customer's documents. The page makes use of web part connections to filter the custom Quotations, Orders, and Invoices views on the customer's documents list based on the value selected in the customers' list displayed on the page. All this magic happens through a few mouse clicks and a simple wizard; no code required. Web part connections are a great feature for building composite applications.

Finally, when it comes to analyzing our sales performance, all we need to do is select the view on the customer documents library we want and hit the **Export to Excel** button on the **Library** tab of the **List Tools** ribbon. From there we can analyze our sales data using Excel charts, pivot tables, and reports that allow us to present the data however we choose.

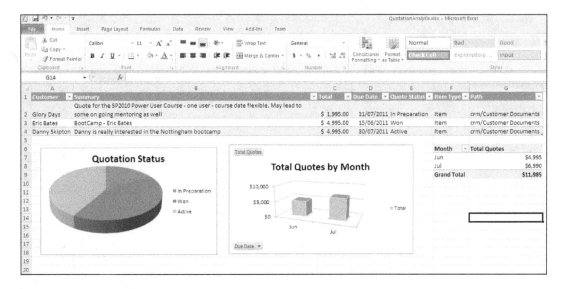

If you want to get really smart, then publish your exported spreadsheet back to SharePoint using Excel Services and then embed the charts and tables into your pages using the Excel Services web part. Every time you refresh the worksheet, all the data displayed in your site will be updated.

What we have learnt

The recipe reinforces the concept that a Team Site makes a great starting point for many composite applications.

In this case, we see the power of content types and how the use of content types helps us store quotation, orders, and invoice documents in the same document list, allowing us to capture different metadata and apply different business rules and workflows for each different document types.

We have learnt how to use web part connections to create connected views of business data, allowing us to quickly view all the customer documents for an individual customer, while at the same time using the summary fields of SharePoint views to automatically display the total values of quotes, orders, and invoices.

The narrative surrounding this recipe is designed to remind you that SharePoint is only one of many tools that you have at your disposal when creating composite applications. It is best used in conjunction with the Office applications such as Word, Excel, and Outlook 2010.

There's more...

There are an almost infinite number of ways that this composite application could be extended. A lookup column could be added to the invoice column to allow the invoices to be related back to orders as well as customers, creating a master/detail view of this data. Meeting workspaces could be used in the calendar to plan each course instance (storing details such as the trainer, location, attendees, and so on). Custom declarative workflows could be attached to each of the content types to perform sales pipeline functionality such as creating tasks to follow up a quote a week after it was sent out or chasing up a customer invoice when it is overdue. The task list could be modified to include a customer lookup and the tasks for a particular customer added to the Customer View page. More views could be added to the customer documents library using more advanced filter criteria such as combining the content type, due date, and invoice status column to create an overdue invoice view and so on.

 When creating any composite application, you may find your imagination getting the better of you. Always start simple and get something working. Then evolve and refine the application as you use it. Only add the features that you really need and don't over-complicate it.

Recipes that will help you build this application

- ▶ *Project Management composite application*
- ▶ *Creating a SharePoint list, Chapter 1*
- ▶ *Creating a content type, Chapter 1*
- ▶ *Creating a Team Site, Chapter 2*
- ▶ *Adding users to a Team Site, Chapter 2*
- ▶ *Adding a new page to a Team Site, Chapter 2*
- ▶ *Creating a SharePoint Contact List and connecting it to Outlook 2010, Chapter 2*
- ▶ *Creating a custom list view, Chapter 3*
- ▶ *Uploading an existing document to a document library, Chapter 3*
- ▶ *Uploading multiple documents to a document library, Chapter 3*
- ▶ *Requiring users to check out a document before they can edit it, Chapter 4*
- ▶ *Enabling versioning on a document library, Chapter 4*
- ▶ *Publishing a major version of a document, Chapter 4*
- ▶ *Enabling content approval on a document library, Chapter 4*

- *Using content types to store different types of documents in the same document library, Chapter 4*
- *Creating an Excel Spreadsheet to run on the server, Chapter 7*
- *Creating a list workflow using SharePoint Designer 2010, Chapter 8*

Human Resources composite application

This composite application is a simple HR application designed to track holiday requests.

The problem

My company needs to be able to track employee holiday requests. Employees require a simple, web-based portal which allows them to:

- See their current holiday entitlement
- Submit new holiday requests
- Review previous requests
- Review the shared holiday calendar

The system must not allow employees to request holidays beyond their current entitlement. All holiday requests must be routed to the employee's line manager for approval. Approved holiday requests must update the employee's holiday entitlement and be added to the shared team calendar. Employees need to be notified of the progress and outcome of their requests by e-mail.

Our solution

Our solution is to create a modified SharePoint 2010 Team Site to serve as a holiday request portal. The home page of the portal is modified to present a personalized view of the leave entitlement, holiday request forms, and previous holiday requests for the current user by making use of the current user filter. Each visitor to the site only sees their leave entitlement and previous holiday requests.

A custom list is used to store details of employees and their current holiday entitlements. An InfoPath form is created to allow an employee to make new holiday requests and submit them to a holiday request form library. We use rules in the InfoPath form to hide its submit button and so prevent a request being modified once it has been submitted.

A modified out of the box approval workflow is automatically triggered for each new request received, first validating the request, then routing it for approval to the employee's line manager (looked up from the employee's user profile). Approved holidays are automatically added to the shared calendar by the workflow. The workflow notifies the employees of the outcome of their holiday requests through e-mail.

Getting ready

This recipe works for:

▸ SharePoint 2010 Enterprise Edition

How to do it...

 These instructions are intended to guide you through the key steps that you should perform to build this composite application. They are not a comprehensive guide like the recipes presented earlier. You will need to apply the knowledge you have learned and refer back to the recipes presented earlier to successfully build this application. Recipes that will be particularly useful to you are listed in the *Recipes that will help you build this application* section at the end of this recipe. This recipe assumes the knowledge presented in the earlier *Project Management composite application* and *CRM composite application* recipes. This recipe joins many of the InfoPath form and workflow approaches previously described in *Chapter 8*. I recommend that you also read the *How it works* section of this recipe first to gain further insight before trying to recreate this application.

1. Create a new SharePoint 2010 Team Site for the holiday request portal. Customize the site's home page to remove the out of the box placeholders. Delete the **Announcements** and **Links** lists, **Team Discussion** board, and **Shared Documents** library. Apply an appropriate security model to the site.

2. Create a new custom list called **Holiday Entitlement**. Create new columns as follows:

Name	Type	Notes
Employee	Person or group	Select from people only (all users). Set the **Show Field** to **Name** (**with picture**). Check the **Add to default view** checkbox.
Entitlement	Number	Set the minimum value and the number of decimal places to zero. Check the **Add to default view** checkbox.
Days Taken	Number	Set the minimum value and the number of decimal places and the default value to zero. Check the **Add to default view** checkbox.
Days Available	Calculated	Use the formula **[Entitlement]-[Days taken]**. Set the data type to **Number**, the **Number of decimal places** to zero. Check the **Add to default view** checkbox.

3. Edit the **Title** column on the list. Set the default value to **Not Used**. Edit the **All Items** view. Remove the **Title** column from the view.

 Title is a required column on all SharePoint lists. You should never delete it as SharePoint assumes it will be there and bad things happen if you do. However, when you have no use for the title column (as in this case), a useful trick is to set a default value for it (to save you from having to fill it in for each item) and then remove it from all your list views. The title column remains in the background to keep SharePoint happy but you no longer need to worry about it.

4. Add some employee details, holiday entitlements, and days taken to the list. Your list should look like the following screenshot:

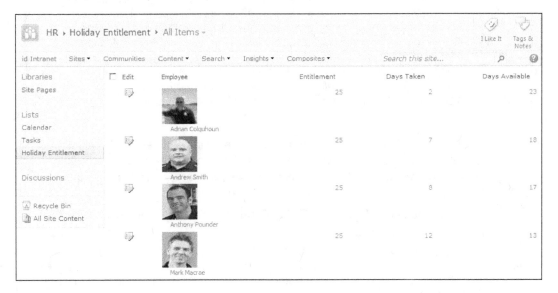

5. Create a holiday requests InfoPath form that includes the fields **Employee** (people or group), **Start Date, End Date, Number of Days, Request Status**, and **Comments**. Set the **Request Status** and **Comments** fields to read-only in the form. Make the comment's field control to multiline.

6. Add a **Submit** button and remove the standard InfoPath from controls.

7. Add a **Cancel** button and configure it with a rule to close the form.

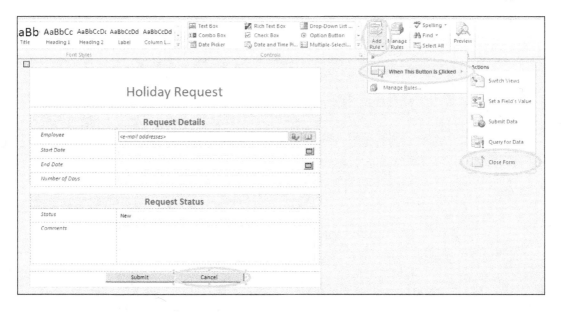

8. Publish the form to the **Holiday Requests** form library. Promote all the fields. Allow the **Request Status** and **Comments** fields to be edited in the form library. Promote the **Display Name** and **Account id** fields for the **Employee**. Ensure that you create a new column in the library for the **End Date** and **Comments** fields (do not use the built-in columns automatically offered in the wizard).

9. Set the **Submit** button to submit to the same form library. Add a rule to the **Submit** button to hide it once the form has been submitted and its request status updated.

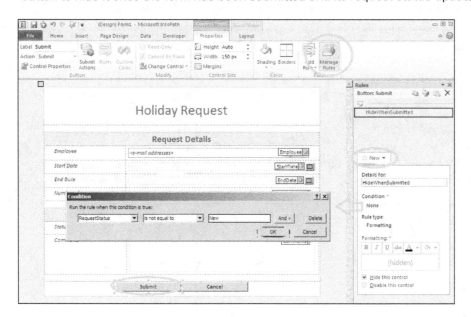

10. Add a naming formula to the form to give each submitted form a unique name. Republish the form. The completed form should look like the following screenshot:

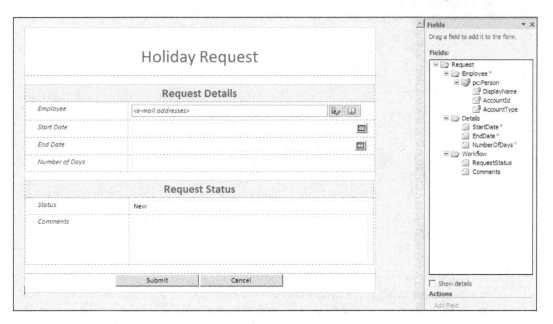

11. Open the site in SharePoint Designer 2010. Create a new **List Workflow** named **Holiday Request Approval Workflow**. Attach the workflow to the **Holiday Requests** form library. Set the workflow to start automatically when a new item is created.

12. Add the following variables to the workflow:

Name	Type	Purpose
Days Available	Integer	Used to store the number of holidays the employee currently has available.
Days Taken	Integer	Used to store the number of holidays the employee has already taken.
Days Remaining	Integer	Used to store the number of days remaining if this request is approved.
Manager	String	Used to store the name of the employee's manager (so that the approval tasks can be routed to them).

13. Add the following steps to the workflow:

Name	Purpose
Initialize Workflow	This step gathers the information required for the workflow to do its work. It reads and stores the employee's holiday entitlements, looks up their manager using their user profile, and updates the **Request Status** field to **In Progress**.
Validate Request	This step checks if the employee has enough days available to satisfy their holiday request.
Seek line manager's approval	This step sends the holiday request to the employee's line manager for approval.
Process manager's response	This step processes the line manager's response, e-mailing the employee to inform them of the outcome, and updating the shared holiday calendar for approved requests.

14. In the **Initialize Workflow** step, add the following activities:

Activity	Purpose	Notes
Set Workflow Variable action	Used to set the **Days Available** variable to the value of **Days Available** in the **Holiday Entitlements** list so that it can be used in the workflow.	To find the correct value in the **Holiday Entitlement** list, the **Find List Item** field must be set to **Employee** and its value must be set to **Current Item:Account Id**.
Set Workflow Variable action	Used to set the **Days Taken** variable to the value of **Days Taken** in the **Holiday Entitlements** list so that it can be used in the workflow.	To find the correct value in the **Holiday Entitlement** list, the **Find List Item** field must be set to **Employee** and its value must be set to **Current Item:Account Id**.
Lookup Manager of a User action	Used to find the manager of the employee making the holiday request.	Pass the **Current Item:Account Id** and store the value returned in the workflow variable manager.
Update List Item action	Used to set the request status to **In Progress**.	Update the **Current Item**.

15. The set workflow variable lookup actions are set as illustrated in the following screenshot:

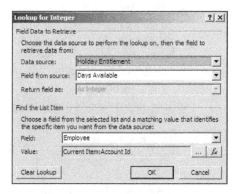

16. The completed step should look like the following screenshot:

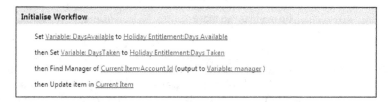

16. In the **Validate Request** step, add the following activities:

Activity	Purpose	Notes
Do Calculation action	Calculates the numbers of days that will remain if this holiday request is approved.	Subtracts the **Current Item: Number of Days** from the **Days Available** workflow variable.
If any value equals value condition	Checks if there are insufficient days available for this request.	Check if the variable **DaysRemaining** is less than 0.
Update List Item action	Used to set the request status to **Request is invalid. Insufficient days remaining**.	Inserted within the **If** branch.
Send an E-mail action	Notifies the employee that their request has been rejected because they do not have enough days remaining.	Inserted within the **If** branch. Set the **To:** field to **Current Item: Account Id**.
Stop Workflow action	Used to stop the workflow as no further processing is required.	Inserted within the **If** branch. Logs the message **Request invalid - Insufficient days**

Activity	Purpose	Notes
Else If branch condition	Contains the activities to be executed if there are sufficient days for this request.	
Do Calculation action	Calculates the numbers of days that will have been taken if this holiday request is approved.	Adds the **Variable: Days Taken** to the **Current Item:Number of Days** and stores the result in the **Variable: DaysTaken**.

The completed step should look like the following screenshot:

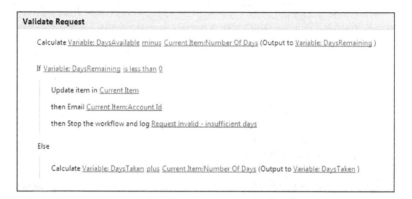

17. In the **Seek line manager's approval** step, add the following activities:

Activity	Purpose	Notes
Start Approval Process action	Uses the built-in approval task process to seek the line manager's approval for the holiday.	Start the process on the **Current Item** with the variable manager. Name the task process "**Approve Holiday Request Process**". See the *How it works* section for more details on this task process.

The completed step should look like the following screenshot:

Seek line manager's approval

Start Approve Holiday Request Process process on Current Item with Variable: manager

18. In the **Process manager's response** step, add the following activities:

Activity	Purpose	Notes
If any value equals value condition	Checks if the manager approved the holiday request. Contains the activities to be run if the manager approved the request.	The previous task process sets the **Current Item:Approval Status** field. Check for the value to be changes to **Approved**.
Create List Item action	Creates a new entry in the **Calendar** for approved requests.	Added within the **If** branch. Set the properties as shown in the following screenshot.
Send an E-mail action	Notifies the employee that their request has been approved.	Added within the **If** branch. Set the **To:** field to **Current Item:Account Id**.
Update List Item action	Used to set the request status to **Approved**.	Added within the **If** branch. Set the **Request Status** column to **Approved**.
Else If Branch condition	Contains the activities to be executed if the manager rejects the request.	
Update List Item action	Used to set the request status to **Rejected** and to record any comments made by the line manager.	Added within the **Else** branch. Set the **Request Status** column to **Rejected**. Set the **Comments** to **Variable: CompletionReason** (this variable contains any comments supplied by the manager).
Send an E-mail action	Notifies the employee that their request has been rejected.	Added within the **Else** branch. Set the **To:** field to **Current Item:Account Id**.

19. When creating a new event in the Calendar, set the properties as shown in the following screenshot:

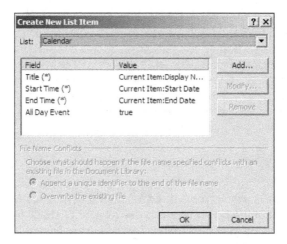

The completed step should look like the following screenshot:

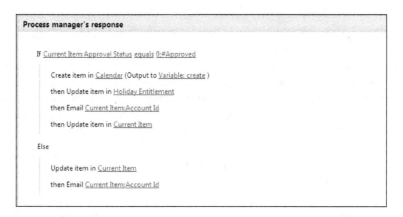

20. Check for and correct any errors in the workflow before publishing it to the site.

21. Modify the home page of the site. Remove all existing information and set the **Text Layout** to **Two Columns**. For a screenshot of the completed home page please refer to the *How it works* section later in this recipe.

22. In the left column, add the **Holiday Requests** form library. In the right column, add the **Holiday Entitlement** list and **Holiday Calendar**.

23. Add a **Current User Filter** web part to the page. Add a web part connection to **Send Filter Values** to the **Holiday Entitlements** list (**Employee** column) and the **Holiday Request** list (**Display Name** column). The lists are now filtered to only show information for the user currently browsing the site.

24. Add an InfoPath form web part to the left column of the home page. Create a web part connection that sends the form from the **Holiday Requests** form library to this web part. Name the web part **Current Request**.

25. Add a new link to the top of the left column. Set the link text to **Create a new holiday request** and the hyperlink to `/hr/_layouts/FormServer.aspx?XsnLocation=http://intranet.id-live.com/hr/Holiday Requests/Forms/template.xsn&SaveLocation=http://intranet.id-live.com/hr/Holiday Requests&Source=http://intranet.id-live.com/hr&DefaultItemOpen=1`. You will need to modify this hyperlink for your own environment. Please refer to the *How it works* section for an explanation of the link format.

How it works...

Tracking holiday requests is exactly the type of function that most users expect SharePoint to be able to perform out of the box. It often comes as a bit of shock to learn that, while all the building blocks are included, unfortunately this is one application that you have to build yourself. The portal described here is intended to give you an idea of how you might go about it. This application, despite being the most complex recipe presented in the book, should be considered a guide rather than a comprehensive solution.

In this application, holiday requests are tracked in the HR portal. Each employee who visits the portal sees a personalized view that shows their holiday allowance, current balance, previous holiday requests, and a shared calendar that displays the team's approved holidays. Users submit new holiday requests through the portal. For each request, a custom approval workflow runs automatically to validate the request before routing it to the user's manager for approval. Approved requests are automatically added to the shared calendar and made visible to the whole team. The functionality is illustrated in the following diagram:

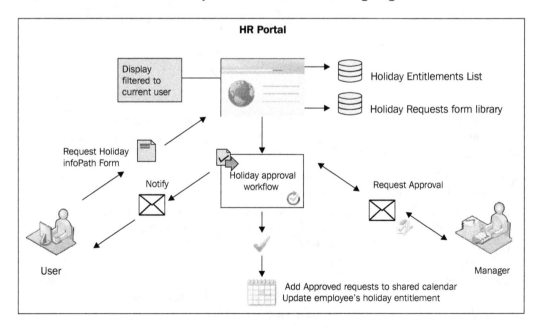

A picture is a great way to communicate key concepts of a composite application, allowing you to discuss and agree them with other users. A few hours in your favorite drawing package can save you a lot of time and effort building the wrong thing in SharePoint!

This application again starts with a customized Team Site. Most of the out of the box functionality is removed, leaving a bare bones site which is then customized into the HR portal.

 Never use the blank site template as a starting point for your composite applications. It has a number of basic SharePoint features turned off, meaning it doesn't always work the way that you expect.

Composite applications work best if they are contextual. Extending the connected web parts approach demonstrated in the previous application, the home page of the HR portal features a number of connected web parts. This page is designed to display holiday request information tailored to each user who visits the site.

The correct context is set through a hidden current-user filter web part, connected to the **Holiday Entitlement** and **Holiday Requests** web parts respectively. Each time a different employee visits the page, the current user filter passes their identity to these web parts, allowing the views to be restricted to only show the holiday entitlement and those requests that belong to them.

The current user filter is a powerful tool for creating contextual composite applications. It is one of a number of filter web parts that SharePoint provides out of the box. It can provide not only the users identity, but a range of properties drawn from their user profile. Other filters you can include are dates, choice fields, query string parameters, and so on.

A second web part connection exists between the **Holiday Request** web part and the **Current Request** InfoPath form web part. Each time a holiday request is selected, the corresponding InfoPath form is displayed directly on the page, allowing its details to be reviewed. Notice that the **Submit** button is hidden on the form, helping prevent its data from being changed once the request is being processed. The request status and comments fields are "read only", their contents being updated by the custom workflow that runs against each submitted request.

The purpose of this recipe is to illustrate the power of the out of the box filter web parts to create context within a composite application. However, conditional formatting, read-only views, and filter web parts are not security features and do not prevent determined users accessing or changing SharePoint data. If your data is sensitive, then apply unique item- or folder-level permissions to it.

Beyond the portal home page, its functionality is delivered through a list, form library, and custom approval workflow. Central to the applications operation is its ability to track an employee's annual holiday entitlements, the holidays already taken, and their available balance. This information is recorded in the **Holiday Entitlements** custom list.

Holiday requests are entered in an InfoPath form. A link on the home page opens a new blank form. The employee fills in the details of their holiday request and submits the form. Pay close attention to the format of the hyperlink used to open the InfoPath form (`/hr/_layouts/FormServer.aspx?XsnLocation=http://intranet.id-live.com/hr/Holiday Requests/Forms/template.xsn&SaveLocation=http://intranet.id-live.com/hr/Holiday Requests&Source=http://intranet.id-live.com/hr&DefaultItemOpen=1`). This contains a number of **query string parameters** (name/value pairs that appear after ? in the link). These control how the form opens and what happens after it is submitted as shown in the following table. You will need to replace the references to my development server (`http://intranet.id-live.com`) with the correct values for your machine.

Parameter name	Value	Notes
XsnLocation	http://intranet.id-live. com/hr/Holiday Requests/ Forms/template.xsn	Specifies the source of the InfoPath form template.
SaveLocation	http://intranet.id-live. com/hr/Holiday Requests	Specifies where this form instance would be saved (not used in this example but still required).
Source	http://intranet.id-live. com/hr	Specifies the page to display after the form is submitted.
DefaultItemOpen	1	Opens the form in the web browser.

Submitted requests are stored in the **Holiday Requests** library. An instance of the **Holiday Request Approval Workflow** is automatically started for each request submitted. This workflow is divided into four steps.

The **Initialize Workflow** step collects and stores all the data required in the workflow, including the employee's current leave entitlement and line manager details. The line manager details are retrieved form the employee's user profile. You will need to make sure these are populated or you will receive an error. Check with your SharePoint administrator for more information if this occurs.

The **Request Status** column on the **Holiday Requests** library is updated to **In Progress**. This change is automatically synchronized back into the InfoPath form, which then ensures that the **Submit** button in the form is to be hidden by the conditional formatting rule we created the next time the form is displayed. This approach helps prevent modifications to the form after it has been submitted.

The **Validate Request** step performs a quick calculation to see if the employee has enough days remaining for their request. If they do not then the request is rejected, the workflow is stopped, and the employee is informed of the outcome through e-mail. When there are sufficient days for the request, the amount of days taken is calculated so that the employee's balance can be updated later after their request is approved by their manager.

Seek line manager's approval step starts an out of the box approval process on the current Item, passing the employee's manager (retrieved earlier) as the approver. The employee's line manager is assigned a task to approve or reject the employee's holiday request. The task is placed in the **Tasks** lists and the manager is notified of the task through e-mail. If the manager rejects the holiday request, then any comments that they make will be added to the **Holiday Requests** library (and form), and so will be visible to the employee concerned.

The single line on the workflow designer surface hides a considerable amount of complexity. If you click through the **Approve Holiday Request Process** hyperlink, then you will find the task process designer.

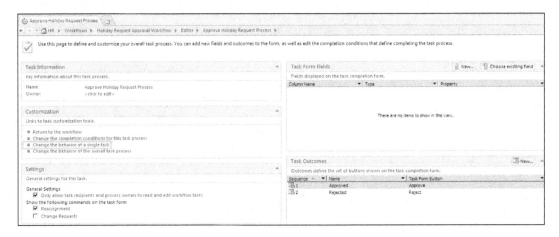

Think of this as a "*workflow within a workflow*". However, in this case the workflow just deals with the approval task processing itself. Everything you find here is configurable. You can configure what happens for each of the task's lifecycle events (completed, rejected, reassigned, and so on). For example, you may want to change what happens when a task expires, such as adding an action that automatically approves the holiday request task if the manager fails to respond.

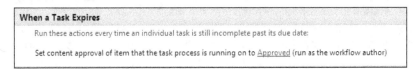

The process manager's response step takes the appropriate actions depending on whether the holiday request has been approved or rejected. Where the request has been approved, the **Calendar** is updated with the holiday details and the employee's amount of days taken (in the **Holiday Entitlements** list) is set to the new value. Their available balance (a calculated field) is automatically adjusted down by SharePoint. Where the request is rejected, the manager's comments are updated in the **Comments** column of the **Holiday Requests** library. These comments are synchronized by SharePoint back into the InfoPath form and will be visible to the employee should they wish to review it. In either case, the **Request Status** is updated and the employee is notified of the outcome by e-mail accordingly.

What we have learnt

This recipe demonstrates the use of the filter web parts to set context in a composite application. By applying the current user filter, we are able to automatically configure the application to only display information relevant to the user viewing the site.

The recipe shows how we can combine the InfoPath forms and workflows, similar to the ones we developed earlier in the book, to automate our business processes. InfoPath is used for the front-end data capture and to apply business rules that we need to enforce. The workflow provides the business process and task management that we need for the logic of our application.

This recipe is necessary, simplistic, and designed to show key concepts. Again there are a near infinite number of ways in which this application could be extended and enhanced. Hopefully it gives you an appreciation of what is possible when creating composite applications. At the same time you should realize that meaningful composite applications can very quickly become quite complex.

Recipes that will help you build this application

- ▸ *Project Management composite application*
- ▸ *CRM composite application*
- ▸ *Creating a SharePoint list, Chapter 1*
- ▸ *Creating a Team Site, Chapter 2*
- ▸ *Adding users to a Team Site, Chapter 2*
- ▸ *Adding a new page to a Team Site, Chapter 2*
- ▸ *Enabling versioning on a document library, Chapter 4*
- ▸ *Creating a holiday request InfoPath form and publishing it to a form library, Chapter 8*
- ▸ *Using the Collect Feedback workflow to receive feedback on a Microsoft Word 2010 document, Chapter 8*
- ▸ *Creating a list workflow using SharePoint Designer 2010, Chapter 8*

Closing thoughts

The recipes in this book have taken you from creating simple SharePoint artifacts such as sites, lists, and libraries through to workflows, InfoPath forms, and complete composite applications. I trust you have picked up lots of techniques along the way that you can now apply in your everyday dealings with SharePoint 2010. By now you should have an appreciation that SharePoint is a large and complex product. While SharePoint provides great power, not every task is as simple and as straightforward as is should be. I hope this book has eased your SharePoint frustrations and inspired you to become a more proficient SharePoint Power User. For those of you who wish to continue your SharePoint journey, I recommend that you visit the book's companion website (http://www.sharepoint-mentor.com), spend some time reading and exploring the official Microsoft SharePoint site (http://sharepoint.microsoft.com/en-us/Pages/default.aspx), subscribe to key blogs such as Get The Point (http://sharepoint.microsoft.com/Blogs/GetThePoint/default.aspx), and take some time out to get involved in your local SharePoint user group or attend a free to attend SharePoint Saturdays conference (http://www.sharepointsaturday.org/default.aspx).

Thanks for reading, and good luck!

Index

A

Active Directory (AD) 54, 264
advanced search
  performing 190-192
alert
  adding, to SharePoint page 30, 31
  providing, on document modification
      135, 136
  search, saving as 194, 195
alerts
  about 8, 32
  managing, in SharePoint 32, 33
announcement
  adding, to Team Site 162-164
  targeting, with audiences 165
announcements list
  working 164
Application pages 56
Approve permission level 178, 181
association 263
audiences
  used, for targeting announcements 165

B

basic search
  about 186
  performing 186, 187
better keyword searches
  building 188, 189
blog
  about 165, 167
  creating, in My Site 166
  posting to, from Word 2010 167-170
business intelligence 199

Business Intelligence centre 50
business intelligence tools 199

C

Central Administration 51
chart
  about 230
  creating, Chart Web Part used 200-205
  creating, PerformancePoint Dashboard
      Designer used 224-230
Chart Web Part
  about 200
  limitations 206
  used, for creating chart 200-205
  working 205
colleagues
  tracking, My Site used 20-22
collect feedback workflow
  used, for receiving feedback on Word 2010
      document 259-265
columns
  removing, from InfoPath form 241, 242
composite application
  about 283, 284
  building 287
  CRM example 296
  designing 287
  features 284
  Human Resources example 306
  Project Management example 287
  testing 287
  types 284
composite application, building
  questions 285, 286
Contacts 48

contacts list
about 69
connecting, to Outlook 2010 84
creating 84
content approval
enabling, on document library 146-149
content type
about 8, 174, 175
creating 14-16
features 15
used, for storing multiple documents in
document library 155-159
content type hub 302
**Contribute permission level 67, 70, 74, 77,
81, 124, 127, 143, 150, 152, 171, 178,
181**
Contributor permission level 83, 84, 212
copy
downloading, of document 134, 135
CRM composite application
about 296
building 297-304
issue 296
solution 296
customer dashboard 303
custom list
about 90
creating 11
creating, from spreadsheet 96
custom list view
creating 98-102
custom workflows 238

D

data
charting, from SharePoint list for displaying
figures 200-205
datasheet view
about 77
accessing 77
tasks, editing in tasks list with 77-80
Designer permission level 55, 57, 60, 90
**Design Permission level 8, 12, 14, 98, 137,
139, 141, 146, 156, 162, 171, 176,
200, 206, 212, 238, 246, 267, 278**

Discussion Board 48
discussion item
adding, to forum 67-69
creating 67-69
tracking 67-69
document
checking out, before editing 137, 138
co-authoring 152-155
creating, in My Site 130, 131
link, emailing to 132, 133
previous version, restoring of 143-145
document copy
downloading 134, 135
document libraries
securing 45
document library
about 9, 64, 124
advantages 126
content approval, enabling on 146-149
existing document, uploading to 124, 125
multiple documents, uploading to 126-129
versioning, enabling on 139-141
working 126
document management 24
document publishing 142
documents
securing 45
downloading
document copy 134, 135

E

Editing Tools ribbon 56
electronic forms 237
Excel
about 215
charting feature 215
data visualization feature 215
Excel services
unsupported features 217
Excel spreadsheet
publishing, on server 212-215
existing document
uploading, to document library 124, 125
experts
searching, people search used 192, 193

explanatory text
adding, to InfoPath form 242, 243
external content type
about 110
creating 111-117
using 121
external list
about 11, 117
creating 118-121

F

features, term set 105
form libraries 9
form library
holiday request InfoPath form, publishing to
246-255
Form Library forms
versus List Forms 256
**Full Control permission level 8, 12, 14, 48,
52, 55, 57, 60, 90, 98, 118, 137, 139,
141, 146, 156, 162, 171, 176, 196,
200, 206, 212, 238, 246, 267, 278**

G

groups
about 54
users, adding to 54

H

holiday request InfoPath form
creating 246-255
publishing, to form library 246-255
submit options, configuring for 257-259
Human Resources composite application
about 306
building 307-320
issue 306
solution 306

I

images
adding, to InfoPath form 242
individual pages
securing 45

InfoPath 2010 237
InfoPath Designer
versus InfoPath Filler 245
InfoPath Filler
versus InfoPath Designer 245
InfoPath form
about 237, 238
columns, removing 241, 242
creating, for SharePoint list 238-240
explanatory text, adding 242, 243
images, adding 242
key concepts 255
rules, adding for data validation 244
tips 256
tooltips, adding 242, 243
InfoPath Form Designer 2010 239
inheritance 38
items
specifying, for publishing 216

K

Key Performance Indicator (KPI)
about 209
creating, status list used 206-209
keyword search 187, 188

L

link
emailing, to document 132, 133
links
adding, to Top link bar 58, 59
list column
creating, term set used 106-110
List Forms
versus Form Library forms 256
list items
securing 45
lists
about 8, 126
Announcements 10
Calendar 10
Contacts 10
creating 9
Custom List 10
Custom List in Datasheet View 10
data storage issues 11

Discussion Board 10
External List 10
Import Spreadsheet 10
Issue Tracking 10
Links 11
Project Tasks 11
Survey 11
Tasks 11
list workflow
   creating, SharePoint Designer 2010 used
     267-275

M

major version
   publishing, of document 141, 142
managed metadata service
   used, for creating term set 103-105
map report 224
media libraries 9
metadata 15, 187
Microsoft Visio 2010
   SharePoint workflow, modeling with 278-281
MS Word 2010
   about 238
   workflows, starting from 266
multiple documents
   uploading, to document library 126-129
My Site
   about 8, 130
   accessing 16
   blog, creating in 166
   creating 16
   document, creating in 130, 131
   used, for tracking colleagues 20-22
   used, for updating user profile 18, 19

N

notes
   about 28
   reviewing, for posts on SharePoint page 28,
     29
notification
   obtaining, during result modification 194,
     195

O

OLAP 230
Online Analytical Processing. *See* **OLAP**
out-of-the-box workflows
   about 238
   customizing 267
Outlook 2010
   contacts list, connecting to 84
   Shared Calendar, managing with 70-73
   SharePoint task list, managing in 81-83
   used, for making document libraries offline
     150, 151

P

page
   adding, to Team Site 55, 56
   creating, on publishing site 171-175
page layouts
   about 56, 174, 175
   modifying, for publishing site page 176, 177
people search
   used, for searching experts 192, 193
PerformancePoint Analytic Chart 230
**PerformancePoint business intelligence
    dashboard**
   building 230-235
PerformancePoint Dashboard Designer
   used, for creating chart 224-230
   working 235
PerformancePoint Services 224
Permission levels
   about 51
   Approve 178, 181
   Contribute 67, 70, 74, 77, 81, 84, 124, 127,
     143, 150, 171, 178, 181, 212
   Contributor 83
   Design 8, 12, 14, 90, 98, 137, 139, 141,
     146, 156, 162, 171, 176, 200, 206,
     212, 238, 246, 267, 278
   Designer 55, 57, 60
   Full Control 8, 12, 14, 48, 52, 55, 57, 60, 90,
     98, 111, 118, 137, 139, 141, 146, 156,
     162, 171, 176, 196, 200, 206, 212,
     238, 246, 267, 278

Read 64, 70, 132, 134, 135, 186, 192, 194
Reader 81, 84, 150
permission levels
verifying, in SharePoint sites 38
permissions
determining, in SharePoint site 34-37
Personal Documents library 131
Picture button 242
PowerPoint 2010 60
Power User 284
previous version
restoring, of document 143-145
project documentation 288
Project Management composite application
about 287
building 289-294
issue 287
solution 288
publishing
items, specifying for 216
Publishing pages 56
Publishing Portal 50
publishing site
new page, creating on 171-175
publishing site page
page layouts, modifying for 176, 177
publishing 178-181

Q

Quick Launch menu 130

R

Reader permission level 81, 84, 150
Read permission level 64, 70, 132, 134, 135,
186, 192, 194
regular lists
features 121
report
creating, Report Builder used 217-223
Report Builder
about 223
used, for creating report 217-223
reusable workflow 276
Root Site 51
rules
adding, to InfoPath form 244

S

Sandbox solution 286
ScreenTip text 244
search
saving, as alert 194, 195
search analytics
used, for viewing people's search 196, 198
securable objects 38
security trimmed 186
sensitive content, securing
alternative ways 45
server
Excel spreadsheet, publishing on 212-215
Shared Calendar
about 48
managing, with Outlook 2010 70-73
SharePoint
alert, managing in 32, 33
alert, providing on document modification
135, 136
colleagues, tracking with My Site 20-22
composite application 284
content type, creating 14-16
CRM composite application, building 297-304
groups 38
Human Resources composite application,
building 307-320
inheritance 38
items, specifying for publishing 216
link, emailing to document 132, 133
lists, creating 9
My Site, accessing 16
My Site, creating 16
page, tagging 25-27
Project Management composite application,
building 289-294
securable objects 38
site, viewing 23, 24
site column, creating 12, 13
user profile, updating with My Site 18, 19
users 38
SharePoint 2010
about 48, 90, 237, 238
document management 124
existing lists 96
key capabilities 49

pages 56
templates 49, 50
SharePoint Designer
about 89
custom list, creating with 90-95
custom list view, creating 98-102
versus Web Browser Interface 95
SharePoint Designer 2010
about 238
list workflow, creating with 267-275
SharePoint Foundation
about 10
list templates 10, 11
SharePoint list
about 8
creating 9
data storage issues 11
InfoPath form, creating for 238-240
unique permissions, applying to 41-44
SharePoint lists 237
SharePoint page
alert, adding to 30, 31
notes, reviewing on 28, 29
tagging 25-27
tags, reviewing on 28, 29
SharePoint search guru 185
SharePoint security 54
SharePoint site
advanced search, performing 190-192
announcement, adding to Team Site 162-164
basic search, performing 186, 187
blog, creating in My Site 166
chart, creating with Chart Web Part 200-205
chart, creating with PerformancePoint
    Dashboard Designer 224-230
collect feedback workflow, used to receive
    feedback 259-265
contacts list, connecting to Outlook 2010 84
contacts list, creating 84
content approval, enabling on document
    library 146-149
custom list, creating with SharePoint Designer
    90-95
custom list view, creating 98-102
discussion item, adding to forum 67-69
discussion item, creating 67-69
discussion item, tracking 67-69

document, checking out before editing 137,
    138
document, co-authoring 152-155
document, creating in My Site 130, 131
document copy, downloading 134, 135
Excel spreadsheet, publishing on server
    212-215
existing document, uploading to document
    library 124, 125
experts, searching with people search
    192, 193
external content type, creating 111-117
external list, creating 118-121
holiday request InfoPath form, creating
    246-255
holiday request InfoPath form, publishing to
    form library 246-255
InfoPath form, creating for SharePoint list
    238-240
Key Performance Indicator (KPI), creating
    206-209
list column, creating with term set 106-110
list workflow, creating with SharePoint
    Designer 2010 267-275
major version, publishing of document
    141, 142
multiple documents, uploading to document
    library 126-129
notification, obtaining during result modifica-
    tion 194, 195
other user's permissions, verifying 39, 40
page, adding to Team Site 55, 56
page, creating on publishing site 171-175
page layouts, modifying for publishing site
    page 176, 177
PerformancePoint business intelligence
    dashboard, building 230-235
permissions, determining in 34-37
previous version, restoring of document
    143-145
publishing site page, publishing
    178-181
report, creating with Report Builder
    217-223
search analytics, using 196, 198
searching, saving as alert 194, 195
slide library, adding to Team Site 60-64

tasks, assigning to users 73-76
Team Site, creating 49
Team Site Calendar, managing with Outlook
    2010 70-73
term set, creating with managed metadata
    service 103-105
used, for storing multiple documents
    155-159
users, adding to groups 54
users, adding to Team Site 52, 54
versioning, enabling on document library
    139-141
viewing 23, 24
web analytics used, for tracking popular pages
    on site 182-184
Word 2010, used for posting to blog
    167-170
workflow, modeling with Microsoft Visio 2010
    278-281

SharePoint sites
permission levels, verifying in 38
SharePoint task list
managing, in Outlook 2010 81-83
SharePoint workflow
modeling, Microsoft Visio 2010 used
    278-281
site
reusing, as template 294
site-level workflow 277
Site Collection level 54
Site Collections
versus Sites 50
site column
about 8, 12
creating 12, 13
Sites
versus Site Collections 50
site templates
about 49
test driving 50
URL, for video previews 50
slide
adding, to presentation from SharePoint slide
    library 65, 66
slide library
about 60, 64

adding, to Team Site for sharing PowerPoint
    slides 60-64
slide, adding to presentation from 65, 66
spreadsheet
custom list, creating from 96
SQL Server Reporting Services. *See* **SSRS**
SSRS 223
Status Indicator
displaying, Status List Web Part used
    210, 211
Status Indicators 210
Status List Web Part
about 210
used, for displaying Status Indicator 210, 211
submit options
configuring, for holiday request InfoPath form
    257-259
Sub Sites 51

T

tags
about 28, 187
reviewing, for posts on SharePoint page
    28, 29
tasks
about 48
assigning, to another user 73-76
creating 73-76
editing, in tasks list 77-80
tasks list
about 69, 73, 76
managing, in Outlook 2010 81-83
tasks, editing in 77-80
Team Discussions forum 66
Team Site
about 48, 162
announcement, adding to 162-164
basic navigation controls 59
creating 49
links, adding to Top link bar 58, 59
page, adding to 55, 56
slide library, adding to 60-64
users, adding to 52, 54
template
site, reusing as 294

Template Parts 256
templates, SharePoint 2010
  Basic Meeting Workspace 50
  Blog 50
  Document Centre 50
  Document Workspace 50
  Team Site 50
term set
  about 105
  creating, managed metadata service used
      103-105
  features 105
  used, for creating list column 106-110
Term Sets 89
Term Store Administrator 103
tooltips
  adding, to InfoPath form 242, 243
Top link bar
  links, adding to 58, 59
track colleagues functionality 23
Tree View navigation control 59

U

unique permissions
  applying, to SharePoint list 41-44
user profile
  updating, My Site used 18, 19
users
  adding, to groups 54
  adding, to Team Site 52, 54
  tasks, assigning to 73-76

V

versioning
  enabling, on document library 139-141
Visio 2010 Premium
  workflow execution status, tracking with 277
Visio Premium 2010 238, 281

W

web analytics
  about 196
  used, for tracking popular pages on site
      182-184
Web Browser Interface
  versus SharePoint Designer 95
Web Part pages 56
Web Part Zones 56
Wiki page
  about 56, 288
  URL, for downloading 56
Wikipedia 56
Word 2010
  about 167, 170
  used, for posting to blog 167-170
Word 2010 document
  feedback, receiving on 259-265
workflow associations 263
workflow execution status
  tracking, with Visio 2010 Premium 277
Workflow Information section 264
workflows
  about 238
  starting, from MS Word 2010 266
  types 276
workflows, types
  reusable 276
  site-level 277
workflow tasks
  allocating 266
Workflow Visualization section 264

Thank you for buying
Microsoft SharePoint 2010 Power User Cookbook

About Packt Publishing

Packt, pronounced 'packed', published its first book "*Mastering phpMyAdmin for Effective MySQL Management*" in April 2004 and subsequently continued to specialize in publishing highly focused books on specific technologies and solutions.

Our books and publications share the experiences of your fellow IT professionals in adapting and customizing today's systems, applications, and frameworks. Our solution-based books give you the knowledge and power to customize the software and technologies you're using to get the job done. Packt books are more specific and less general than the IT books you have seen in the past. Our unique business model allows us to bring you more focused information, giving you more of what you need to know, and less of what you don't.

Packt is a modern, yet unique publishing company, which focuses on producing quality, cutting-edge books for communities of developers, administrators, and newbies alike. For more information, please visit our website: www.PacktPub.com.

About Packt Enterprise

In 2010, Packt launched two new brands, Packt Enterprise and Packt Open Source, in order to continue its focus on specialization. This book is part of the Packt Enterprise brand, home to books published on enterprise software – software created by major vendors, including (but not limited to) IBM, Microsoft and Oracle, often for use in other corporations. Its titles will offer information relevant to a range of users of this software, including administrators, developers, architects, and end users.

Writing for Packt

We welcome all inquiries from people who are interested in authoring. Book proposals should be sent to author@packtpub.com. If your book idea is still at an early stage and you would like to discuss it first before writing a formal book proposal, contact us; one of our commissioning editors will get in touch with you.

We're not just looking for published authors; if you have strong technical skills but no writing experience, our experienced editors can help you develop a writing career, or simply get some additional reward for your expertise.

Microsoft SharePoint 2010 Administration Cookbook

ISBN: 978-1-84968-108-7   Paperback: 288 pages

Over 90 simple but incredibly effective recipes to administer your Microsoft SharePoint 2010 applications

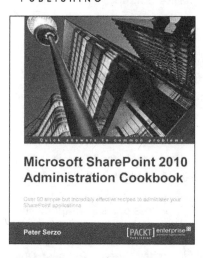

1. Solutions to the most common problems encountered while administering SharePoint in book and eBook formats

2. Upgrade, configure, secure, and back up your SharePoint applications with ease

3. Packed with many recipes for improving collaboration and content management with SharePoint

SharePoint Designer Tutorial: Working with SharePoint Websites

ISBN: 978-1-847194-42-8   Paperback: 188 pages

Get started with SharePoint Designer and learn to put together a business website with SharePoint

1. Become comfortable in the SharePoint Designer environment

2. Learn about SharePoint Designer features as you create a SharePoint website

3. Step-by-step instructions and careful explanations

4. Follow a step-by-step tutorial to create a feature-packed media-rich Plone site

Please check **www.PacktPub.com** for information on our titles

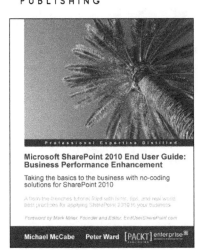

Microsoft SharePoint 2010 End User Guide:
Business Performance Enhancement

Taking the basics to the business with no-coding
solutions for SharePoint 2010

A from-the-trenches tutorial filled with hints, tips, and real world
best practices for applying SharePoint 2010 to your business

Foreword by Mark Miller, Founder and Editor, EndUserSharePoint.com

Michael McCabe   Peter Ward [PACKT] enterprise🍀

Microsoft SharePoint 2010 End User Guide: Business Performance Enhancement

ISBN: 978-1-84968-066-0   Paperback: 424 pages

A from-the-trenches tutorial filled with hints, and real world best practices for applying SharePoint 2010 to your business

1. Designed to offer applicable, no-coding solutions to dramatically enhance the performance of your business

2. Excel at SharePoint intranet functionality to have the most impact on you and your team

3. Drastically enhance your End user SharePoint functionality experience

4. Gain real value from applying out of the box SharePoint collaboration tools

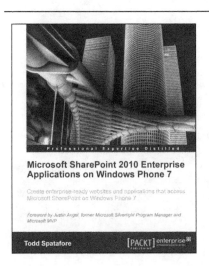

Microsoft SharePoint 2010 Enterprise
Applications on Windows Phone 7

Create enterprise-ready websites and applications that access
Microsoft SharePoint on Windows Phone 7

Foreword by Justin Angel, former Microsoft Silverlight Program Manager and
Microsoft MVP

Todd Spatafore   [PACKT] enterprise🍀

Microsoft SharePoint 2010 Enterprise Applications on Windows Phone 7

ISBN: 978-1-84968-258-9   Paperback: 252 pages

Create enterprise-ready websites and applications that access Microsoft SharePoint on Windows Phone 7

1. Provides step-by-step instructions for integrating Windows Phone 7-capable web pages into SharePoint websites

2. Provides an overview of creating Windows Phone 7 applications that integrate with SharePoint services

3. Examines Windows Phone 7's enterprise capabilities

Please check **www.PacktPub.com** for information on our titles

www.ingramcontent.com/pod-product-compliance
Lightning Source LLC
LaVergne TN
LVHW062304060326
832902LV00013B/2049